The Real and
Imagined Role of Culture
in Development

The Real and Imagined Role of Culture in Development

CASE STUDIES FROM INDONESIA

EDITED BY
Michael R. Dove

HAWAI University of Hawaii Press • Honolulu

Library of Congress Cataloging-in-Publication Data

The Real and imagined role of culture in development: case studies
   from Indonesia/edited by Michael R. Dove.
     p. cm.
   Includes bibliographies and index.
   ISBN 0-8248-1080-5
   1. Community development—Indonesia—Case studies. 2. Social
institutions—Indonesia—Case studies. 3. Culture—Case studies.
4. Social change—Case studies. I. Dove, Michael.
HN710.Z9C6529   1988   87–35567
304.1'4'09598—dc19   CIP

To my parents

CONTENTS

Part IV: Social Relations/Social Change

Part V: Evaluation

ILLUSTRATIONS

FIGURES

PHOTOGRAPHS

TABLES

ACKNOWLEDGMENTS

The idea for this volume was born in a conversation with Ivan Kats, director of the Obor Foundation, in October of 1979. To his concern for the plight of traditional societies goes primary credit for my undertaking this project. For support during the years since in which this volume slowly took shape, I am indebted to the Rockefeller Foundation, the Ford Foundation, and the Environment and Policy Institute of the East-West Center (none of these organizations, however, is responsible for the final product). To each of the authors, I am indebted for their alacrity in responding to editorial suggestions and for their patience in awaiting publication. Finally, I would like to thank B. S. Eko Prakoso and Josie Herr for assistance in drawing the volume's maps and Noegravidha Prasetyanti for her uncomplaining typing and retyping of the manuscript.

MICHAEL R. DOVE

Islamabad, December 1986

Introduction: Traditional Culture and Development in Contemporary Indonesia

MICHAEL R. DOVE

In Indonesia, as in many other developing countries, development is widely interpreted as meaning and necessitating change. That which is old and unchanged is reflexively categorized as undeveloped. This especially applies to culture. Traditional cultures and lifestyles are regarded as clear signs of underdevelopment and as formidable obstacles to necessary socioeconomic advancement. Accordingly, one ubiquitous element in development planning is the deprecation and attempted alteration or elimination of traditional culture.

It is my thesis that this view and treatment of traditional culture is in error and is itself inimical to the process of development in Indonesia. The error, I suggest, lies in viewing culture as excess baggage that is borne by society but has no relationship to its basic processes of self-perpetuation, except insofar as it disrupts them. In contrast, I maintain that traditional culture is intimately bound up with and directly supports the basic social, economic, and ecological processes of society. I further maintain that traditional culture is dynamic, is always undergoing change, and as a result is not inimical to the process of development per se. The aforementioned erroneous view of traditional culture is due, I suggest, to the absence from development planning of empirical evaluations of either the planning itself or the traditional cultures to which it is applied.

This thesis is developed in this volume through the presentation by eleven authors of case studies from different parts of Indonesia (see Fig. 1). Each case study focuses on a traditional culture, or a traditional aspect of some culture, that has been the object of development efforts. In each case the function or meaning of the traditional culture is analyzed in detail, and then the attendant development efforts are described and their impact discussed. Throughout, an attempt is made to

1

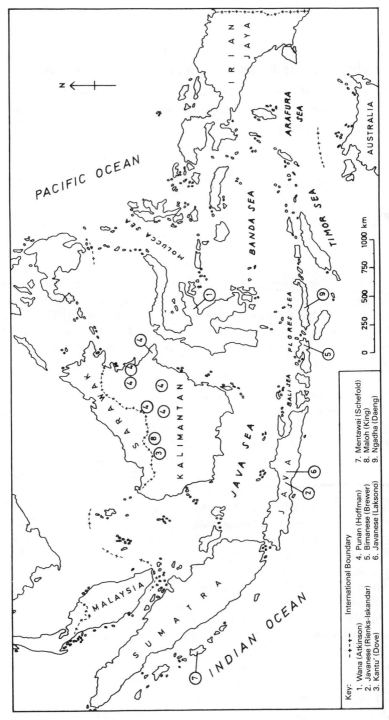

Figure 1 Location of the Case Studies within the Indonesian Archipelago

Key: -·-+-·- International Boundary

1. Wana (Atkinson)
2. Javanese (Rienks-Iskandar)
3. Kantu' (Dove)
4. Punan (Hoffman)
5. Bimanese (Brewer)
6. Javanese (Laksono)
7. Mentawai (Schefold)
8. Maloh (King)
9. Ngadha (Daeng)

discuss not only the intended impact but also the actual impact of development efforts, separating their latent functions from their manifest ones. These discussions, along with the case studies themselves, are grouped under five headings: ideology, economics, ecology, social change, and evaluation.

Ideology

One of the most salient of the controversies pertaining to the development of traditional societies in Indonesia is the issue of religion or, to be more precise, the issue of the lack of religion. According to the national government, those Indonesians—mostly members of minority tribes in the outer islands—who do not profess belief in one of the "world religions" (viz., Christianity, Islam, Hinduism, or Buddhism) do not have a religion; this is seen as an obstacle to their socioeconomic development and possibly as a threat to the country's political stability as well. The government's response to this perceived situation is to encourage the peoples involved to adopt one of the world religions. In terms of the national census and other government records, this encouragement amounts to obligation: there are no categories for "atheist," "agnostic," "animist," or "other" for the questions regarding religious affiliation.

This is the topic of Atkinson's chapter on the Wana of Sulawesi. The Wana have come under considerable pressure from government officials, missionaries, and others because their traditional belief system is not recognized as a religion. As Atkinson points out, one of the reasons that the Wana system of belief may not "look" like a religion is that it permeates the rest of their culture, rather than being separated from it institutionally. In Weberian terms, it is a traditional as opposed to a rationalized system. This distinction has become clear to the Wana themselves, as pressure from both missionaries and the government has heightened their consciousness of this topic, for the Wana now refer to their belief system as *agama yang belum jadi agama* (a religion that has not yet become a religion). This reference shows that the Wana implicitly understand something that the government officials do not, namely, that the dispute between them involves not the presence or absence of Wana religion, but rather the official accreditation or recognition of Wana religion.

Although the Wana recognize that their religion has no official status, they do not regard it as in any sense inferior. Quite the contrary, based on its undisputed historical priority—even their Christian and Muslim neighbors agree that the Wana belief system is historically prior to their own in this part of Sulawesi—the Wana believe that their system is superior to all others. That is, while government officials place greatest value on the modernity of a belief system, the Wana place greatest value on its antiquity, or more specifically its seniority. The government and the Wana, then, have very different conceptions of what religion is or should be. Religion for the government, with its emphasis on modernity, is a sign as well as an agent of progress. With their emphasis on antiquity, religion for the Wana is more a matter of accumulated tradition and lore.

These two conceptions of religion have very different implications for the strength or quality of belief. Since adherence to a world religion is valued by the government at least in part for its contribution to development, and since development is a major element in the government's political philosophy, adherence or conversion to a world religion often has political overtones.[1] Indeed, allegiance to one of the world religions often has the quality of allegiance to a political party, with all the connotations of expediency and impermanence that this implies. Public awareness of this quality is expressed in the phrases, commonly heard in Indonesia today, *Kristen statistik* (statistical Christian) and *Islam statistik* (statistical Muslim). They refer to people who claim allegiance to one of these religions for "statistical" purposes only, meaning to secure government favor and avoid its censure, but whose true allegiance is to some other system of belief that is not officially recognized. (Perhaps the most common example of this are the Central Javanese who claim allegiance to Islam, but who depend on the traditional *kejawen* system of belief for their existential needs.) In contrast, there are no "statistical" believers in Wana religion or in any of the other traditional belief systems of Indonesia. Their adherents believe implicitly in the precepts of these religions, with a certitude that is lacking among many of the followers of Indonesia's world religions. An important but as yet completely unaddressed question is whether statistical allegiance to a world religion or genuine allegiance to a traditional minority religion better serves the cause of Indonesian national development. While an authoritative answer to this question is beyond the scope of this book, there certainly does not appear to be any basis for assuming that the former is preferable to the latter in this regard.

The government's unremitting pressure on adherents of minority religions is puzzling, therefore, since the impact of conversion to a world religion on national development and stability is at best debatable and is at worst detrimental. This puzzle is perhaps best explained by the aforementioned fact that allegiance to world religions is perceived not so much as a religious statement as a political one. Consequently, pressure for this allegiance is influenced by the exigencies of national politics, in which the statistics of belief—and their short-term impact—can indeed be more important than the genuineness—and longer-term impact—of belief.

Evidence of this politicization and deculturation of religion is given in the unique role that missionaries play in the nation's religious development. This role is pervasive: in each case study in this volume in which much discussion is given to traditional belief systems—namely, the Wana, the Maloh, the Ngadha, and the Mentawai—the role and impact of missionaries is salient.[2] Especially in the case of postindependence work by foreign missionaries, this role is anomalous, for in no other aspect of Indonesian cultural life is intervention by foreign creeds as tolerated, much less as actively supported by the government, as the foreign missionaries are. This singular lapse in the cultural pride or chauvinism that otherwise characterizes Indonesia's relations with the rest of the world is, again, attributable to the political light in which religious matters have come to be viewed. Because the government views adherence to minority religions as a political issue, so does it view the role of foreigners in the conversion of these adherents as politically expedient, instead of culturally and morally repugnant.

This deculturation and devaluation of traditional religion is made possible by extremely simplistic and literal interpretations of traditional beliefs. For example, most development officials will dismiss as superstition a shaman's attribution of illness to a neighbor's sorcery—without investigating the possibility that conflict with a neighbor has indeed created tension and even illness in the household in question. It is not necessary to believe in sorcery, that is, in order to accept that there may be some empirical congruent that has the same effect (viz., illness). However, rarely if ever do development officials attempt to translate indigenous beliefs into the adopted language and logic of Western science before evaluating them. Rienks and Iskandar's study of the health cadre program in Central Java presents a good example of this. Although the indigenous system of shamanic curing is well known to most development officials, and although it can be shown to be a sophisticated, coherent, and functional way of dealing with illness, no attempt was made to evaluate it in terms of the principles of ethnomedicine, psychology, sociology, so as to incorporate its more readily usable elements into the planned cadre program. Rather, this indigenous system of curing was ignored in the planning of the cadre program, and this omission, as Rienks and Iskandar convincingly argue, has proven to be a major flaw in the program.

In short, it is at least a useful heurism for development planners to assume that there is an empirical basis for traditional beliefs, even those that at first glance appear to be nonfunctional or dysfunctional. In addition to the Javanese system of curing just cited, several other of the case studies present compelling evidence of this assumption. For example, Laksono's analysis of traditional beliefs regarding Merapi volcano in Central Java shows that many of them have a valid basis, such as the prediction of eruptions based on what are in effect environmental clues. Similarly, Schefold's study of the Mentawai of Siberut shows that traditional beliefs regarding the stability of the natural environment and the need to protect it through observance of ritual proscriptions on hunting help to conserve the natural resources upon which the existence of the Mentawaians depends.

Among all of the case studies, Daeng's study of the Ngadha of Flores represents the most sustained attempt at a functional interpretation of a belief system. In his analysis of the Ngadha's historic system of potlatch-type feasting, he convincingly argues that this seemingly extravagant practice functioned to both optimally redistribute land among the population and absolutely reduce the population/land pressure. The former was achieved through awarding disputed sections of land to the clan that had the most livestock to slaughter—and hence had the greatest need for more grazing land—and the latter was achieved by virtue of the slaughter itself, which immediately and for some years thereafter reduced the size of the herds of the clans involved. These demonstrations of the economic and ecological functions of ritual—and in particular, of ritual expenditure and consumption—are of great relevance in Indonesia today, given the reflexive condemnation by government officials of all such expenditures as wasteful and antithetical to the goals of national development.

The case studies in this volume support the thesis that there is not just an empirical basis to traditional systems of ritual and religion but, more generally, that there is an empirical basis to all traditional systems of knowledge. As already noted, the study by Rienks and Iskandar makes it clear that the Javanese (especially their shamans) know a great deal about sickness and healing (especially their psychological dimensions), while the study by Laksono makes it equally clear that the Javanese know a great deal about the ecology of volcanos. Similarly, the studies by Schefold and Hoffman demonstrate that the Mentawai of Siberut and the Punan of Kalimantan are experts in exploiting the resources of the tropical rain forest. This last point is forcefully put in the study by Appell as well: he claims that contemporary development is destroying not only the botanic gene pools of the tropical forests, but also the traditional knowledge of how to exploit this gene pool. (For an example of what is being lost, note Hoffman's reference to the grass that the Punan traditionally ate as a contraceptive.)

The idea that the villager, the peasant, the tribesman is an expert is old hat to anthropologists, for whom traditional societies have for long been an object of sympathetic study; but it is not old hat to those from other disciplines—particularly development planners—for whom traditional societies have been primarily a subject for planned intervention and change. The problem here is structural. It is difficult for the typical, highly educated, and highly paid development planner to accept that the typical, poorly educated, and poorly paid villager knows far more about his own local economy and environment than the expert knows or is likely to learn. This fact is threatening to those development experts who mistakenly interpret "expert" as "all-knowing," as opposed to the more modest but more realistic "all-resourceful" (viz., having access to special financial and technological resources). Hence, in Indonesia as elsewhere in the developing world, the overwhelming majority of development experts (including foreigners as well as nationals) treat the rural villagers as their students as opposed to their teachers. It is an article of faith in these circles that in the space of a few hours or at most few days, any expert can enter an unfamiliar village, survey it, and then be capable of instructing its inhabitants how better to order their lives.[3]

This stance is based upon an extremely high valuation of formal education. The advanced formal education of the development planners is regarded as a guarantee of the validity of their observations and conclusions. In contrast, it is assumed that because the villagers have little or no formal education, that they literally "know nothing." Their nonformal education, traditional lore, oral literature, and so on are accorded little if any value. A logical extension of this outlook is the belief that any young person with some formal education is capable of instructing any elderly villager with none. This is the rationale behind the government's KKN (*Kuliah Kerja Nyata* [Real Work Study]) program, under which all graduating university students are obliged to serve in rural areas of the country for three months. The students entering this program are instructed not to learn from the villagers in the areas to which they have been assigned, but rather to teach them—teach them how to improve their agricultural practices, diet, cooking, sanitation, environment, and so on.[4] The government expects this association with "educated" youth to benefit the village peoples, because it attributes the latter's purported underdevelopment in large (perhaps, largest) part to their lack of education.

There is no recognition in government quarters that modern formal education might even be a cause of some of Indonesia's developmental problems.[5] Some problems stem from removing the student from his rural environment to continue his schooling. This removal prematurely terminates the student's informal schooling in the technical aspects of his local economy and ecology. As a result, the average educated inhabitant of Java's or Bali's cities is far more ignorant of and insensitive to the principles of a balanced rural ecosystem, for example, than the average uneducated inhabitant of Java's or Bali's countryside. Nonetheless, it is the former not the latter to whom the government solely entrusts development planning for the rural environment—with the result that much of this planning is wrongheaded and unsuccessful. This will continue to be the case so long as traditional systems of knowledge and belief are regarded as obstacles to development, to be destroyed wherever possible, as opposed to resources for development, to be studied and utilized wherever possible.

Economics

The case studies in this volume suggest that the attitudes of development planners need to be changed not only with respect to Indonesia's traditional belief systems, but also with respect to its traditional economic systems. Three such systems—swidden agriculture, sago collecting, and hunting and gathering—are treated in some detail in the case studies. The most detailed treatment of swidden agriculture is contained in Brewer's case study from Sumbawa.

Brewer states that one of the principal objectives of government land reform in Bima, from colonial times to the present, has been to eliminate or restrict the practice of swidden agriculture. In fact, as he goes on to show, the practice of swidden agriculture actually increased under the government programs in question. Brewer attributes this irony, in part, to the persistent failure of government officials to incorporate into their programs the views and desires of the Bimanese farmers themselves. In addition, he says, swidden cultivation is one of the only practical ways of farming the steep and rocky slopes of Bima's hinterland. In former times, swidden cultivation could be practiced on these slopes without causing any damage to the environment, the government's fears notwithstanding. There is somewhat greater basis for these fears today, because of growing population/land ratios and shrinking fallow periods. Nevertheless, swidden cultivation still persists, in large part because the government, although it continually pressures the farmers to abandon this form of cultivation, has not yet offered them a viable alternative.

The alternative that government officials most often propose to swidden agriculture, namely, irrigated rice agriculture, is anathema to most swidden cultivators. The difference between their perception of this system of agriculture and the government's perception of it is due to a fundamental difference in value systems: the government's is based on capital or land, and the swidden cultivators' is based on human labor.

Hence, officials focus on and praise the relatively high returns per unit of land in irrigated rice agriculture, while the swidden cultivators focus on and criticize its relatively low returns per unit of labor (Dove 1983, 1985a).[6] The fact that swidden agriculture yields, by comparison, high returns on labor and hence demands less of the farmer's time (cet. par.), is sufficiently important to have become encoded in language: the Javanese word *ladhang*, which is cognate to the common Indonesian/ Malay term for swiddens, *ladang*, means *ada waktu luang*, "there is extra time" (Prawiroatmojo 1981:284).

A particularly interesting variant of swidden agriculture is found among the Mentawaians of Siberut, who are the subject of Schefold's case study. They cultivate bananas and root crops using swidden agricultural techniques, but with one unusual omission: they clear the forest for their swiddens, but they do not burn it (cf. Maas 1902; Spencer 1966:44). This practice should be of particular interest to the Indonesian government, since the supposed threat of fire to valuable forests is its principal stated reason for opposing the practice of swidden agriculture. In fact, the government has taken no apparent notice of the fireless character of the Mentawaian's swidden agriculture and is treating them the same as it treats other forest-dwelling swidden groups elsewhere in the archipelago. The government is attempting to resettle them out of the forested interior of Siberut and onto its coast—a policy that Schefold suggests is related less to government concern to minimize the Mentawaians' exploitation of the island's forests than to a desire to maximize its own.

The Mentawaians, in addition to making root crop swiddens (and tending taro gardens and fruit groves), exploit naturally occurring stands of sago. Sago is exploited elsewhere in Indonesia as well, most notably in the Moluccas and Irian Jaya (Ruddle et al. 1978:47–48); but nowhere does it receive much attention from development planners. Provincial forestry officials often do not know whether forests under their supervision contain sago or, if sago is present, whether it is being exploited by local peoples or not. There are several reasons for this ignorance. First, sago is a relatively abundant, naturally occurring plant. Second, it can be cultivated and exploited with no capital inputs whatsoever. Third, although it has commercial potential, it is largely exploited for subsistence purposes in Indonesia.[7] Fourth, it is largely exploited by groups that are regarded by the government as backward and undeveloped, existing on the fringes of civilized society. None of these characteristics of sago cultivation recommends it very highly to development officials, whose perceived job consists of introducing new plants as opposed to working with indigenous ones (Dove 1986c), whose personal income is often linked to the capital intensity and commercial applications of the projects in which they are involved, and who respond first and foremost to the needs of politically powerful and conspicuous groups—which definitely do not include Neolithic, swamp dwelling, sago eaters.

Natural stands of sago are also exploited by the Punan of Kalimantan, discussed in Hoffman's study. The Punan gather a variety of other forest products for their subsistence, and they are heavily involved in hunting as well, but (at least traditionally) they did not engage in agriculture. Scholars and government officials alike have tended to regard such peoples—nomadic, forest-dwelling hunters and gatherers—as possessing the most primitive, subsistence-oriented economy possible. Hoffman convincingly argues that a radical revision of this view is in order. He suggests that the Punan economy is basically oriented not toward subsistence consumption, but toward the market, through trade in forest products. He further suggests that the distinguishing characteristics of Punan life—their location in the forest, their noninvolvement in agriculture, and their nomadism—are all essential to this involvement in trade.

Hoffman maintains that the Punan are, in short, specialists in the collection of forest products, including such products for the international trade as rattan, resins, and edible birds' nests. The other ethnic groups of Kalimantan—whose involvement in agriculture forces them to be sedentary, consumes most of their time, and obliges them to live outside the primary forest—cannot participate in the collection of these products except in a periodic and incidental way. Indeed, Hoffman argues, the settled agriculturalists and the Punan exploit completely different ecological niches. As in other parts of the world, however, the two groups have extensive ties with one another—for example, through the trade of food crops for jungle products—that allow each side to reap the advantages not only of its own economic specialization, but to some extent of the other's as well. These relations, Hoffman suggests, are the key to the cultural and historical origin of the Punan: they represent not one distinct ethnic group, but rather the forest-based "wings" of many different, settled agricultural groups.

The reality of Punan life is greatly at variance with the official perception of it. The official perception is that the Punan have a primitive economy with few if any links to the outside world. The reality is that the Punan have a highly specialized and productive economy, which feeds directly into the export sector of the national economy.[8] (Atkinson makes a similar point in her study of the Wana.) The Punan economy is more directly linked to the outside world than the insular economy of the wet rice cultivators of Java, for example, yet it is the latter—as noted earlier—that the government treats as the model of and for developed agriculture. Based on this misperception, the government is attempting to move the Punan (and all similar peoples) out of the forests, settle them in permanent villages, and turn them into agriculturalists. In light of Hoffman's analysis, it is clear that this policy, if successful, will severely reduce or even terminate the role of the Punan in the collection of forest products, with a similar impact upon the not unimportant contribution of forest products to Indonesia's export sector. Such an impact would run directly counter to the government's all-out effort to find exportable commodities to replace the country's dwindling supplies of oil and gas.

This is not an isolated case: there is a general tendency in development circles in Indonesia to overlook the contribution of all tribal economies to the national economy. Perhaps the best example of this tendency involves those tribal economies that incorporate both swidden food crops and smallholder export crops (Dove 1983; Pelzer 1978). This combination of subsistence and market-oriented agriculture has proven to be extremely successful: most of the smallholder crops for Indonesia's export markets (e.g., rubber, pepper, coconuts) are today grown by farmers who depend on these crops for access to consumer goods but who depend on the swidden cultivation of food crops for their daily subsistence. This success has received no recognition in government planning for the development of either swidden agriculture or smallholder export crops. All current programs to develop smallholder crop production focus on large, highly centralized and heavily capitalized government plantations (Dove 1985a, 1985b, 1986a).

Far from believing that tribal peoples can contribute to the national economy, most development officials do not believe that they can even satisfy their own basic economic needs. Thus, a primary rationale for all government programs for these groups is the purported need to "increase their standard of living." It is noteworthy, however, that these developmental imperatives are never supported with comparative data on the extant standards of living of the target groups. Whenever such data have been gathered, they have not supported the developers' perception of people on the thin edge of subsistence. Thus, the case studies by Hoffman and Schefold show that the Punan and the Mentawaians have many and varied sources of foodstuffs. Indeed, at least in terms of consumption of meat and fish, and most probably in terms of diet in general, it is clear that the Punan and Mentawaians eat far better than the lower classes in the highly developed urban areas and wet rice lowlands of Java and Bali.

The development myth that tribal peoples are economically deprived is associated with another set of myths about why they are deprived. One of these myths faults the organization of village-level production, in particular its supposedly "communalistic" character. In almost all cases, this belief in peasant communalism represents a false inference from the physical appearance of joint houses, work parties, or feasts. For example, one of the most well known "communal" structures of Southeast Asia, the longhouse of the Dayak of Kalimantan, is actually no more than an aggregation of the privately owned houses of its constituent but independent households (Dove 1982). The chief advantage of this aggregation is to facilitate participation in agricultural work parties. These parties represent not communal labor, however, but reciprocal labor, which enables individual households to maintain a high rate of utilization of labor in the face of time constraints imposed upon them by the environment. Similarly, what development officials perceive as communal consumption typically represents either a loan or a wage labor payment from a household that is temporarily enjoying an agricultural surplus to one that is temporarily suffering from a deficit. When the tables are turned, the favor must also be returned. This pattern of consumption represents an adaptation to the unpredictability of the rain forest environment. This unpredictability guarantees that even the most prudent and industrious household occasionally will have to turn to other, simply luckier households for assistance. This is why, as Schefold notes in his chapter on Siberut, a single Mentawaian household is not a viable economic unit. This is not to say that the individual Mentawaian (or other Indonesian peasant) household is not a discrete socioeconomic unit, but only that it must cooperate with other such units to assure its own long-term survival. (In my case study of the ceremonial consumption of alcohol among the Kantu' of Kalimantan, shortly to be discussed, I analyze one of the traditional ways in which such cooperation is regulated.)

While this sort of reciprocity is common among Indonesia's traditional communities, true communal consumption is not, with one or two exceptions. One involves the village-wide consumption of wild game. This custom, which is described in Schefold's case study of the Mentawai and has been reported on throughout the Indonesian archipelago, represents (in some cases) an adaptation to the historic lack of a means for preserving animal flesh (Dove 1981). A second exceptional instance of communal consumption, which is found among all of the societies discussed in this volume, involves the provision of food and drink to guests at ceremonies. Daeng's case study and mine discuss such consumption in detail.

Daeng, as noted earlier, argues that historic ceremonial consumption among the Ngadha functioned to reduce both pressure on land and imbalances in its distribution. In my study of the Kantu' of West Kalimantan, I argue that contemporary ceremonial consumption of alcohol functions to create and maintain social and economic relations among otherwise separate and autonomous households and longhouses—relations that are of critical importance to the viability of the society as a whole. Every year in every longhouse, some households reap poor harvests and some reap good ones, and the former have to trade their labor for the grain of the latter in order to survive. Similarly, every few years or so, some longhouses in the region uniformly reap poor harvests while others reap good or, at least, better ones, and the former similarly must trade their labor for the latter's grain. These labor-grain exchanges are facilitated by the participation of different longhouses in dyadic, ceremonial drinking relationships.

In spite of their functional value, all such instances of communal consumption are criticized by development officials in Indonesia. The officials maintain that communal consumption in general, and ceremonial consumption in particular, is a waste of scarce resources that could otherwise be more productively employed. Based on this belief, the government in West Kalimantan, for example, has periodically issued official restrictions on the number of days on which major ceremonies can be held. To the extent that these restrictions are effective, the regional economic linkages that are made possible by the ceremonies will be disrupted.

The disruption of local economies is certainly not in keeping with the government's ostensible commitment to economic development. It is, however, in keeping with a de facto commitment to the development of those sectors of the economy in which government officials themselves participate and with which they are therefore both more familiar and more interested. These sectors do not include regional tribal networks for the exchange of labor and grain. They do include regional trade in manufactured and consumer goods. Hence the common observation by development officials that it would be better "for development" if the resources that are devoted to ceremonial expenditure were devoted instead to the purchase of agricultural chemicals or implements (Dove 1985a:28–31). It is not at all clear that such purchases would contribute to the economy of the villagers; it is clear that they would contribute to the economy of the national entrepreneurial class, to which government officials themselves belong.

In addition to traditional patterns of consumption, traditional patterns of ownership, especially of land, are another major subject of misunderstanding and conflict. This is the focus of Brewer's study of Bima, in which he presents data on indigenous land tenure and government land policy during the colonial and postcolonial eras. During both eras there have been two major sources of contention between government and farmers. The first is the failure by all governing authorities to comprehend traditional patterns of land use, particularly under swidden agriculture. There has been a pervasive and tenacious tendency on the part of government to view fallowed swidden land, lying under a cover of secondary growth, as "abandoned," "unowned," and, therefore, as belonging to the state by default.

In reality, not only among the Bimanese but also among all of the other swidden groups in Indonesia (including the Kantu' whom I studied [Dove 1983, 1985c:55–62]), tenurial rights do not lapse when swidden land is fallowed and naturally reforested. Such land can be bought, sold, swapped, rented, and passed on to one's heirs, just like any other type of property. Among a minority of swidden groups in Indonesia today, when swidden land is fallowed, tenurial rights to it revert from the individual household to the village or community as a whole. Thereafter, every household in the community has an equal right to recultivate that land when its fallow period is finished. Households from other communities have no such right, however. Not even in this minority of cases, therefore, is fallowed swidden land "unowned."

In the cases in which tenurial rights to fallowed swidden land do not revert to the community as a whole, the community still holds *hak ulayat* (residual rights or rights of avail) to this land (Holleman 1981:278), in contrast to the individual household's *hak milik* (ownership rights). These residual rights give the community authority to forbid, for example, the sale of land outside the community. They do not supplant but rather complement the individual household's rights of ownership; they are part of the same tenurial system. This subtlety has been lost on successive Indonesian governments, which have tended to believe that ownership rights and residual rights are mutually exclusive, and that only the latter apply to unregistered peasant lands. This is a crucial determination with respect to the interests of the government versus the peasants, because residual rights were granted far less protection than ownership rights under both colonial law and national law (viz., the 1960 "Basic Agrarian Laws"). As a result of this determination, countless privately owned peasant lands have been appropriated by the government, without compensation, for transmigration sites, reservoirs, logging concessions, and so on.

The appropriation of these lands is usually protested by the erstwhile owners. While this is a natural enough reaction, the government has tended to interpret all such protests as being politically motivated, as reflecting antigovernment or subversive attitudes.[9] This interpretation is completely belied by the facts, as, for instance, in the case of a tribesman in Kalimantan who owns some forested land that has been appropriated by a government plantation. If this tribesman reacts to the appropriation with anger, clearly it is for no other reason than his perception that his legitimate rights to his private property have been violated by his government. His reaction, that is, is based on beliefs in the sovereignty of the individual and his property vis-à-vis the state—which is an essentially conservative political philosophy. How then can the government view this protest as evidence of radical leftist sympathies? How can a protest based on the sanctity of private property be viewed as subversive in a noncommunist (indeed, vehemently anticommunist) state? I suspect that the answer to this question has to do with the fact that if the peasant's anger is attributed to subversion, the correctness of the development planning that gave rise to it will not be questioned, whereas otherwise it would be.

Ecology

As in the example just discussed, a great many of the development issues in Indonesia involve man-land relations. A major source of controversy in this regard is the virtue of traditional peasant adaptations to the environment. Most government officials (as well as physical and natural scientists) in Indonesia view these adaptations at best as uninformed, and at worst as destructive. They support this view with documented cases of peasant destruction of the local environment. In fact, such cases prove little. In particular, they prove nothing about the ability of peasants to conserve their environment when they have some incentive to do so. The importance of incentives in peasant conservation of the environment is routinely overlooked.

For example, a recurrent topic in discussions of the state of Indonesia's forests is peasant burning of lands that have been reforested by the forest department. Forest department officials attribute this destruction either to ignorance or to a "poor mental attitude" on the part of the peasants involved. The possibility that the peasants have some rational basis for wanting to destroy rather than protect the forest department plantings is never mentioned. In fact, some such basis usually exists. Reforestation projects are all carried out on state land, which in many if not most cases has been appropriated from the proximate peasant communities, by whom it was previously used for agricultural purposes. In such cases, therefore, the peasants have both a moral and a material basis for obstructing the government's reforestation efforts and pursuing their traditional title to and use of the land in question. This is not to say that the peasants are right and the government is wrong in such cases (e.g., one can imagine an instance in which regional ecological interests might take priority over local economic ones), but only that the peasants' behavior is no less reasoned or rational than the government's. Peasants are destructive of government plantings (action construed by the government as being destructive of "the environment," although this is not the same thing at all) when it serves their best interests, not because they are ignorant or have poor mental attitudes.

In some cases, the peasants' incentive for destructive behavior is provided by the broader "developed" society. For example, forest department officials in Java constantly accuse peasants of illegal felling of trees in state forests. These same officials levy no accusations, however, against the city-based entrepreneurs who stimulate most of this cutting by sending trucks into the state forests and offering what in local terms are irresistible sums of money for illegally felled timber. (These entrepreneurs do not—indeed, could not—operate without the collusion of forest department personnel, which explains the lack of criticism by the latter.)

Another striking example of an ecological problem with origins in the broader society is the practice of swidden agriculture along logging roads in the commercial timber concessions of Kalimantan and the other outer islands. After the concessionaire has built an access road and selectively logged off the forest, these swidden farmers follow the road in, clear and burn the remaining forest, and then plant their crops in the ashes. They usually crop the land again during the second, third, and sometimes fourth following years, after which the land's plant cover is reduced to a fire-climax stand of *Imperata cylindrica*—whereupon these farmers then move on up the logging road to a fresh stand of forest and begin the cycle all over again (see also Vayda and Sahur 1985). To date, the government's principal response to this singularly destructive variant of swidden agriculture has consisted of trying to resettle the farmers involved into model villages. This response is based on the assumption that the guilty farmers are the *suku terasing* (isolated tribes) who originally inhabited the remote interiors of the logging concessions.

In fact, few if any of these logging-road cultivators come from such tribes (most of whom continue to practice traditional, "integral" swidden agriculture [Conklin 1957:2] in whatever corner of their traditional territories is left to them by the loggers). Most of them are lowland truck farmers, whose operations are financed by urban entrepreneurs. The latter provide chain saws, hired laborers, and seed to open up and plant the "truck swiddens," and then they provide vehicles to transport the harvest to the markets of Kalimantan's lowland cities. In short, the direct sponsors of this destruction of the forests are members of the urban elite (and the consumers of its fruits are the urban population as well). The indirect sponsors of this destruction are the logging concessionaires, whose contracts with the government typically make them responsible for controlling public access to the concession. In contrast, the forest-bound tribes, who to date have borne all of the blame for this destruction, neither sponsor, participate in, nor benefit from it. They are involved only in the sense that it is their traditional lands that are being ravaged—first, by the loggers, and second, by the truck farmers.

When destructive uses of the environment are investigated, therefore, the much maligned peasant is usually found to have either just cause for this destruction or else no role in it. On the other hand, when traditional uses of the environment by peasants are investigated, they are usually found to embody sound principles of utilization and conservation—which are often expressed through the idiom of ritual. This finding is well illustrated by several of the case studies in this volume. For example, Schefold shows that the impact of man on the natural environment is a matter of major and explicit concern to the Mentawai and is carefully regulated by them through ritual means. In his study of the Ngadha, Daeng shows how an optimal balance among the human population, the animal population, and the land resources is similarly maintained through ritual means. In my study of the Kantu', I show how ritual drinking helps to achieve an optimal distribution of grain and labor resources among the human population. Finally, Laksono shows how the central Javanese on Mount Merapi use ritual to interpret and respond to volcanic hazards. These examples are not aberrant: throughout Indonesia (and indeed, among traditional societies throughout the world), the proscriptions and prescriptions that are critical to the harmonious interaction of humans with their natural environment are expressed and enforced through ritual means.

This traditional role of ritual has been overlooked by the national government in its current campaign to protect the environment and promote rational, long-term utilization of natural resources. Instead of studying and making use of the traditional ritual systems for regulating critical environment relations, the government is attempting to create and impose an entirely new regulatory system based upon civil law. In practice, this has succeeded only in eliminating a traditional system that worked and introducing a new one that does not. Whereas fear of certain supernatural sanction resulted in strict observance of the traditional regulations, the lack of fear of uncertain civil penalties is resulting in widespread disregard of the new laws. This disregard is heightened by the fact that many government officials themselves do not take some of the new laws too seriously. Many of the military and police stationed in rural areas regard the shooting of wildlife for personal consumption or even resale as one of the perquisites of their office—regardless of whether such wildlife is protected by law. The ultimate impact of such attitudes can be disastrous for the environment. In the dry savannah of northwest Sumbawa, for example, there formerly was a traditional and strictly observed rule against killing does of *Cervus timorensis* during the annual foaling season. Today, the local subsistence hunters no longer observe this rule. With locally garrisoned soldiers using automatic weapons to slaughter dozens of deer at a time (which they then transport by army truck to urban markets), the local hunters see little point in its continued observance.

Just as tradition had (and in many cases still has) a role to play in regulating man's impact on the environment, so too is this true in the case of the environment's impact on man. In my study of the Kantu', for example, I note that the nature of the physical environment (given the extant swidden technology for exploiting it) necessitates the dispersal of the human population among semiautonomous socioeconomic units at the same time as it necessitates the periodic cooperation of these units in grain-labor exchanges. The traditional Kantu' system of ceremonial drinking makes these exchanges possible in spite of this dispersal, thereby mitigating the impact of environmental constraints on socioeconomic development.

A more dramatic example of how traditional culture mitigates the impact of environment on man is contained in Laksono's study of the Javanese on Merapi volcano. Laksono shows how, by means of a complex system of ritual belief, these Javanese deal with the psychological problems of life on one of the world's most dangerous volcanos. Of greater importance, he also shows that they can minimize this danger by means of a system of folk knowledge concerning the signs, types, and timing of volcanic eruptions. This system, he notes, has enabled the population of his study village to weather four major eruptions during the past forty years with just three fatalities. In contrast, twenty-nine of these villagers reportedly died of disease during their first two months of residence in the transmigration site in Sumatra to which they were sent for safety (in 1961) by the government. This is a good example of governmental underestimation of a traditional culture's ability to adapt to its old environment—albeit a dangerous one—and overestimation of its own ability to comprehend and master a new one.

The high initial mortality at the Sumatran transmigration site reflects not just a lack of information and preparation on the part of the transmigrants and (especially) the government, it also reflects the fact that any such radical transformation of the circumstances of life entails a cost in the health of the population involved. This is one of the principal theses of Appell's study, namely, that change is essentially traumatic for human populations. The more changes that occur at one time, the greater the trauma and the greater the threat to health. This threat, Appell maintains, is a major but largely ignored cost of social change. Certainly this cost has received little if any attention in Indonesian development, one of the guiding principles of which is that it is better to change a lot than a little. For example, government projects to improve and intensify agriculture typically involve not merely attempts to introduce new genetic material and methods of cultivation but also attempts to reorganize production and marketing along cooperative lines, resettle the population into model villages, implement family-planning programs, reorganize religion along orthodox lines, and so on. According to Appell's analysis, such a number of changes in the way of life of a people cannot be made without impairing their health. Consequently, such a number of changes should not be attempted—and these serious health costs not incurred—unless the development benefits expected are indeed extraordinary. This is rarely the case: most of the development schemes that entail such serious costs offer only modest benefits in exchange.

This imbalance is usually obvious to the intended beneficiaries, and where they have the option, they act accordingly. A good example of such action is the government's much troubled *Resetelmen Penduduk* (Population Resettlement) program, to resettle tribal swidden cultivators. A significant percentage of the resettlement villages built under this program have simply been abandoned (if, indeed, they were ever inhabited at all) by the tribal peoples for whom they were intended. Again, development officials tend to blame this on the "poor mental attitude" of the tribesmen. Appell's study suggests that the real problem is that the officials in question are asking their subjects to change too much, too fast, in exchange for too little.

Because of the great amount of change entailed in any resettlement scheme, the success of such schemes is—as just noted—highly problematic. Nevertheless, resettlement is a major tool of development policy in Indonesia. Development officials view it as the optimal solution to a wide variety of different purported problems in the rural areas, involving the welfare of both the rural environment and the rural peoples themselves. The most often cited problem of the first sort is the purported destruction of valuable forests by swidden cultivators. This was the principal rationale for many resettlement programs under the Dutch, as noted by Brewer in his study of Bima, and it is no less important today. Thus, forest protection is one of the manifest motives in the current government program to resettle the Mentawaians, as described in Schefold's study. The latent motives of this program, as noted earlier, may well be to increase not the protection but the exploitation of the forest.

As regards problems involving the welfare of the rural peoples, the one most often cited in connection with resettlement programs is the purported isolation of forest-dwelling tribesmen. The official government view is that the isolation of these peoples prevents them from sharing fully in the benefits of national development and that the best remedy is to resettle them in nuclear villages closer to centers of government administration. This is another of the principal stated motives in the government's plan to resettle the Mentawaians discussed above, as well as the Wana discussed by Atkinson and the Punan discussed by Hoffman. A second problem of social welfare that government planners try to remedy through resettlement involves environmental hazards. As noted earlier in the discussion of Laksono's case study, for example, one of the government's principal strategies for protecting the Javanese on Merapi volcano from the threat of eruptions has been to resettle them elsewhere.

The government's reliance on resettlement as a development panacea has not been justified by the results. In terms of the objective of improving human welfare, for example, many resettlement projects clearly fall short. Whereas safety from environmental hazards is supposed to be one of the justifications for resettlement, many resettlement sites—such as the one in Sumatra discussed by Laksono—prove to be equally if not more hazardous than the place of origin. Similarly, whereas resettlement is supposed to offer opportunities for agricultural intensification and development, the sites selected often prove to be less capable of supporting intensive agriculture than the places of origin. This last point, a basic albeit completely ignored constraint on most resettlement projects, is a simple function of the fact that population densities tend to be higher near centers of government administration than farther away, good land tends to be scarcer, and the soil tends to be more overworked (Burbridge, Dixon, and Soewardi 1981:241; Dove 1986b:119).

In terms of improving or safeguarding the quality of the rural environment, many resettlement programs also come up short. Whereas many resettlement programs are justified by the government as a way of ending peasant destruction of the rain forest, destructive use of the forest is not common among Indonesian peasants. Far more common is destructive use of the forest by the government itself, following resettlement. While the government usually presents watershed protection or nature conservation as its planned alternative to the extant peasant exploitation, in fact, the actual alternative is often industrial logging. Especially in Indonesia's outer islands, the resettlement of forest-dwelling peoples is often followed by—and hence is clearly stimulated by as well—the granting of commercial logging concessions.

It is doubtful whether industrial logging, even when accompanied by all possible measures to minimize its impact on the environment, is less destructive than the systems of traditional exploitation (e.g., integral swidden agriculture) carried out by Indonesia's tribesmen and peasants. In any case, in a majority of concessions, few if any of these measures are actually carried out: destructive extraction techniques are employed, soils are compacted, replanting is not done, and truck farmers are allowed into the concessions. In such cases, there is no question that the new use of the forest, made possible by the resettlement of its indigenous human population elsewhere, is more destructive of it than the old one was.

In short, there is real uncertainty as to how beneficial resettlement programs are for either the human communities or the natural environments involved. This uncertainty is great enough to suggest that the real motives for the resettlement program differ from the announced ones. One of the implicit motives, I believe, involves government suspicion of forest-dwelling peoples.[10] This suspicion can be traced back to the historic kingdoms of Java, which were unable to exercise either political or economic control over people who lived in and from the forest (Dove 1985a). This included people who by custom lived in the forest (viz., autochthonous Javanese tribesmen) as well as people who fled there to escape the king's authority (including criminals, pretenders to the throne, and peasants fleeing onerous tax burdens).

Over the centuries, the severity of this forest-based threat to central governments on Java has greatly diminished. Occasionally, criminals and opponents of the government still seek refuge in inaccessible forest areas. However, it is no longer possible for any indigenous forest community to operate beyond the political authority of the government simply by virtue of its location in the forest. Nevertheless, military and police posts in the rural areas of Indonesia's outer islands still routinely categorize forest-dwelling tribal peoples as their greatest "security" problem, calling them "communists" or "primitive communists" or "people susceptible to communist influence." There is no empirical basis for this categorization. The traditional peoples who still live in Indonesia's forests are, in fact, far more law abiding and politically conservative than the people who live in Indonesia's settled agricultural and urban areas. This point is borne out by recent Indonesian history: the supporters of the attempted coup against the government in 1965 came largely from the cities and lowland areas of Java and Bali. None were tribesmen from the remote, forested areas of the outer islands.

This confusion in official circles as to why people live in Indonesia's forests represents in part confusion over how they live there—in economic terms. As Hoffman notes in his study of the Punan, for example, development officials and other outsiders think that the Punan live in the forest in order to hunt pig. They do not realize that you do not have to live in the forest in order to hunt pig, although you do in order to engage full-time in the gathering of forest products for the international markets. There is just as little understanding in official circles of how people such as the Wana or Mentawaians wrest their living from the forest. This lack of understanding is clearly reflected in the kinds of development plans that are made for the forest peoples. Only by being ignorant of how people obtain a living from the forest and of how good a living is thereby attained could development officials recommend the resettlement of a group out of the forest and into a marginal agricultural area "in order to raise their standard of living."

The lack of knowledge among development planners of traditional uses of the forest returns us to a point made earlier, namely that the most knowledgeable person about this (or any other) environment is the tribesman or peasant who grew up in it and who depends on it for his livelihood. No outside observer can hope to acquire more than a fraction of the total botanical, zoological, and climatological knowledge of the tropical rain forest that is possessed, for example, by the average Punan or Mentawaian. Appell rightly notes in his study that this store of indigenous knowledge is a resource of great value and should be better utilized by development officials and scientists than it has been in the past. The future utilization of this kind of knowledge will be influenced by two conflicting trends in contemporary Indonesian society.

One trend is based on the elevation of formal schooling above all other sorts of knowledge, an elevation that leads to the extreme situation of university students being sent into the villages in the capacity of "experts." The second, contrary, trend is based on a newly revised opinion of traditional knowledge among some academics, and also on the reverence for traditional herbal lore and like types of knowledge that never entirely disappeared among the Indonesian (especially Javanese) elite. This latter trend is arguably reflected in the newly created presidential award (the *Kalpataru,* "Tree of Life") for villagers who have, using local ideas, resources, and knowledge, and without direction or remuneration from the government, distinguished themselves in the study, protection, and conservation of the natural environment.

Social Structure/Social Change

As I stated earlier, development officials in Indonesia see themselves first and foremost as agents of change. One apparent corollary of this self-image is an inability to believe that change can take place spontaneously, in the absence of their efforts and inputs. The mere possibility of such change is missing from the discourse of development in Indonesia. Never does one hear of a project expressly designed to quicken or strengthen some wholly indigenous and spontaneous development effort; and never does one see officials assuming the role of merely guiding some such indigenous effort. Always, theirs is the role of creating and initiating development projects from scratch. It is, indeed, an article of faith in official circles that the process of development is absent from and in fact alien to traditional societies in their natural state. In the absence of stimulation from the government's development bodies, it is assumed that these societies are static. Nothing could be further from the truth.

The traditional societies of Indonesia, as of other developing countries, are essentially dynamic. They are constantly evolving and changing, in response to both internal forces and changes in their external social and physical environments. Such evolution is readily seen in the historical data in this volume's case studies. Thus, Atkinson shows how the Wana have recently developed a new, more self-conscious and comparative view of their belief system, in response to criticism by outsiders of their purported lack of religion. Brewer shows how the Bimanese have adapted their land use practices to the policies and perceptions of successive central governments, always with the goal of trying to strengthen their claims to the land in the eyes of the government.[1] In his study of the Maloh, King describes how their traditional system of rank changed and diminished in importance under the influence of first the Dutch colonial government and Catholic missionaries, and then later the nationalist government. Daeng shows how, when the system of competitive feasting in Ngadha came under pressure from both the government and the Catholic church, resources that formerly went into feasting came to be channeled instead into the functional alternative of adjudication.

Not all of the changes cited in these case studies are due to the influences of outside forces. For example, Daeng shows that Ngadha society has also changed internally, in particular in terms of the relative importance of people versus land. This change has had its own impact on the traditional feasting system, by making people a new object of competition and brideprice/dowry a new means. Internally generated change also is evident in my study of the Kantu'. In the course of this century, their ceremonial system has diminished in both intensity and regional scope because—as I argue—of the development of rubber cultivation. Rubber provides each household and longhouse with a cushion against periodic failures of the rice harvest, thus reducing the need to seek assistance from other households and longhouses and thereby reducing as well the need for integration through ceremony.

Whether in response to internal or external forces, therefore, the norm for Indonesia's traditional societies is not stasis, but rather continual evolution and transformation. As a result, far from being inherently resistant to the adoption of innovations, they are characteristically open to it (see Johnson 1972). The readiness of even the most isolated and subsistence-oriented farmer to experiment with new cultigens is well known to all scholars who have taken the time to observe farmer behavior. Readiness to experiment is not, however, the same thing as readiness to assume risks. A farmer who is willing to plant a new cultigen on a small fraction of his field as an experiment can be said to be open to innovation; but one who is willing to plant his entire field with a new and untried cultigen—even at the behest of agricultural extension officers—is not being open to innovation, he is being foolhardy, and foolhardiness is a rare trait among Indonesian peasants.

Two good examples of this openness to innovation are discussed in the case studies in this volume. In his study of the Maloh, King describes how, when the traditional system of rank came under pressure from external forces and began to lose its former functional importance, alternate forms of socioeconomic differentiation were developed, in particular by the nonaristocratic classes that had fared worst under the traditional system. Similarly, when the competitive feasting of the Ngadha came under pressure from external forces and when its functional role was undercut by the waning power of the rajahs and the waxing power of the civil bureaucracy, the Ngadha abandoned it and shifted their energies to competition within this bureaucracy, concentrating their resources on education and litigation. The Ngadha and Maloh cases exemplify how traditional societies accept fundamental innovation when it is in their best interests. Readiness to accept such innovations can, indeed, be taken as a heuristic principle in the study of peasant development.

The corollary heuristic principle is that change or innovation that is not in the peasants' best interests will be rejected. A good example of this is presented in Laksono's study, involving the transmigration by the government of the Javanese on Mount Merapi to a site in Sumatra. When the villagers realized that they were being moved from an environment with a low mortality rate to one with a much higher rate, they reacted by returning to their original homes on Mount Merapi. Another example involves the health cadre program of Banjarnegara, as studied by Rienks and Iskandar. The selection and training of the cadres was carried out with no regard for local concepts of sickness and healing. As a result, the program failed to address the needs of the villagers and ultimately was rejected by them. A third example involves the ceremonial system in my study of the Kantu'. The government has condemned this system in ignorance of its pivotal role in the regional economy, as a consequence of which its efforts to restrict the system have been stoutly resisted by the tribesmen.

Although the grounds for rejection of development programs vary somewhat from case to case, there are some common elements. One of the most salient of these is the attempt to change, restrict, or eliminate some aspect of traditional culture before the government is willing or able to replace it. Because of the emphasis on change for its own sake, the possibility that traditional institutions are performing valuable functions that will have to be performed by some other institution if they are eliminated is rarely considered by development planners. If functional alternatives are needed and not provided, however, the society will suffer—a point that is elaborated theoretically in Appell's study and substantively in Brewer's. Brewer shows how government efforts to weaken village control over land, in the absence of simultaneous efforts to create alternative control institutions, greatly increased local inequities in land distribution and ownership. Schefold also addresses this problem in his study of the Mentawaians. After discussing the ecological function of traditional ritual proscriptions on hunting, he discusses the probable ill consequences if these proscriptions are abandoned and replaced with government regulations that do not address the same local ecological imperatives. In my study of the Kantu', I predict similar unhappy consequences if the government succeeds in eliminating the tribesmen's system of ceremonial feasting without creating its own institutions to regulate the regional flow of grain and labor. (This latter step is unlikely, because it presumes prior recognition of the function of the feasting system, a recognition that is obviously lacking.)

In all of these cases, the likelihood of ill consequences plays a role in the peasants' rejection of the development programs in question. Development officials in Indonesia, however, uniformly attribute such rejection to the peasants' poor *pola berpikir* (way of thinking) or *terbelakang* (backward) culture. The utility of this explanation, for the officials that promulgate it, is that it precludes any investigation into whether their own planning and execution of the development programs is to blame or not. The disutility of this explanation, for the peasants as well as officials, is that it encourages the belief that Indonesian peasants are mentally stubborn and backward, and consequently it offers no solution to development impasses with the peasantry other than "reeducation." As a result, enormous resources of time, labor, and money are devoted to *penyuluhan* (extension or training) for the peasants involved in development programs. The amount of resources devoted to this can indeed be taken as a reverse barometer of the quality of development planning: the worse the planning, the louder the calls for "extension" for the recalcitrant peasants.[12]

Evaluation

This tendency to blame all development problems on recalcitrant peasants is part of a broader pattern of poor evaluation, or even the complete lack of evaluation, of development programs in Indonesia. Rienks and Iskandar explicitly address this topic in their study of health cadres in Central Java. While undertaking this study, they observed that the government was giving ever-increasing support to the cadre program despite the fact that the selection, utilization, and even self-perception of the cadres was clearly at variance with the professed goals of the program. This discrepancy was made possible, they suggest, by an over-production of "normative" literature—describing and urging support for cadre programs—and an underproduction of empirical literature—evaluating how cadre programs have actually performed vis-à-vis their stated goals. There are other such examples among the case studies in this volume. Thus, Laksono shows that the transmigration of the Gimbal villagers from Central Java to Sumatra resulted in increased environmental threats to their health, despite the fact that the explicit purpose of the program was to reduce such threats. Similarly, Brewer shows that while the stated purpose of government intervention in land use and tenure in Bima was to promote social equity and intensify agricultural practices, the actual effect was to promote inequity, with little effect on intensification. In none of these cases did the development authorities themselves conduct the kind of studies that would have told them what effect their programs were actually having, as opposed to the effect they were supposed to be having.

Evaluative studies are needed not just to measure the actual performance of development programs, but also to weigh the merits of the traditional institutions that they threaten. Thus, Atkinson writes convincingly of the merits of the officially unsanctioned traditional religion of the Wana, as do Rienks and Iskandar of the officially ignored traditional system of curing in Central Java. Hoffman documents the economic merits of the much disparaged Punan nomadism, while Brewer does the same for Bimanese land tenure. The merits of traditional adaptation to volcanic hazards and the tropical rain forest are discussed by Laksono and Schefold, respectively, while Daeng and I discuss the merits of traditional ceremony and feasting, and Appell provides an evaluation of the merits of traditional society in general. In none of these case studies were the merits in question recognized by the development authorities, and in all cases this lack of recognition has gone hand-in-hand with their efforts to change or eliminate the traditional institutions.

Empirical evaluations of traditional institutions, as well as development alternatives, are an essential part of development planning. Many development planners in Indonesia appear to believe that "good intentions" obviate the need for such evaluations: they do not. The planner's pronouncement that a program is designed "for the good of the people" should not excuse it from critical scrutiny. The planner, after all, may simply be misinformed or uninformed, as is the case among the planners involved with virtually every traditional institution discussed in this volume. In addition, the planner may have unstated motives for supporting a program that differ from his stated ones. For example, a development official who proposes a program to replace grass roofs with corrugated iron ones may say that he is concerned about fire hazards; but if he also happens to control the sale of corrugated iron in the area, there is reason for suspecting that his stated concerns are not his only ones. To distinguish between manifest and latent motives in such cases, it is necessary not only to investigate any obvious self-interest on the part of the official involved, but also to make a comparative evaluation of both the traditional practice and the proposed alternative—for example, the actual incidence of grass-roof fires and the deleterious effects that corrugated iron has on health because of its lesser ability to insulate and its greater ability to condense water vapor. Such evaluations will help to reveal the role in development planning of latent motives, those that are known to the planners themselves as well as those of which even they are unaware (see Dove 1985a:32).

Some reports on development programs—in particular the largely quantitative reports on every aspect of development that are continually being produced by the Indonesian government—appear to be evaluative but in fact are not. An example of such reports, as cited in the study by Rienks and Iskandar, consists of the number of people that have been signed up for cadre training, the number of posts that have been established for weighing infants, the frequency with which weighing sessions are staged, and so on. Development officials favor these sorts of data because they are easily gathered and also, and more importantly, because they are inherently supportive of the projects that they describe. A recitation of the number of cadres, weighing posts, and weighing sessions, in a village implies the existence of a functioning health cadre program—even if such is not actually the case. As Rienks and Iskandar point out, not all of those who are signed up to become cadres attend the training sessions, nor do all of those who attend subsequently put their training into practice; not all weighing posts that are built are utilized; and not all weighing sessions that are held are attended.[13] Rienks and Iskandar suggest that it is the inherently deceptive nature of these sorts of data that enabled a poorly planned and poorly performing cadre program to receive ever greater support from the government. Another example in this volume is the transmigration program discussed by Laksono. This program has also been evaluated primarily in terms of simple numerical measures—the number of people moved, the number of houses built, the number of schools and mosques built, and so on. None of these measures the most important variables of all, the physical health and economic welfare of the transmigrants—both of which are known to have fallen drastically among some groups of transmigrants.[14]

Sound planning requires not just numerical reports on development projects, therefore, but analytic reports that assess their costs as well as their benefits. Extant planning and reporting tend to focus far more on project benefits than costs. A clear example of this is, again, the government's plan to transmigrate the villagers of Gimbal from Merapi volcano, as reported by Laksono in his study: the benefits of this transmigration—primarily freedom from the hazard of volcanic eruption —were the sole focus of attention; the possible hazards of this transmigration—psychological stress, a lowered standard of living, and the hazards to health at the transmigration site—received no attention whatsoever. The other studies in this volume contain similar examples. Thus, Brewer demonstrates that government reform of the Bimanese system of land tenure had the unintended and apparently unnoted effect of increasing inequities in land distribution and ownership. In her study of the Wana, Atkinson shows that attempts to acculturate tribal minorities through evangelical programs are having the opposite effect of alienating them from the government. In my study, I show that government efforts to abolish the Kantu' system of ceremonial feasting, if successful, will have an unforeseen and debilitating impact on the vital system of regional exchange. Hoffman similarly demonstrates that if the government succeeds in its efforts to resettle the Punan, there will be an unintended and detrimental impact on their valuable trade in forest products. Appell argues in his study that these unintended costs of development and change can be threatening to both personal and social health and that much greater efforts must be made to predict them, and weigh them, in advance.

The failure to predict such costs in advance, or to perceive them after the fact, may be due to simple ignorance or to what might be called "structural ignorance." I define "structural ignorance" as the failure to perceive that which is not in one's own best interests.[15] One of the most important examples of structural ignorance involves the failure of Indonesian planners to perceive the true opportunity costs—or any opportunity costs at all—of taking land out of peasant production for use in development schemes.[16] Many schemes that would be rejected as uneconomic if true opportunity costs were calculated (and this would include most of Indonesia's transmigration projects) are approved and funded when these costs are drastically lowered or eliminated altogether. The peasants whose costs and interests are thus depreciated do not always accept the situation passively, and their resistance—in effect, their insistence upon the developers' recognition of true opportunity costs—is one of the major problems besetting development projects in Indonesia today.

The developers' equally fervent insistence upon a false view of the economic costs of their projects is reflected in their reflexive tendency to attribute all peasant resistance to the peasants' *salah pahaman* (incorrect understanding). According to this view, peasant resistance to development projects is due not to the possibility that a project was planned without regard for the peasants' own interests, but rather to the fact that the project was simply not completely understood by (or adequately explained to) them. In a characteristically Indonesian (or, more accurately, Javanese) fashion, the possibility of government error is thereby categorized out of existence: there are no bad projects and mistreated peasants, but only "misunderstood" projects and "misunderstanding" peasants.[17]

This view of the peasants is dependent upon the special character of development research as carried out in Indonesia today. With rare exceptions, this research is structured so as to prevent any knowledge of either the actual impact of development projects on the peasants or their reaction to this impact. In most government sponsored studies of development, face-to-face contact with the peasants is actively (albeit unconsciously) avoided, as is actual inspection of their houses, gardens, and fields. If peasants are interviewed, it is almost always in the presence of local officials, thus precluding any possibility of eliciting candid opinions of the local development projects in which these same officials are involved. In any case, the very idea of asking peasants for their opinions of development projects is seen by most Indonesian academics as presumptuous—as treating the peasants as though they too were *ahli* (experts), on the same level as the academics themselves. In most studies, only the offices of local officials are visited, and only the officials themselves are interviewed. Most field time is devoted to copying the secondary data with which such offices are invariably well blessed. Statistical summaries of these data form the basis of most "field reports," notwithstanding the fact that all or most of these data will already have been sent to the sponsoring agency by the local offices themselves. Thus, the typical development study tells the sponsoring agency nothing new about its most troublesome constituency, the peasantry. This supports the status quo and hence is welcomed by the large majority of development planners.

This type of research is supported by the character of Indonesia's academic culture, in particular by the absence of peer review. The majority of research reports on development projects are reviewed only by the sponsoring government agency, between whom and the authors there is a collusion of interests in not being critical of uncritical analysis. The presentation of such reports in public seminars attended by scholars with no vested interest in either the project or research in question is the exception rather than the rule. Even more exceptional is the publication of such reports in one of the country's scientific journals—not one of which, in any case, uses peer review to evaluate papers submitted for publication. In short, the scholarly evaluation of development projects in Indonesia is carried out in the near total absence of the sort of review by fellow scholars that is usually deemed essential to maintaining standards not only of excellence, but of objectivity as well.[18]

These deficiencies in development research are both easy and difficult to remedy. The easy part is including the peasants' perspective in development studies. This involves no more than talking with them about their wants and needs, their hopes and fears, in an atmosphere free of coercion or intimidation. The difficult part is providing the incentive to do this. Before Indonesia's academics will carry out genuine studies of the impact of development on the country's peasants, they will have to know that this is what the developers want and what their peers expect. Before the developers will demand this, in turn, they must come to the realization that their own long-term interests will suffer if they do not get reliable and candid feedback on the impact of their projects on the peasant population. I believe that some of Indonesia's development planners are now coming to this realization.

Summary and Conclusion

I began this discussion with the proposition that traditional culture is not inimical to socioeconomic development, the fears of most development planners in Indonesia notwithstanding. I examined this proposition with respect to several different aspects of Indonesian culture, drawing data from each of the ten case studies in this volume. The first aspect discussed was ideology. In this section, I suggested that traditional Indonesian systems of belief merit recognition both as "religions" and as empirically valid systems of knowledge about the real world. In the succeeding section on economics, I suggested that a reassessment of Indonesia's much disparaged traditional systems of subsistence (including swidden agriculture, sago cultivation, and hunting-and-gathering) is in order. I went on to critique prevailing misconceptions regarding production, consumption, and land tenure in tribal and peasant economies. Next, in reviewing ecology I discussed the wisdom of most traditional adaptations to the environment, as well as the lesser wisdom of many developmental solutions to environmental problems—in particular those solutions predicated upon population resettlement. In the fourth section, I discussed the dynamic character of traditional cultures. I noted that these cultures are characteristically open to change, whether generated internally or externally in the course of development, except (in the latter case) for change that purports to be beneficial but in fact is not. In the fifth and final section, I discussed the need for more evaluative reporting on the planning and implementation of development programs. I suggested that such reporting should look at latent as well as manifest functions, at costs as well as benefits, and at the perspective of the peasants as well as that of the government planners. I ended this discussion with a comment on the relationship between the way traditional peoples are perceived by Indonesia's development community and the way they are studied by Indonesia's academic community.

In summary, most development planners in Indonesia view traditional culture, before the fact, as at best no asset to development and at worst as a hindrance to it; after the fact, they blame it for many of their failures. Since there is little or no empirical basis for this view, the question arises as to how it has come into being. Indonesian history throws some light on this question: officials of the Dutch colonial administration held a view of traditional culture that is very similar to that held by officials today. For example, like contemporary officials, the colonial officials viewed ceremonial consumption as a waste of scarce resources that would be better devoted to surplus production or investment. In her study, Atkinson notes that both the colonial and the contemporary governments deemed it advisable to try to resettle the Wana out of the interior of Sulawesi. Brewer, in his study of the Bimanese, demonstrates that the colonial and contemporary governments intervened in their system of land tenure for the same reasons, namely, to constrain the practice of swidden agriculture and to lessen village control over land. These and other similarities in colonial and contemporary government policy (more marked yet in agriculture and forestry; see Dove 1985a) clearly cannot be ascribed to similar cultural backgrounds, so they must reflect similar economic and political objectives.

One such objective appears to be misrepresentation of the true purposes of development policies. During both colonial and contemporary times, it has been common practice for officials to justify in terms of the "national interest" development policies that in fact benefited the interests of only a single person, group, or industry. Whereas peasant resistance to such policies has been attributed to treasonable sentiments or ignorance, in reality it has often been a simple matter of the peasants defending their personal interests against the equally personal interests of the policy makers. The public politics of both eras have made it impossible for officials to admit (or even perceive) this, however: hence conflicts between the self-interests of the two different groups (viz., officials and peasants) have been framed as conflicts between the welfare of the country as a whole and the self-indulgence of one particular group, as conflicts between national development and backwards peasant culture. Because this has been going on for so long in Indonesia, and because the conflicts of interest involved are so pervasive, this way of framing relations between the peasantry and the government has become embedded in the culture of officialdom: it has become a latent, preattentive trait.

All of the contemporary government's objectives in dealing with traditional cultures were not shared by the colonial government. One revealing exception involves the separate identities of Indonesia's many ethnic groups. This diversity presented no special problem to the colonial government: itself non-Indonesian and ethnically homogeneous, it could with perfect equality "represent" (in fact, oppress) all of the country's ethnic groups. Ethnic diversity has presented a problem to the postcolonial government, however: although it necessarily purports to represent all of the country's ethnic groups, the government has been dominated by Javanese and Malays. As a result of this dominance, Javanese and Malay cultures have been accorded a political legitimacy that has not been accorded the other cultures of the archipelago; and deviance from this politically superordinate culture has come to be seen as political deviance, as subversion.[19] As a result, political coercion has come to be seen as an appropriate government response to continued cultural differentiation. As examples of such coercion, both Atkinson and Schefold describe the apparently dire threats made against tribal peoples who continue to wear beads and loincloths and follow traditional religious practices.

To the extent that the insignia of regional tribal identity reflect the continued heterogeneity of Indonesia's population, they do reflect a potential source of political tension. However, to attempt to deal with this tension by, for example, outlawing loincloths is to mistake a symbol for its referent. And this referent itself, namely ethnic diversity, has in fact not proven to be a great threat to Indonesia's national security. During the aborted communist coup of 1965, none of those who raised arms against the central government were loincloth-clad, spear-carrying tribesmen. The country's tribal minorities supported the central government during this time of need or stayed out of the conflict altogether. For example, the Dayak tribes of West Kalimantan, who are today suspected of subversive tendencies because they live in longhouses and oppose ill-planned development projects, beheaded many of the supporters of the 1965 coup who, after its collapse, fled into the jungle.[20]

As this last point demonstrates, the misinterpretation and misrepresentation of traditional cultures in development planning is made possible by, and indeed necessitates, a profound lack of knowledge about them. It would not be possible in the face of abundant, publicly held, empirical knowledge of these cultures. To make it possible, two things are necessary. One is the effective lack of empirical study of traditional cultures by development planners and scientists. As discussed earlier, many studies are carried out, but they are so structured as to ensure that almost no worthwhile data are obtained. The second prerequisite to misinterpretation and misrepresentation is the effective lack of any feedback or input from the members of these cultures. (The absence of any such input in development planning is mentioned in the case studies by Brewer, Laksono, and Rienks and Iskandar; and it is implicit in most of the rest of the studies as well.) The reason for its absence is implicit in the official term for the principal interface between officials and peasants in Indonesia, *penyuluhan* (extension)—meaning a situation in which the officials talk and the peasants listen (or pretend to listen, as is more often the case). So long as this is the case, development planners will not hear what they apparently do not want but nevertheless need to hear from their peasant clientele, namely, the peasants' own accounting of what they need—and what they do not need—to improve their way of life.

Notes

1. President Suharto is officially known as the *Bapak Pembangunan* (Father of Development) and his cabinet as the *Kabinet Pembangunan* (Development Cabinet).

2. The two Javanese case studies are exceptions, due to the predominance within Indonesia of the Javanese people and culture. An associated cultural chauvinism makes the work of missionaries relatively more difficult among the Javanese than among the country's minority cultures.

3. This faith has received unwitting support from the development of a special subfield of rural sociology devoted to assessing the basic economic, ecological, and social parameters of a given area or society in periods of several days to several weeks. When employed by the foremost academicians and development scientists, these extremely sophisticated and demanding techniques—commonly referred to by the rubric of "rapid rural appraisal"—can produce sound, useful empirical data. When employed by the average scholar or development official, as is typically the case, these techniques usually produce data that are at best innocuous and irrelevant, and at worst, flawed and potentially destructive.

4. The students' own expectations appear to have little to do with either teaching or learning. The acronym *KKN* is sarcastically interpreted in student circles as *Kisah Kasih Sayang* (love story) or *Kawin Kemudian Nikah* (sex before

marriage), referring to the hopes of the male students for sexual liaisons with village women.

5. The one exception to this is increasing government anxiety over the potential political threat from educated and underemployed urban youth.

6. The labor-based value system of subsistence farmers has long been known to anthropologists (e.g., Leach 1949), for whom farmers—and their likes and dislikes—are a major object of study; but it is still unknown to many agricultural scientists, whose object of study is not farmers per se, but farms.

7. This was not always the case (Ruddle et al. 1978:134–135).

8. The productivity of the Punan economy, like that of all hunting and gathering economies, is based on high returns to labor—higher even than in the swidden economies discussed earlier (see Sahlins 1972:chap. 1).

9. This has long been the standard reaction of Indonesian government officials to any opposition to their plans or programs on the part of the peasants. For example, Javanese wet rice farmers who refused to participate in *Bimas* rice production programs in the late 1960s were labeled "pro-communist" (Hansen 1973:113).

10. Another implicit motive for resettlement programs is their financial attraction: any such program involves the sale and purchase of land, the awarding of contracts for land improvement and house construction, and the procurement of equipment and commodities. All of this activity presents the broader development community with opportunities for participation and profit.

11. This sort of adaptation to government perceptions of reality, in particular the reality of land use and tenure, is pervasive throughout Indonesia (see Dove 1983:87).

12. One of the longest-running examples of this in Indonesia is the national rice intensification program. Originally established in the belief that the peasants would not respond to simple economic incentives because of "cultural constraints," its so-called *penyuluhan terpimpin* (guided extension) employed frankly coercive measures to get them to behave as the government wanted them to (Hansen 1973:5–6, 11–12).

13. See Mubyarto, Soetrisno, and Dove (1983) for further discussion of the gap between the statistics and the reality of development in Indonesia.

14. It would be relatively easy to measure the physical and economic health of the transmigrants using more complex numerical measures, such as infant mortality rates and per capita caloric intakes. These could be compared with measurements at the transmigrants' point of origin, to yield a clear, empirical measure of the program's success. However, I have never seen nor heard of such a comparison in any government literature or speeches pertaining to this program.

15. Wallerstein (1974) felicitously called this an "ideological deflection" from reality. See Dove (1985a) for further discussion of such deflections in Indonesian officialdom.

16. For example, when the government forest department decided to plant pine trees on *Imperata* grasslands in South Kalimantan, it assessed the existing economic use or value of the grasslands as negligible, completely ignoring the

extant use of these grasslands—under an intensive system of dry rice agriculture and animal husbandry—by the resident peasants (Dove 1986b).

17. An early example of this is cited by Hansen (1973:117n): "On December 28, a spokesman from the provincial Department of Agriculture in West Java told the press that *Bimas* was achieving its production targets. When asked about reports that peasants were rejecting the program, the official explained that this was not true; he said that if some peasants were in opposition, this was because they did not understand the purpose of *Bimas.*"

18. These criticisms apply with equal if not greater force to the international development community in Indonesia. Its members infrequently present the results of their work for discussion in public seminars, and they even less frequently publish them in international scholarly journals. For reasons that are incomprehensible to me, the scholarly publishing that is required of Western scholars who teach, as proof of their continued development and competence, is not required of Western scholars involved in development—despite the fact that the latter have the lives of Third World peoples in their hands and hence should be held to the highest standards of all. In the absence of some other explanation, this distinction between university-based scientists and development scientists suggests that Western society places a higher value on the education of its youth than it does on the development of the Third World.

19. This view of tribal minorities appears to be a function of the highly centralized character of the Indonesian government, rather than the particular political philosophy that this government embraces. The communist government of Vietnam, for example, although espousing a very different political philosophy, regards its own tribal minorities with equal suspicion, although the purported rationale for this suspicion is different: whereas the Indonesian government suspects its tribesmen of being communist subversives, the Vietnamese government suspects its tribesmen of being imperialist diehards (Hickey 1982).

20. Admittedly, not all of those who fled into the jungles in the aftermath of the coup were supporters of it. Many otherwise innocent Chinese shopkeepers and farmers were forced to flee, and some of them doubtless fell victim to the Dayak as well. However, since the Dayak attacks on the refugees were implicitly (and in some cases explicitly) supported by local government officers, the error was not theirs. What is important in the context of the current discussion is that the Dayak allied themselves with the central government against its perceived enemies.

References Cited

Burbridge, Peter, John A. Dixon, and Bedjo Soewardi
1981   "Forestry and Agriculture: Options for Resource Allocation in Choosing Lands for Transmigration Development." *Applied Geography* 1:237–258.

Conklin, Harold C.
  1957   *Hanunóo Agriculture: A Report on an Integral System of Shifting Cultivation
          in the Philippines.* Rome: FAO (Forestry Development Paper No. 12).

Dove, Michael R.
  1981   "A Tribal Pork Taboo in Local and Regional Perspective." Paper
          read at the 80th Annual Meeting of the American Anthropological
          Association, Los Angeles, 2–6 December.

  1982   "The Myth of the 'Communal' Longhouse in Rural Development:
          The Kantu' of Kalimantan." In *Too Rapid Rural Development,* edited
          by Colin MacAndrews and L. S. Chin, pp. 14–78. Athens: Ohio
          University Press.

  1983   "Theories of Swidden Agriculture and the Political Economy of
          Ignorance." *Agroforestry Systems* 1:85–99.

  1985a   "The Agro-Ecological Mythology of the Javanese, and the Political
          Economy of Indonesia." *Indonesia* 39:1–36.

  1985b   "Plantation Development in West Kalimantan I: Extant Population/
          Land Balances." *Borneo Research Bulletin* 17 (2): 95–105.

  1985c   *Swidden Agriculture in Indonesia: The Subsistence Strategies of the Kaliman-
          tan Kantu'.* Berlin: Mouton.

  1986a   "Plantation Development in West Kalimantan II: The Perceptions
          of the Indigenous Population." *Borneo Research Bulletin* 18 (1): 3–27.

  1986b   "Peasant versus Government Perception and Use of the Environ-
          ment: A Case Study of Banjarese Ecology and River Basin Develop-
          ment in South Kalimantan." *Journal of Southeast Asian Studies* 17 (1):
          113–136.

  1986c   "The Practical Reason of Weeds in Indonesia: Peasant versus State
          Views of *Imperata* and *Chromolaena.*" *Human Ecology* 14 (2): 163–190.

Hansen, Gary E.
  1973   *The Politics and Administration of Rural Development in Indonesia: The Case
          of Agriculture.* Berkeley: Center for South and Southeast Asian Stud-
          ies, University of California (Research Monograph No. 9).

Hickey, Gerald C.
  1982   *Free in the Forest: Ethnohistory of the Vietnamese Central Highlands, 1954–
          1976.* New Haven: Yale University Press.

Holleman, J. F., ed.
  1981   *Van Vollenhoven on Indonesian Adat Law.* The Hague: Martinus Nijhoff
          (Koninklijk Instituut voor Taal-, Land- en Volkenkunde, Transla-
          tion Series No. 20).

Johnson, Allen W.
  1972   "Individuality and Experimentation in Traditional Agriculture."
          Human Ecology 1 (2): 149–159.

Leach, Edmund R.
1949   "Some Aspects of Dry Rice Cultivation in North Burma and British Borneo." In "Techniques and Economic Organization Among Primitive Peoples," edited by Adrian Digby, pp. 26–28. *The Advancement of Science* 6 (2): 23–28.

Maass, A.
1902   *Bei liebens wurdigen Wilden: Ein beitrage zur Kenntnis der Mentawei-Insulaner.* Berlin: Susserott.

Mubyarto, Loekman Soetrisno, and Michael R. Dove
1983   "Problems of Rural Development in Central Java: Ethnomethodological Perspectives." *Contemporary Southeast Asian Studies* 5 (1): 41–52.

Pelzer, Karl J.
1978   "Swidden Cultivation in Southeast Asia: Historical, Ecological, and Economic Perspectives." In *Farmers in the Forest: Economic Development and Marginal Agriculture in Northern Thailand,* edited by Peter Kunstadter, E. C. Chapman, and Sanga Sabhasri, pp. 271–286. Honolulu: East-West Center.

Prawiroatmojo, S.
1981   *Bausastra Jawa-Indonesia* [Javanese-Indonesian dictionary.] 2 vols., 2d ed. Jakarta: Gunung Agung.

Ruddle, Kenneth; Dennis Johnson; Patricia K. Townsend; and John D. Rees
1978   *Palm Sago: A Tropical Starch from Marginal Lands.* Honolulu: East-West Center.

Sahlins, Marshall
1972   *Stone Age Economics.* Chicago: Aldine/Atherton.

Spencer, J. E.
1966   *Shifting Cultivation in Southeastern Asia.* Berkeley and Los Angeles: University of California Press.

Vayda, Andrew P., and Ahmad Sahur
1985   "Forest Clearing and Pepper Farming by Bugis Migrants in East Kalimantan: Antecedents and Impact." *Indonesia* 39:93–110.

Wallerstein, Immanuel
1974   *The Modern World System I: Capitalist Agriculture and the Origins of the European World-Economy in the Sixteenth Century.* New York: Academic Press.

PART I: IDEOLOGY

1. Religion and the Wana of Sulawesi

JANE M. ATKINSON

Abstract

While the majority of Indonesia's citizens today are ensured religious freedom, the situation is less clear for members of Indonesia's ethnic minorities who hold to traditional ways. This paper examines Indonesian religious policy from the perspective of pagan members of the Wana population of Poso district in Central Sulawesi. By insisting on conversion to a world religion as a prerequisite for development and full participation as citizens, it is argued, the nation is hampered in dealing effectively with its traditionally minded ethnic minorities.

Introduction

The status of traditional religions is an issue that affects a number of Indonesia's traditional minorities. Rather than treating the issue in general terms, this paper focuses on the religious situation of the Wana people of East Central Sulawesi with whom I conducted research from 1974 through 1976.[1] It is hoped that this case will illuminate some aspects of Indonesian religious policy by exploring reactions to that policy on the part of one of the groups it is designed to affect.

Before turning to the details of the case, some introductory remarks about the approach to be taken are in order. Anthropology has a popular reputation among many as an antiquarian field dedicated to the preservation of curious but inconsequential information about obscure peoples. But cultural anthropology has moved far from its nineteenth-century role as a repository of data about supposedly vanishing cultures. Today, the cultural anthropologist seeks to investigate systems of thought and action through which people in a society deal with experience. Details of custom once collected as oddities or survivals from a prehistoric past are now examined in terms of their significance for social actors and the insights they offer into the workings of social systems. Ethnography, the investigative process used for anthropological research, therefore requires an extended field stay and serious efforts to learn the language, concerns, and perspectives of the people being studied. The anthropologist does not go to the field to impose his/her cultural understandings unreflectively on informants, but rather to explore how people in another society make sense of the world. This paper is dedicated to that end.

The preceding paragraph may suggest how contemporary anthropology, far from being a storeroom of dusty curios, can offer some critical perspectives essential to development planning. Designers of policy need to know not only what their own objectives are but also how their programs will be received by the people they are designed to affect. Sometimes the view from the planners' office does not match the realities of the situations they wish to change. Rather than relying simply on their own view of the world, policy makers can draw on the insights provided by ethnographic research in communities they hope to influence. Such insights can provide helpful and corrective feedback for development plans.

While this paper may therefore be of some interest to policy makers, it will not address specific government programs regarding religion and *suku terasing* (isolated tribes). There are several reasons for this. First, most of my research was conducted in the Wana area, far from the agencies responsible for formulating policy. Second, policies as formulated in national and provincial centers are not necessarily the policies actually applied in local areas. Finally, my focus here concerns Wana understandings of national attitudes regarding religion, not the intentions of policy makers. I want to show how national religious concerns are actually perceived and received by the Wana, as opposed to what policy makers intend to convey. It is my hope that an analysis of Wana interpretations of national and religious policy will be of more value than any comments I could give about its formulation in Jakarta or Palu (the latter the capital city of Central Sulawesi).

A final word concerning the tone of this article. Because I am treating religion from the Wana perspective, much of what is said may seem critical of the dominant society and its religious views. No disrespect is intended by the inclusion of such material. This is merely an attempt to convey as accurately as possible the views of the Wana, in the hope that this may prove thought-provoking for those (in government and elsewhere) who are used to seeing these issues in a different light. As an American and a cultural anthropologist, I have yet another set of perspectives, and these will be identified where relevant in the following discussion.

The Wana and Their Relations with the Broader World

Because the Wana people are not well known beyond their rather isolated region, a brief ethnographic introduction is in order. The Wana are swidden farmers who inhabit the mountainous interior of the sub-districts of Ulu Bongka, Bungku Utara, and Barone in the district of Poso. Exact census figures do not exist, but the Wana may number as many as 5,000 people. While they are relatively isolated by virtue of their location, the Wana have by no means remained untouched by events in the wider world. In the last century, the Wana were partially incorporated into coastal sultanates. Portions of the population paid tribute to Raja Bungku to the south and Raja Tojo to the north. In the first decade of the twentieth century, the Dutch moved into the area to administer the Wana directly. Finding the geographical isolation of the Wana to be an administrative problem, the Dutch tried to ease the task of governance by moving the Wana population into coastal settlements, just as the Indonesian government much later attempted to do (I refer here to the *suku terasing* projects developed in the 1970s under the auspices of the social department). Then, as now, Wana resisted the move, objecting to relocation to inferior farmland and alien surroundings. The Dutch administration eventually abandoned their efforts to relocate the population and decided to permit the Wana to remain in their homeland on the condition that they register with the government and establish permanent, nucleated *kampung* (villages). Many Wana cooperated with these demands. Villages were built and schools begun at a number of sites in the interior. Dutch control ended with World War II. During the war, a small group of Japanese soldiers were posted in the interior with plans to build an airfield, but their plans were never realized. Since 1945, the Indonesian government has had jurisdiction over the area. Its administration has varied in effectiveness and scope depending on local officials and policy, as well as time and place.

Though they live in the hilly interior, Wana have been integrated into coastal trade networks for generations. Dependent on coastal sources of cloth, salt, and metal tools, they have relied on trade to obtain these necessities. During Dutch times and in the early years of the Republic, Wana engaged in a thriving damar trade. When I did my research in the mid-1970s, the damar market had sunk into a serious decline, as the widespread use of petroleum-based synthetics freed foreign industries from reliance on natural sources of resin. To compensate for the de-

A Wana Shaman at a Healing Ceremony

A Wana Man Arranges Chickens for a Farming Celebration

pressed damar market, Wana have come to rely on other sources of cash and trade goods, including rice, rattan, and a variety of other products from forest and garden.

Politically and economically, then, Wana have had dealings for generations with coastal populations. Over the years, some Wana have been assimilated into coastal society. The To Ampana, Muslims who speak another dialect of the Wana language, are regarded as close relations. In addition, members of other ethnic groups, most noticeably Mori, have moved and married into Wana communities. During my fieldwork I encountered quite a few Wana who, as individuals and families, had moved back and forth between coastal and interior regions.

In conjunction with their familiarity with other ethnic groups, the Wana have been acquainted with Islam for a century at least, and probably longer. A. C. Kruyt's (1930:418) account of the Wana, based on his tour of the area in 1928, contains a Wana tale of two brothers, one pagan and elder, the other Muslim and younger. (The term "pagan" is used here to refer to someone who has not converted to one of the "world religions.") The Muslim brother, offended by the life of his pork-eating brother, tries to convince him to convert to Islam. A better life on earth and in heaven are the reasons he cites. The brothers take their debate before God, who upholds the worthiness of the pagan brother's earthly and heavenly existence on the grounds that he is the elder. The story serves as evidence that conversion to Islam has long been an issue for the Wana. Over the years many Wana have entered Islam, some temporarily, others permanently. In other ways as well, Islam has had a considerable impact on Wana culture.[2]

Christianity is a newer import to the region. Prior to World War II, some Christian Mori had arrived in the area, and a Dutch missionary named Perdoc spent some time in Lemo in the southern Wana region, but most of my informants regard Christianity as a postwar phenomenon. Asked what religion the Dutch had, older informants speculated that the Dutch probably possessed their own traditional religion just as the Wana do. Whatever the Dutch religion was, they indicated, the Dutch did not force it upon the Wana. Since World War II, there have been efforts by Protestants in Central Sulawesi to spread their religion through the Wana area, and Wana converts have assisted in these efforts. In 1979 a new group, the New Tribes Mission, an evangelical organization based in the United States, stationed a missionary family in an interior Wana community.

It is difficult to say just how many Wana are Christian or Muslim, or just how permanent and meaningful these labels are. Most Wana converts with whom I am acquainted say that they adopted a world religion out of fear of government reprisals. A common pattern is to convert when afraid, then revert to traditional ways when the threat of persecution recedes a little. The picture to be presented below derives primarily from pagan Wana communities and from people who may have at one time converted but have since given up the adopted practices. Still, because of the fluidity of religious affiliation in the area, the positions outlined here are familiar and meaningful not only to pagans but to many Muslim and Christian Wana as well.

With the increasing presence of world religions in their area, Wana have become distinctly aware that the government and the nation at large wish them to convert. This realization has caused considerable consternation. Fueling this consternation have been threats and rumors forecasting dire consequences for those who resist conversion. The sources of these threats and rumors include Muslims and Christians (some of them Wana) who wish to frighten pagans into accepting a world religion. They also include pagan Wana themselves who speculate that violence will be their fate for not converting. Fears of aerial bombings and military squads bent on death and torture were rampant in the Wana region during my study. Informants claimed to have heard that pagans would have their necks slit like chickens and their genitals cut open and rubbed with salt if they refused to convert. Apart from the physical threats, pagan Wana are very conscious of the scorn with which they are regarded by many Muslims and Christians. Some report having been told to their face that they lack the personal worth of a dog or a chicken because they have no religion. Such threats and abuse do not endear many Wana to the new faiths.

Traditional Wana Religion

In response to claims by the larger society that they lack a religion, pagan Wana assert that they do possess a religion. What I wish to examine in the remainder of this paper is the way in which Wana have formulated a response to their Muslim and Christian critics. In order to do so, it will be necessary to examine the premises that underlie Indonesian views of religion, as well as the premises on which Wana construct their rejoinder. This study will demonstrate that a religion cannot be studied in a vacuum. Instead, its analysis requires detailed consideration of the social and historical context in which it has evolved. For example, if one were to examine the rise of Indian Buddhism, one would need to consider as well Hinduism and other aspects of the Indian society out of which Buddhism grew and to which it was a response. Similarly, the Near Eastern religions—Judaism, Christianity, and Islam—can each be studied as responses to particular social and historical conditions, including the presence and influence of other religions in the area. In short, religions do not arise *ex nihilo*. Viewing their development as attempts to grapple with issues current in their time can offer considerable insight into the forms they take. Here, what the Wana term their religion will be examined as the Wana side of an exchange with Indonesian society at large.

Put another way, this paper explores a conflict phrased in terms of a debate over suitable definitions of religion. My task as an anthropologist is to unravel what is meant by people on both sides of the argument. My task is emphatically not to pronounce once and for all what religion is. For me religion is, in methodological terms, a matter of what informants say it is. Yet as an anthropologist I too have my culture, which furnishes me with a working definition of religion, one which it is only fair to make explicit. Following Clifford Geertz (1966), I approach religion as the system of symbolic forms that give profound expression to the fundamental nature of existence and serve to orient individuals and communities to their world. This definition is deliberately very broad and presumably very open-minded. It does not presume or deny the objective truth of any given religious system. Its value is that it permits examination of the way people in a given society find ultimate meaning in their world.

Often, an anthropologist studying a culture finds in it no indigenous word for religion. I suggest that a distinct term for religion arises only in societies with specialized professional hierarchies dedicated to the management of the sacred or in societies that have come in contact with other societies possessing such institutions. The Wana today, like their fellow Indonesians, have adopted the word *agama* as the result of such contact.[3] To my knowledge, there is no term with the same meaning in their own language. Religion, as an institution set apart from the rest of cultural life, appears to be an introduced idea. But to say that formerly the Wana did not have religion (in the general sense outlined above) is like saying the Balinese traditionally lacked art because they had no specific term for it (Black and Hoefer 1974:84). Just as art is an integral part of everyday life in Bali, so one can perceive something "religious" inextricably bound up in Wana cultural experience.

If I apply the definition of religion presented above to Wana society, some central features of what may be called "traditional Wana religion" emerge. Wana cosmology defines the nature of the world and its inhabitants with reference to their creation by a single God known as *Pue*, "Owner" or "Lord." It posits a subsequent division of reality into hidden and apparent dimensions. Whereas at one time in the past humans had access to all facets of experience, they are now ordinarily excluded from certain realms because of their corporal being. Yet those hidden realms of reality are the sources of the knowledge, power, and other influences that critically affect human existence. Justice and goodness

as well as evil and suffering all derive from the hidden reality. In order
to cope with these powerful but unseen influences over their lives, people must rely on the mediation of shamans, individuals who can gain
access to the hidden sides of experience to tap the knowledge and
powers that originate therein. Human health and well-being depend on
the shamans' negotiations with the hidden world. And because the
physical and spiritual states of individuals and their communities are
affected by the behavior of individuals, because a person's thoughts and
actions can have serious consequences for the well-being of others and
vice versa, shamans negotiate not simply matters of physical health, but
also social, moral, and spiritual concerns as well. (Those who mock the
naïvete of shamanic healing as unscientific and ineffectual fail to recognize that shamans are treating more than physical symptoms; they are
the moral and spiritual arbitrators of the society.[4])

So far I have treated religion in anthropological terms and asserted
that the Wana have something that functions as religion in their society
although they themselves have not self-consciously set it apart institutionally or intellectually as such. In Weberian terms, it is a traditional
rather than a rationalized system. That is, it has been embedded in
everyday life and has not been subject to the institutional specialization
and systematization chracteristic of world religions. But as I noted at
the beginning of this paper, an anthropologist must not simply impose
the categories of his/her culture, anthropological or otherwise, and
ignore the categories and perspectives of informants themselves. The
complex system sketched above is not the first thing that comes to mind
for Wana when they discuss the nature of *agama* (which they do a great
deal). When Wana use the term *agama,* they allude to something rather
different from what I have outlined here. Indeed, their concept of *agama*
represents a dramatic reworking of traditional cultural concepts. It represents the transformation of a traditional religious system provoked by
challenges from representatives of world religions. The picture to be
presented here runs counter to the view that small-scale, nonindustrial
systems are static and unchanging, stagnant holdovers from antiquity.
Wana religion cannot be pigeonholed as primitive animism. It is not an
ossified survival of a paleolithic past, but instead a dynamic system that
has developed and adapted to cope with changing circumstances. The
following analysis will trace this process as it was evident in the 1970s.

The Concept of Religion in Indonesian National Society

Following the approach being proposed here, in order to examine the
recent development of Wana religion one needs to consider the wider

context in which it has occurred. Particularly important are wider Indonesian assumptions about the nature of religion and the association of religion and national identity.

The word *agama* derives from Sanskrit and no doubt was imported along the early Indonesian-Indian trade routes. Historians have speculated that local Indonesian rulers adopted elements of Hindu and Buddhist culture to validate their status and enhance their prestige. Indian religion in this period was a hallmark of the royal courts. Literacy entered the archipelago at this time as well. Perhaps this was the beginning of the strong association Indonesians draw between writing and religion. Islam, a later arrival along the trade routes, intensified respect for religion and scripture through its universalism and the supreme importance it places upon the Koran. What is more, Islam brought with it a sharp distinction between heathens and "people of the Book." While less influential in terms of religious conversions, the Dutch colonial presence in its later years may have reinforced the view that true religion is very different from pagan beliefs, and that the former is a part of progress while the latter is only a cause for shame. For well over a millennium, then, *agama* has been associated with sophistication, education, power, and internationalism.

The central place religion occupies in Indonesian values is best expressed in the *Pancasila,* the five principles of the Republic. One of these principles is *bertuhan* (belief in God), which thus stands out as a fundamental tenet of Indonesian society. The formulation of this principle is liberal and tolerant. While the overwhelming majority of the population is Muslim, the *Pancasila* upholds religious freedom for those belonging to other faiths. In principle, Indonesia's tolerance toward religious minorities is exceedingly generous, but this generosity applies only to those systems of belief already recognized as world religions, which excludes the traditional Indonesian religions. The former are classifed as *orang yang beragama* (people who have religion) whereas the latter are classifed as *orang yang belum beragama* (people who do not yet have religion), a phrase that implies a deficiency and asserts the inevitability of conversion. While they may personally feel their own religion to be superior to those of other "people who have religion," most Muslims, Christians, Hindus, and Buddhists uphold the rights of the adherents of other world religions to their own religious choice. But the right to adhere to a traditional religion, rather than converting to a world religion, is not extended to the "people who do not yet have religion."[5]

Several criteria support the distinction Indonesians draw between religions and nonreligion, a distinction anthropologists would rephrase as one between world religions and traditional religions. One criterion is monotheism, belief in the existence of one God. Monotheism is a feature characteristic of certain Near Eastern religions (e.g., Judaism, Christianity, and Islam)—although some Muslims might dispute the monotheistic claims of Christianity because of the doctrine of the Trinity. Hinduism and Buddhism are less rigorously monotheistic than their Near Eastern counterparts, although there is some evidence that, in Indonesia, members of these two religions conform in their discourse to the nation's monotheistic ideal (Geertz 1973:188). As will be explained below, the Wana assert the existence of a single God and claim that the God they recognize is the God worshipped by Muslims and Christians as well. To dismiss contemporary Wana religion today as not meeting a monotheistic standard would, therefore, be difficult.

A second criterion important to Indonesians is the existence of a written scripture. As noted above, the advent of Indian religion in the archipelago was accompanied by writing. The coming of Islam and Christianity intensified the respect given to sacred texts. These world religions all developed in literate cultures, and indeed literacy played a major role in their diffusion. On the other hand, Wana religion, like most traditional religions, developed in a nonliterate society. The argument can be made, therefore, that the presence or absence of written scripture reflects not the ultimate truth or wisdom of a religion, but rather the technological sophistication of the society from which it comes.

A third criterion is transcendence of ethnic boundaries. World religions unite members of diverse cultures in a single faith, whereas traditional religions often reinforce the unity of a single culture. Attempts to coerce traditionally oriented minorities to convert to world religions can be seen in large part, therefore, as an effort to draw them into mainstream Indonesian society. However, other means besides religion could be used to effect the same end. The association of a particular religion with a particular ethnic group is not unknown elsewhere in Indonesia, nor has it been an insurmountable problem in achieving national unity. The fact that all Indonesian citizens believe in *Tuhan* (God), albeit in different ways, can symbolize unity and cooperation, while at the same time permitting religious freedom, a flexibility represented by the *Pancasila*.

There is a final criterion implicit in Indonesian concerns about religion, namely the criterion of progress. The distinctions between religion and nonreligion in Indonesia sometimes seem to be not so much an evaluation of the beliefs themselves as an assessment of the social development of their adherents. Those classed as "not yet possessing a religion" are people regarded as *terbelakang* (backward), and unintegrated into the nation-state. Religion thus becomes a badge for the educated, the progressive, and the nationalistic. According to such usage, to say that a people lack a religion is not a statement about their spiritual values, but rather a comment upon their social and economic sophistication.

The Concept of Religion among the Wana

I have outlined some of the assumptions that characterize the religious climate of Indonesia and shape attitudes—both popular and official—toward people like the Wana. The Wana are not oblivious to these attitudes. Rather, they are acutely aware of and sensitive to the way they are regarded by others more powerful than themselves. What they call *agama Wana* represents a self-consciously constructed response to the judgments of the dominant society. This response builds on the images of what constitutes a religion that the Wana have received in their dealings with Muslims and Christians. Their own conception of religion has been shaped through these exchanges and reflects the issues central to them.

First of all, religion is interpreted by Wana as something highly political. This is not surprising, given that they have been told that the government demands that all people adopt a religion. The Wana find nationalist preoccupation with their religious status difficult to comprehend. They are conscious of being classified by Indonesian officialdom as *suku terasing* (isolated tribes), which to them associates the perceived lack of religion with a refusal to be governed. To those Wana who have paid taxes, performed government labor, registered as village residents, and even attended school or held village office during Dutch times or in the first two decades of the Republic, being labeled ungovernable because of their traditional religion causes great distress. Religion thus takes on for them ominous political overtones, and religious conversion becomes a highly charged political matter. Their suspicions are heightened by their awareness that recent Indonesian history has been marred by bloody conflicts involving religion. Fueling their anxieties are popular Muslim and Christian predictions about religious wars, impending cataclysm, and an expected end to the world. Such factors contribute to Wana apprehension that there is a menacing agenda behind other people's concern over their religious status. Thus, many Wana suspect that the nation is awaiting the day when everyone has converted to either Christianity or Islam, at which time religious war will erupt.

Clearly, the Wana interpret Indonesia's religious policy quite differently than do the majority of Indonesian citizens. The Wana perceive it not as a strategy for national unification but rather as a divisive instrument promoting social upheaval. This perception is logical enough, given that their own traditional consensus is being shattered by

pressures to divide their allegiance between two alien and poorly understood belief systems.

Pagan Wana respond to the claim that they have no religion by insisting that they do. They label their religion with terms that reflect their
awareness of the dominant society's view of them, namely, *agama yang
belum jadi agama* (a religion not yet a religion), and *agama kapir* (pagan
religion). As noted above, religion (as an anthropologist would define
it) is embedded in all aspects of Wana experience. For purposes of
characterizing their religion, Wana have selected certain elements of
their culture that match what they—based on their experience of Islam
and Christianity—have come to regard as definitive components of religion as recognized by the larger society. The elements they have
selected reflect quite strikingly their impressions of characteristic Muslim and Christian behavior. Diet, burial practices, healing techniques,
farming rituals, sexual propriety, religious offices, and relationship to
government all figure prominently as religious issues in Wana discourse, no doubt because they represent salient distinctions that the
pagan Wana see between themselves and their Muslim and Christian
neighbors. A few examples will illustrate this process of religious deline-
ation.

Religion to the Wana immediately connotes dietary practices. This is
not surprising, given the profound impression that Islamic food prohibitions make on a boar-hunting hill population.[6] The Wana term for
Muslims is instructive in this regard. They call them *tau puasa* (fasting
people), after the name for the month-long Muslim fast of Ramadan.
The Islamic ban on pork has spawned a rich assortment of Wana stories
that seek to explain the affinity between Muslims and that forbidden
animal. For example, one prominent story locates the origin of the pork
taboo in a contest between two brothers, one pagan, the other Muslim.
The Muslim put his two children in a chest, then challenged his elder
brother to guess the contents. The brother guessed that the chest contained two pigs. As seniority confers authority in Wana thought so, fit-
tingly, when the chest was opened, two pigs bounded forth. The event
both upheld the position of the elder brother and served as a charter in
Wana eyes for the Muslim ban on eating pork—literally the flesh of the
Muslim brother's children. If Islam is the religion that prohibits all
manner of foods, it follows in the Wana view that Wana religion is one
that expressly declares all food edible, especially pork and rat, both
viewed as highly unclean by Muslims. Christianity is said to be like the
Wana religion in that it prohibits no foods.

The link between food and religion is underscored by the special significance both carry for physical health and well-being. Religions, like
the foods they permit or prohibit, are thought to affect the body.

Whether religion agrees or disagrees with a person will therefore be reflected in one's state of health. Many Wana who deconvert from Islam or Christianity cite chronic sickness or sores as the reasons for returning to their traditional ways. Susceptibility to a particular religion's effects on the body is determined largely by one's heredity, they feel. Thus, a Bugis whose ancestors for generations have scorned pork is understandably wise to adhere to traditional dietary prohibitions, whereas for a Wana descended from a long line of pork eaters to do the same is thought ludicrous and unseemly.

Since food is such an important issue to Muslims, diet is taken to be the way in as well as out of Islam. According to Wana, one may deconvert from Islam by wringing the neck of a chicken and eating it—in violation of Muslim butchering techniques. Wana call this procedure *maluba.* Christianity, which lacks dietary laws, offers no such easy exit. Once in it, a person is stuck. Simply reverting from Christianity to pagan ways is considered ritually insufficient and a possible source of sickness. Thus, informants explained that a sensible course for those under pressure to convert is to enter Christianity first, then switch to Islam, then wring the neck of a chicken and eat it in order to return safely to their original state of paganism.

Burial practices are a second focus for religious definition, no doubt because conversion involves changes in deeply meaningful ways of coping with serious life crises. Popular accounts that Muslims bury their dead wrapped only in a shroud horrify the Wana, who demonstrate their love for the dead by careful dressing of the corpse. (My informants were unaware that Muslims typically dress a corpse in good clothes before shrouding it.) Christian custom, which unlike Islamic or Wana practice does not observe a long mourning period, is cited as callous for treating humans like dogs by simply burying them.

Healing is a third concern. Here, too, religious prescriptions and proscriptions apply to practices that offer emotional security in times of crisis. According to my informants, Islam permits traditional Wana shamanistic practices, but Christianity declares them sinful. Christianity is regarded as a rich man's religion, for it requires access to hospitals and Western medicine. Christianity puts a poor Wana in a bind, people say, for either one must sit by and watch loved ones die or one must commit a sin by calling on traditional forms of aid.

As these examples illustrate, Wana have identified Islamic and Christian practices that strongly contrast to their own, and they have determined the dimensions of contrast to be the defining features of religion. It follows from this view that the corresponding Wana practices must be key elements in Wana religion. On the surface, then, religion for the Wana appears to be a catalogue of ethnic markers, customs that distinguish pagan Wana from Christian Mori and Muslim Bugis. But beyond attention to superficial differences in custom, Wana religious concerns reveal a more profound side. Challenges to Wana culture and way of life have prompted deep reflection and major shifts in religious conceptions of reality and destiny. Three issues—rewards in the afterlife, the historical priority of Wana religion, and Wana monotheism—will be treated here as evidence of this process.

The first, rewards in the afterlife, represents a case in which a borrowed concept has been embraced and reworked by the Wana in accordance with their own world view. Whatever indigenous notions of an afterlife were once present in Wana culture, they have been radically transformed by the concept of *saruga,* the Wana rendering of the Indonesian term *surga* (heaven), itself a borrowing from Sanskrit. Wana cultural conceptions of reality are predicated on a division between apparent reality and hidden realms of existence. Most mortals ordinarily lack direct access to the hidden dimensions of experience, where special knowledge and powers are to be found. *Saruga,* a "heavenly paradise," is included in this latter dimension. Contemporary Wana explain this division of existence into hidden and apparent realities in a historical framework that refers specifically to *saruga.* In the past, Wana stories say, people freely moved between earth and heaven; but as heaven grew overcrowded, the two were divided, and death was introduced as the transition between the two. The present world, in which mortals are cut off from heaven and their loved ones by death, is thus explained as a degeneration from a once ideal past. Accordingly, Wana religion shares with some world religions a sense that the present order represents a decline or fall from a prior paradise or golden age. The separation of *saruga* from the ordinary world represents just one instance in Wana thought of this decline.

Besides being a marker of historical decline, *saruga* represents hope for the future as well. Strongly influenced by the millenarian outlook of Islam and Christianity, Wana anticipate a time, following a series of cataclysms, when heaven and earth, the dead and the living, will be reunited. Just when and how this might come about is the subject of much debate and occasional collective action. *Saruga,* therefore, has been adapted to fundamental Wana visions of reality. It is a guide by which Wana orient their lives as individuals and as a people.

Wana conceptions of paradise have not been formulated in isolation. Rather they have been forged through dialogues with Muslims and Christians. Informants cite discussions with respected coastal inhabitants, such as Muslim traders, who have confirmed their hopes that heaven exists. No doubt representatives of both Islam and Christianity have used images of heaven as enticements to convert (witness the story

cited earlier by Kruyt [1930:418]), but Wana have reworked the proffered promise of paradise to confirm the value of their own traditional
ways. This has come about in the following manner. Wana are fully
aware that they are at the bottom of an ethnic ladder, dominated and
despised by their neighbors—Bugis, Mori, Pamona, Gorontalo, and
others—who subscribe to one or another world religion. Wana represent themselves as poor and degraded. But their poverty and degrada-
tion are for this life only, they believe. In the next world, *saruga,* they
will be rewarded for their earthly suffering with comfort and leisure.
They are less sanguine concerning the heavenly rewards of their Muslim and Christian neighbors. For example, they assert that Muslims
live their heaven on earth. Muslim wealth (compared to Wana poverty)
and preoccupation with purity (as evident in their dietary code, lustra-
tions, and dress) are cited as testimony for this assertion. In their afterlife, Wana surmise, Muslims will accordingly find themselves living in
filth (pointedly portrayed as pig excrement); and they will be so hungry,
some say, that their souls will take the form of wild boars and go rooting
through Wana gardens. As for Christians, they will have only scraps of
clouds to eat, possibly a reference to pictures of Jesus and angels float-
ing about on clouds.

Heaven is thus taken to be compensation for life on earth. For the
Wana, who suffer so much in their mundane mortal existence, the afterlife offers deserved leisure and comfort. For those whose earthly life is
heavenly, the afterlife is less appealing. The very popular story of
Pojanggo Wawu illustrates this use of *saruga* to validate Wana life and
values. I have abridged it somewhat for inclusion here.

> The hero of the tale is a Wana named Pojanggo Wawu, whose name means
> one who wears a beard full of pig grease. Pojanggo Wawu is a symbol of
> unequaled generosity. When people pass by his house to gather thatch, he
> insists that they take some of his own; he can find more for himself. Likewise,
> he dismantles his floor and disperses his household furnishings to those in
> need. He is a man generous to a fault.
>
> Now there was a man named Pohaji, literally, a Muslim who has made the
> pilgrimage to Mecca. Pohaji lived in a well-appointed house at the coast.
> Pohaji died one day, and as his body was being readied for burial, his soul
> arrived in heaven. Looking around, he saw a beautiful house. "Whose house
> is that?" he inquired. "It belongs to Pojanggo Wawu," he was told. Pohaji
> asked after his own abode and was shown to a filthy hovel. At that, Pohaji's
> soul departed from heaven and rejoined its body on earth. Awakening,
> Pohaji asked his wife to make him coffee (a treat identified with coastal
> living). Once revived, Pohaji assembled his family and went off to find
> Pojanggo Wawu. The story details Pojanggo Wawu's amazement at the
> arrival of Pohaji, who treats him like a brother, insists upon sitting on

Pojanggo Wawu's grease-stained mats, and refuses chicken meat in preference to wild boar. Pohaji lived out his life in Wana style and, when he died,
took up residence in Pojanggo Wawu's heavenly home.

This story reveals quite clearly the ethnic and religious characteriza-
tions current in the Wana area. Pojanggo Wawu represents an ideal
Wana, a successful hunter who, despite his own material poverty, demonstrates ungrudging generosity and hospitality to everyone who comes
his way. His name testifies to his success as a hunter and his unabashed
love of pork (he's even encrusted with pig grease). Pojanggo Wawu is
unequivocally a pagan. By contrast, Pohaji represents a stereotypic
coastal Muslim—a pilgrim to Mecca, a rich man (from a Wana perspective), and presumably one who looks down on Wana ways. The delight
Wana take in the story comes from the dramatic turnaround in Pohaji's
attitudes when, thanks to his deathbed revelation, he is awakened to the
virtues of Wana life, which his own religion denies. The story is then an
answer to the challenge and the scorn of the "people who have religion."

Saruga offers a clear instance of a shared concept receiving sharply different interpretations from pagans, Muslims, and Christians, each
interpretation supporting the ultimate values of a chosen way of life.
The same process can be seen at work in another tenet of Wana religion.
Muslims, Christians, and pagan Wana are all agreed that Wana religion
is the earliest religion. While not accepting Wana religion as a true religion, Muslims and Christians will assert that Wana animism is prior to
their own revealed faiths. To Muslims and Christians, Wana customs
are akin to the animistic beliefs of their own forebearers before the
advent of the world religions. They believe that their own religions, in
contrast to such primitive beliefs, represent an important advance from
former ignorance to current enlightenment.

Pagan Wana accept the idea that their own religion is historically
prior to Islam and Christianity and call their religion *agama ruyu* (first
religion). But for them priority does not connote inferiority. Instead, it
testifies to a special validity. As do some other pagans of upland insular
Southeast Asia (cf. Ileto 1970), Wana conceive the relations among religions in terms of siblingship. Their stories tell of two brothers who
parted ways. The elder followed the Wana religion; the younger
adopted Islam. The elder remained in the Wana land to perpetuate the
old religion, while the younger departed coastward to follow Islam. No
doubt this scenario has been played out historically many times as traditional Wana remain in the interior, while converts to Islam and coastal
ways move off to seek a new life. (The story has been altered in recent
years to accommodate a third sibling, the youngest, who represents the
Christian faith.) For Wana, being the oldest does not mean being the

most primitive. Instead, seniority commands honor and respect. Just as children should defer to parents, so younger siblings should defer to older siblings. The scorn of "people who have religion" toward an older tradition is thus unseemly to the Wana. They foresee a time when their now despised religion will be restored to its acknowledged position of seniority and high regard.

To summarize, while members of all religions in the area consider the pagan traditions of the Wana to be historically prior to Islam and Christianity, they diverge sharply on the interpretations they place upon this assertion. For "people who have religion," priority implies primitive backwardness, the antithesis of progress and development. For Wana, priority carries a special claim to validity and calls for privilege and respect.

The concept of God is perhaps the most critical issue in the religious debates between pagan Wana and representatives of world religions. As noted earlier, Indonesia's religious ideal is monotheistic. Wana beliefs conform to the ideal quite well. While aspects of their cosmology assign roles to two lords—one above and one below the earth—and certain healing rites concern a vengeful lord of thunder, all of these roles are subsumed by the term *Pue* (Owner or Lord), creator and overseer of the world. I suspect that *Pue* has assumed a more central place in Wana discourse as a result of contact with Muslims and Christians, but this requires further documentation.[7] My informants in the 1970s uniformly asserted that there is but one God and that God is the same for all religions. While Wana religion clearly reinforces Wana ethnic identity, the concept of God therein is not used to distinguish Wana as unique, but rather to unite them with the rest of humankind. Wana religion thus appears to be completely in accord with the spirit of Indonesia's *Pancasila,* which makes God a symbol of unity rather than ethnic division. Unfortunately for the Wana, this is not enough. Informants claim that Muslims and Christians deny that the Wana God is the same as their own, just as they deny that Wana forms of worship have the same validity as their own. The sophistication of Wana response to such prejudice is brought out fully in the following account I received from Apa E., an old Wana shaman.

> Once on his way home from a coastal market, Apa E. encountered a Christian minister talking with the head of the village in which Apa E. paid taxes. The minister took note of the raggedy old Wana and asked the village head who he was. Learning that Apa E. was a Wana from the hills, the minister exclaimed in Indonesian, "Oh, this man is one of the still ignorant, one not yet possessing a religion, an animist, one who worships at trees, one who worships at stones." Apa E., who understands some Indonesian, answered the man in a conciliatory fashion. "Yes indeed, it is true, sir, I am a stupid person, an animist. I don't know anything. I worship at trees, I worship at

stones. But sir, if you worship in a house made of wood, you sir, worship also at trees. If you worship inside a church made of stone, sir, you also worship at stones. It is the same if one worships outside in the open, for God is everywhere."

As this story reveals, the Wana apply a more universal and all-embracing notion of God than do their neighbors, for the Wana seek recognition for their religion only as one among other legitimate forms of belief, whereas their neighbors, using religion as a measure of progress, wish to limit the definition of religion to those who conform to their notions of socioeconomic development.

To summarize, religion is being applied to different uses by the Wana and their neighbors. The Wana seek to represent their cultural heritage as a religion; other Indonesians use religion as a badge of citizenship and development. For the Wana, religion is an inclusive concept—every people has one. For most Indonesians, religion is a concept reserved for the progressive and the literate. By demanding conversion as an expression of willingness to participate in their national vision, the nation may have added a serious obstacle in relations with at least one (and probably many others) of its traditional ethnic minorities, many of whose members are strongly committed to defending their heritage as a symbol of their cultural identity.

The three issues treated here—heaven, history, and monotheism—reveal how Wana, in the face of challenges from the larger society, have revised and examined the meanings behind their cultural traditions. Their responses suggest a sophistication and dynamism, a process of rationalization not unlike that which Clifford Geertz (1973) discovered to be underway in Bali in the late 1950s. Ortner (1978:152) has recently defined religion as "a metasystem that solves problems of meaning . . . generated in large part . . . by the social order." What this paper has shown is that Wana religion today is addressing problems of meaning generated not by the Wana social system in isolation, but rather by that system's encapsulation within the Indonesian nation-state. Wana religion is not a static, primitive religion, neatly attuned to its social structure. Instead, it should be seen as a historical transformation of a cultural system in response to challenges from the larger social order in which it is a part.

Discussion and Conclusion

This paper demonstrates that an ethnographic approach can provide insight into social planning for Indonesia's ethnic minorities. In it, I have presented and examined Wana interpretations of, and reactions to, Indonesian attitudes toward religion. I have shown how the Wana, possessing a traditional religion (as defined anthropologically), have evolved a concept of what a religion is supposed to be, based on their experience of Islam and Christianity. In response to Indonesian preoccupation with the linkage between religion and national citizenship, the Wana have interpreted religion as a highly political concept, one which generates considerable fear and anxiety. They have turned to their own religion as a way of coping with concerns about their identity and their future. They regard attacks on their religion as threats against their very survival as a people. Religion has come to represent to them both their vulnerability and their protection in a menacing world.

From the point of view of an educated Indonesian citizen, the conversion of *suku terasing* to a world religion may seem benign and beneficial. However, we should recollect what happened in the beleaguered country of Kampuchea several years ago when the Communist regime demanded that the nation's Buddhists give up their religion. But, one may argue, there is a world of difference between Buddhist Kampucheans being ordered to convert to atheism and pagan "isolated tribes" being asked to convert to a world religion. The details of the two cases differ, as do the methods being used; but structurally the situations are identical. The similarity lies in the fact that in both cases people in power regard their own world view to be positive and progressive, while regarding the world view of the subject peoples to be backward and benighted. Both cases represent challenges to the religious systems by which people make sense of their world.

An assumption of modern Indonesian society has been that religion and development go hand in hand. But is there in fact a necessary link between the two, or does it just happen that religion in Indonesia has been used to symbolize progress and modernity? There is no inherent reason why Wana cannot remain pagan but still advance technologically, economically, and educationally. Most members of the world's great religions no longer live under the same technological and social conditions that prevailed when those religions originated. Like other aspects of culture, therefore, religion can change and adjust to new circumstances over time. The present paper demonstrates how Wana religion has been revolutionized in the last few generations. There is no reason to think that it cannot be used by the Wana to face new challenges in the future.

Notes

1. Sponsorship for this research by the Indonesian Institute of Science (LIPI) is gratefully acknowledged. So too are the hospitality and assistance offered by

the authorities of the provincial government of Central Sulawesi, the district of Poso, and the subdistricts of Ampana, Ulu Bongka, and Bungku Utara. This research was supported by a National Science Foundation (NSF) predoctoral fellowship, a National Institute of Mental Health (NIMH) training grant administered by Stanford University, and the Gertrude Slaughter Award from Bryn Mawr College.

This paper has benefited from discussion with Samuel Patty, Ward Keeler, Daniel Maltz, and Richard Rohrbaugh, as well as useful comments from Michelle Rosaldo, Michael Dove, Tim Babcock, and Virginia Dominguez. I, of course, take full responsibility for the use to which their advice has been put.

2. Kruyt's (1930) account reveals that some Islamic words had been incorporated into the Wana language in the 1920s. Comparing Kruyt's account to my own work in the 1970s, it would seem that the process of incorporation has gone much further. This is not to say that Wana culture is becoming Islamicized. Rather, Islamic terms and concepts have been reworked to have new meanings in the Wana context.

3. Because the connotations of the word *agama* are so highly charged, some Indonesian academics favor using the more neutral term *religi.*

4. For further details on the complex subject of Wana religion, see Atkinson 1979.

5. Since the early days of the Republic, the definition of religion has gradually widened. In the 1960s, the Hindu religion of the Balinese was accorded recognition. More recently, *Aluk To Dolo,* the religion of the Sa'dan Toraja, and *Kaharingan,* the religion of some interior peoples of Kalimantan, have received similar approval. Significantly, both the Balinese and the Toraja are prospering peoples with educated and influential representatives in positions to press for official recognition. The Wana lack such leverage.

6. In Kruyt's (1930:418) account cited above, the Muslim brother's distaste for the pagan way of life reflects a disgust for the pagan diet of pork. The Muslim will not enter his brother's house, the walls of which are characterized as consisting of layers of pig fat. In their audience before God, the Muslim brother refers to the pagan's heaven as that of a swine.

7. My impression, based on a comparison of Kruyt's account and my own data, is that informants in the 1970s were more general and more consistent in their use of the unmarked term *Pue* (Owner or God) than were Kruyt's informants in the 1920s.

References Cited

Atkinson, J. M.
1979 "Paths of the Spirit Familiars: A Study of Wana Religion." Ph.D. dissertation, Stanford University. Ann Arbor: University Microfilms.

Black, Star, and Hans Hoefer
1974 *Guide to Bali.* 3d ed. Hong Kong: APA Productions.

Geertz, Clifford
   1966   "Religion as a Cultural System." In *Anthropological Approaches to the Study of Religion,* edited by M. Banton, pp. 1–46. London: Tavistock.

   1973   " 'International Conversion' in Contemporary Bali." In *The Interpretation of Cultures,* C. Geertz, pp. 170–189. New York: Basic Books.

Ileto, Reynaldo Clemena
   1970   "Magindanao 1860–1888: The Career of Datu Uto of Buayan." M.A. thesis, Cornell University.

Kruyt, A. C.
   1930   "De To Wana op Oost-Celebes." *Tijdschrift voor Indische Taal-, Land-, en Volkenkunde* 70:398–625.

Ortner, Sherry
   1978   *Sherpas through their Rituals.* Cambridge: Cambridge University Press.

2. Shamans and Cadres in Rural Java

ADRIAAN S. RIENKS AND PURWANTA ISKANDAR

Abstract

Government officials in Indonesia have pursued a policy in which modern medical services are delivered separately from, instead of convergent with, indigenous modes of health care. They have persisted with this policy despite recent findings that the rural health centers—the foci of primary health care—are performing far below expectations. The government's response to these findings has been to create a new category of health personnel, the village cadre, to promote health education and to address undertreated diseases. In the light of preparations to establish a nationwide system of cadre programs, it is important to assess whether these programs can actually reach the village poor. Anthropological research into cadre programs and the indigenous Javanese system of medicine suggests that they cannot. First, the actual goals of cadre programs have in practice less to do with health than with politics and bureaucracy, and the actual results of the program are unsatisfactory from the standpoint of both cadres and villagers. Second, substantial differences exist between the cadre programs and the indigenous system of health care in rural Java, with respect to the cosmology of health, the principles of diagnosis, and the types, qualifications, and roles of healers. These differences account for most of the problems encountered by the cadre program. In conclusion, it is suggested that the cadre program be integrated into (and not expected to replace) the indigenous system of health care.

Introduction

Primary health care activities in Indonesia started to expand about a decade ago. Since then simple units for child and maternal health have evolved into more or less well-staffed rural health centers at the subdistrict level and, presently, preparation is underway for a nationwide system of cadre (viz., village health worker) programs. Primary health care is the lowest level of modern medical services in the country. It is an attempt to share some benefits of modern health care with, especially, the urban and rural poor. Health administrators want the poor to view primary health care as (1) the services to which they turn first in the event of illness and (2) a basis for recognized referral to higher levels of health care. Core assumptions in the introduction of primary health care are that the proximity of modern health services will lead to their use by the population and that the indigenous form of health care is easily replaceable. In this paper, an attempt is made to evaluate these core assumptions through a comparison of the structure and content of the government's system of health care and the indigenous Javanese system. This comparison is based on anthropological research into cadre programs and the indigenous system of medicine carried out in the Central Javanese district of Banjarnegara during 1978–1981 (cf. Iskandar, Rienks, Soesartono, and Sunarsih 1979; Rahardjo, Rienks, Slamet, and Soesartono 1979).[1]

The Expansion of Primary Health Care in Indonesia

In spite of the present attention being given to primary health care in Indonesia, the country's health system remains persistently urban and hospital-oriented. The health sector receives an average 3–4 percent of the national budget, which equaled approximately US$1.10 per capita per year for the third five-year-plan (1979–1984) (Government of Indonesia 1979).[2] Moreover, it is estimated that only 25 percent of this amount was allocated for the 80 percent of the population living in rural areas. With respect to manpower, there are currently 10,000 physicians in the country, half of whom live in the four largest cities. In these cities doctor-patient ratios almost equal Western levels, but in rural areas there is only one doctor for every 40,000 to 100,000 persons.

It was not until the second half of the first five-year-plan (1969–1974) that primary health care began to receive any attention at all. The initial assumption that the urban-oriented network of facilities would spontaneously spread to the countryside had been proven incorrect. It became clear that a special effort to develop rural health care would be necessary. This led to the creation of the *Puskesmas (Pusat Kesehatan Masyarakat)* or community health centers, which were designed for the delivery of primary health care. The creation of these centers was facilitated by the positive response of the rural populations to previously established miniclinics for child and maternal health *(BKIA, or Balai Kesejahteraan Ibu dan Anak)* in preceding years. The informal contacts in these units between motivated health educators and expectant women had proved beneficial to all concerned. As a result, the majority of them, about 7,000 in 1973–1974 and 2,500 in 1977–1978 were further developed into full-fledged rural health centers (the *Puskesmas*). These centers became the focus of other related activities as well, namely out-patient treatment, communicable disease control, dental care, laboratory work, family planning, community health education, and the health of school children. The aim to establish a health center in each of Indonesia's 3,500 subdistricts (the average population of which was 43,000 in 1980) was achieved in the course of the second five-year-plan (1974–1979). By 1979, the number of health centers in subdistrict capitals and the number of auxiliary posts in remote parts of subdistricts totaled 4,350. However, the ideal of a well-staffed center headed by a physician was far from reached. In 1978 approximately 50 percent of the centers in Java and about 60 percent of those outside Java did not yet have a doctor (Subekti 1978:2).

As soon as the rural health centers were established, the Ministry of Health began to monitor their utilization. It soon discovered that the centers were used only by approximately 20 percent of the target population (Department of Health 1980). Even more serious, the majority of clients in rural areas was found to be of the upper and middle class as opposed to the poorer, lower class. Thus, the centers appealed mostly to the better educated, to owners of means of transportation, and to people already familiar with modern medicine. With respect to geographical coverage, the centers mainly attracted persons within a range of five kilometers. Beyond that distance, transportation costs were too heavy a burden for potential clients. The cost of treatment itself was relatively low, only Rp 150 (about US$ 0.21) per visit. In addition, very poor villagers could request from their village chief a declaration of poverty, which exempted them from payment. However, the village chiefs did not encourage this practice because such affirmations of poverty reflect poorly on their administration.

The government's awareness that the rural health centers were failing to reach the lower income strata gave rise to the "crucial link" notion. According to this notion, special efforts had to be made to reach the village poor. Two phases can be distinguished in the attempt to establish this crucial link. In the first phase, selected members of the health centers' staff were encouraged to operate as fieldworkers and, occasionally, special fieldworkers were added to the staff. However, the relative scarcity of paramedical personnel proved to be a handicap (for each ten physicians, there were only sixteen nurses, fifteen midwives, and thirty-six medical assistants). In the second phase, an attempt was made to overcome this problem by designating village health workers or "cadres" as a support group. Their proposed role in forging the crucial link to the village poor is illustrated in Figure 2.1.

One of the first attempts to involve cadres in primary health care was undertaken by rural health center physicians in the district of Banjarnegara in the early 1970s.[3] The preparation of these initial cadre programs was necessarily both slow and careful, given that rules and methods had not yet been developed. The following steps were taken in the village of Sirkandi, for example. During the first year, members of the health center's staff manned a medicine post in this isolated village on two afternoons per week. Gradually their involvement expanded to such non-health sectors as road building, mosque construction, and sewing courses. Local confidence in the good intentions of the health center staff grew steadily and, when they asked for volunteers to be trained in health and agriculture at the center for a period of three months, two candidates were easily found. With the help of these two core cadres, in the following two years the staff trained fifty additional cadres in the village, focusing on such skills as manning simple medicine posts, weighing infants, and stimulating among their fellow villagers greater awareness with respect to nutrition and sanitation. This program received support from the subdistrict head, who instructed the village chief to cooperate fully.

The work of this dedicated health center staff, and the surprisingly good results of their cadre program, soon attracted the attention of other health officials. The head of the district's medical service decided to give special emphasis to cadre programs, and within the relatively short period of seven years (1973–1979) such programs were established in 136 of the 281 villages in the Banjarnegara district (which had a population of 670,000 as of 1979). According to the service's records, in that period about 1,900 villagers were trained as health care cadres (who each manage a simple medicine post and insurance program), and

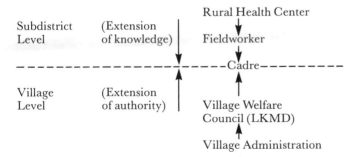

Figure 2.1 Proposed Role of the "Cadre" in Rural Health Care

1,600 others were trained as nutrition cadres (whose primary concern is for children under five years of age).

As this cadre program was developing in Banjarnegara, it acquired a national and even international reputation as a remarkable innovation in the field of rural health care. It gave direction to the growing feeling in Indonesia that something had to be done about primary health care. In 1973–1974 the Health Ministry became interested in the concept of rural, health care cadres, and in 1975 it established a cadre program in the Karanganyar district (also in Central Java). In mid-1979 the ministry decided to gather additional experience by creating an additional 220 programs all over the country (based on selecting two districts per province, two subdistricts per district, and two villages per subdistrict). One weakness has persisted throughout this development, however—a lack of evaluation. Going back to the pioneering cadre program in Banjarnegara, the effects of the programs have never been monitored nor, hence, reliably evaluated.

A Provisional Appraisal of Cadre Programs

The Absence of Data on Cadre Programs

The current optimism in Indonesian medical circles with respect to the value of cadre programs is based on four considerations: (1) the worldwide trend toward involving village health workers in primary health care; (2) the awareness that many common and serious diseases can be dealt with by nonprofessionals (Hull and Rohde 1980); (3) the expectation that a cadre program may achieve popular participation in modern health care; and (4) the fact that a cadre program lessens rather than increases primary health care costs. Based on these considerations, the national government, under the third five-year-plan (1979–1984), embarked on a nationwide effort to establish cadre programs in 20,140 villages in 27 provinces (constituting about one-third of Indonesia's villages) by the year 1984.

One crucial input not considered when the government made this major commitment to cadre programs was data on the preparation, implementation, and results of extant programs. The reason for the omission is simple: such a body of data does not yet exist. Banjarnegara's image as a success story is not backed by any verifiable, evaluative data. Nor, in the case of Karanganyar, has a report as yet been made public that covers all the possibilities and problems of the cadre program there. Various aspects of these two cadre programs have been reviewed in progress reports and other studies, but not in a manner that would show whether they have in fact succeeded or failed. It is even more difficult to evaluate the attempted creation of 220 programs nationwide—how many actually have been created, how many are successes or failures, and why.

This absence of scientifically sound, empirical studies of cadre programs contrasts sharply with the abundance of normative literature on them (stating the need for them, their feasibility, their manner of execution, etc.). This gap may be a structural characteristic of the introductory phase in community development, at which time the emphasis is typically on promotion and defense of the new program. As a blend of hopeful expectation and observation, normative literature serves these purposes well, and so it is given priority at the expense of any actual research into the new program. The development of the concept of the health cadre in Indonesia is a revealing case study of the use and abuse of normative literature.

This normative literature was developed in three distinct stages or "waves." The first wave consisted of the initial reports from the health center physicians in Banjarnegara on their experiments with cadres. To legitimate their work in the eyes of their immediate superiors, the top officials in the district medical service, these physicians wrote positively biased reports in which outstanding cadres were presented as typical and in which the enthusiasm of the villagers for this program was exaggerated. In addition, each physician based his reports (as he did his programs) on his own, often idiosyncratic notion of what a cadre program ideally should accomplish. After several years these reports achieved recognition by the district government of the health cadre concept, as expressed in its incorporation into district medical policy (Haliman 1977).

Once the cadre concept was accepted at the district level, final recognition and legitimation still depended upon the interests of the central government. Banjarnegara's medical service had to demonstrate to the central government not only that a cadre program was manageable in that one district, but that the experience was potentially replicable in other districts as well. This resulted in the second wave of normative literature, in which the idiosyncratic experiences of individual health center physicians were ignored and emphasis was placed on the standardization of aims and procedures. This normative literature was supplemented with seminars and study tours of the Banjarnegara district, all with the aim of gaining acceptance of the health cadre concept by the central government. This was achieved in 1975, when the Health Ministry decided to establish a cadre program in a second Central Java district, Karanganyar.

The cadre program in Karanganyar was established under the direction not of individual health center physicians, but of the central gov-

A *Dalang* Receives an Infant in a Curing Ceremony

Part of the Ritual Offerings in a Curing Ceremony

ernment's research center for health care *(P4K,* or *Pusat Penelitian Pengembangan Pelayanan Kesehatan)* in Surabaya. As a result, the program was necessarily designed in accordance with central government policy on rural health care. The cornerstone of this policy is the rural health care center, and the explicit aim of this policy is to maximize the center's utilization by the local population. Consequently, this too became the explicit aim of the cadre program in Karanganyar; the central government researchers tailored it to address perceived shortcomings in utilization of the rural health centers (Boutmy 1979:115–132). To this end they wrote detailed manuals for the program supervisors (who were usually village leaders and members of the paramedical staff at the rural health centers). These manuals represented the third wave of normative literature on the cadre program ("normative" because, as in the first two waves, it did not address the actual performance of cadres). With these manuals in hand, the program supervisors enveloped the Karanganyar cadres in a web of job descriptions and procedural outlines, making the program much less responsive to the varying circumstances of individual villages than was the case in the Banjarnegara program.

These three waves of normative literature on cadre programs in Indonesia have given them an aura of credibility and feasibility. In the first wave, individual health center physicians tried to legitimate their experiences to district-level officials. In the second wave, the district government tried to legitimate its cadre program to the central government. In the third wave, the central government tried to ensure that its rural health care policy would be supported by the developing cadre systems. None of this literature contained empirically based evaluations of the use of cadres. This has resulted, minimally, in two problems with the cadre programs. First, it is often not clear just what is the empirical referent of the term "cadre program." In Banjarnegara, the term initially referred to an attempt to address the greatest needs of the village populations, regardless of whether these were health-related or not. Subsequently in Karanganyar, this term referred to an attempt to improve the utilization of the rural health center, regardless of whether this constituted the highest priority of the local population or not. A second problem arising from the normative literature is the illusion that—given the existence of this literature—the development of the cadre program has been carefully monitored and evaluated all along. The reverse of this has been the actual case, and yet the need for such monitoring and evaluation is just as marked as has been its absence. A lesson can be learned here from the "Green Revolution" programs in Indonesia: designed to benefit the rural poor, they may have provided more benefit to the middle and upper classes. There is a real danger that the same fate will befall the health cadre programs. The further development of these programs must be based on more empirical evidence of their worth than presently exists.

We carried out evaluative research on the cadre program in Banjarnegara during 1978–1981. This comprised (1) anthropological research in four villages, of which three then had cadre programs, (2) execution of a survey among both cadres and noncadres in the same four villages, (3) long-term medical anthropological research in one village where indigenous healers are still all-important (despite proximity to a rural clinic), (4) attempts to formulate parameters for cadre performance, and (5) attempts to improve data recording techniques at the family, cadre, and clinic levels. This research was complicated by the earlier mentioned lack of clear, official goals for the cadre program or a baseline for evaluating the extent to which they have been achieved. We were obliged to take as a starting point rather ill-defined goals cited by the program officials in Banjarnegara. These specify that (1) a cadre program should be an effort to help the poor and to improve the problem solving capacity of the community, (2) it should start in the sector (not necessarily health) most important to the local population, (3) it should be carefully introduced through village and neighborhood meetings, (4) cadre candidates should be chosen by the inhabitants of the neighborhood they are going to serve, and (5) potential cadres should have a stable source of income, have ample opportunity to receive and visit clients, and be willing and able to follow the training.

Actual Goals of Cadre Programs

Our anthropological research in the three villages with cadre programs demonstrated that the character of these programs is largely determined by the villages' political and economic elites in conjunction with the staff of the local clinics. The input of the average villagers in program formation is minimal. They do not begin to participate in the program until long after it has been announced and candidates acceptable to village leaders and clinic staff have been selected and trained. The lack of participation of the villagers in this initial phase represents a major weakness of the cadre program, because the goals of the clinic staff and the village leaders, while complementary to one another, are actually inimical to the villagers' acceptance of the program. The goals of the clinic staff are speedy establishment of the program and a referral service to the clinic, and the goals of the village leaders are quick, manifest results and the protection of vested interests.

The health center staff usually cannot visit the villages frequently enough, for enough time, or at the right time because of several constraints: the trips from clinic to village often take several hours, and they need to be made in the evening, when villagers are normally available for meetings with visitors. This timing ill-suits the clinic doctors, however, most of whom run private practices in the evening. In consequence, the clinic staff usually consult only the formal leaders of the village during daytime meetings at the clinic itself. These meetings are typically dominated by the staff members, who display their medical authority, refer to the backing of the subdistrict head, and ask for cooperation. The village officials display their compliance, express interest in the program, and promise to explain it to their villagers. A date is then set for the start of the training—usually two or three months after the initial meetings between staff members and village officials. The procedure of choosing suitable cadre candidates is left to the discretion of these village officials. The health center staff does not concern itself with whether or not candidates are chosen by and acceptable to their fellow villagers. Their sole concern is with the candidates' capacity to follow the training.

This training, despite the clinic doctors' avowed belief that cadre programs should focus on the sector (even if a nonhealth sector) of greatest importance to the local population, has focused on rural health care, as delivered by the rural clinics. During the initial experimentation with the cadre concept, it was not uncommon to find health center staff involved in agriculture, fisheries, road construction, and sewing courses. However, with the recognition of the cadre concept by the district medical service and with the development of a districtwide cadre system, the training of health cadres received first priority, and priority was given in this training to support of the operations of the clinics. Thus, the cadres are trained to execute those tasks and treat those diseases of greatest importance to the clinic. This is reflected in their training manuals, which discuss at length such topics as malaria, tuberculosis, and cholera. The cadres are taught to treat simple cases at home, to refer serious ones to the clinic, and to support follow-up treatment by the clinic. This referral function is complicated, however, by the fact that the referrers (viz., the cadres) are typically the villagers who are the most familiar with the health center and, hence, the least comprehending of the need to act as intermediaries with those villagers who are least familiar with the center.

The goals of the village officials differ little from those of the clinic doctors. The village officials also want the program started as soon as possible. They are well aware that officials at higher levels of government judge progress in terms of manifest, physical tokens. Subdistrict officials actually encourage competition between villages with respect to the number and quality of public buildings erected, the capital improvement of arable land, the quantity of livestock, the condition of roads, houses, and yards, and so on. Based on these visible signs of development, all of the subdistrict's villages are ranked along a scale of *swadaya* (self-help), *swakarya* (self-production), and *swasembada* (self-supporting). Cadre programs are the latest addition to this intervillage competition and, as such, they are self-promoting. Thus, many cadre programs in Banjarnegara were started upon the request of village heads who envied the establishment of a program in an adjoining village. In such cases, the village head is interested only in trained cadres (whether they feel motivated to attend the training and finish it or not), the number of infant weighing posts and the frequency of weighing sessions (whether they are attended by the poor or not), and the number of medicine posts (whether they are utilized or not). Impressive lists of the quantifiable aspects of each program are kept in the village council hall, where they are shown to visiting subdistrict officials. Since the latter seldom probe beyond these records, the facade of successful development remains intact.

In addition to using the cadre programs to improve their relations with powers outside the village, the village leaders use it to improve their power base within the village as well. The cadre program has a serious impact not only on health-related aspects of village life, but also on political and economic aspects. There is little official recognition of this fact, however. It is convenient for the health center's staff to downplay the program's potential political impact, based on the official view of the village as a harmonious community and of its officials as ready to sacrifice personal interest for the interest of the group. This naïve belief also justifies the staff's confidence in the village officials' ability to implement the program properly. Key program elements (e.g., the communication of the cadre concept, the selection of cadre candidates, the daily management of the program) receive little supervision by the clinic staff. It is left to the discretion of the village leaders whether candidates are appointed or elected and whether informal leaders are consulted or not. Their response to this opportunity is in general to secure and maintain the status quo. They realize that a cadre program represents potential for political competition between themselves and any opposing factions in the village. Whichever faction gains control of the program through the appointment of loyal cadres receives a unique chance to increase its status and power, by using these cadres to strengthen their ties to the common villagers. The degree of political competition within a program of course varies according to a variety of different factors, many of which are determined by factors outside the program. These include the strength of the village head, the ties among the formal leaders, the extent of informal leadership, and the quality of the *Lembaga Sosial Desa* (village welfare council), which is a board of advisors to the village head on matters of community development. Typically, however, the village's formal leaders manipulate the selection of candidates to increase their influence and reduce the potential influence of any of the informal leaders. As a result, the majority of the candidates belong to (or have close connections with) the existing political and economic elite.

Actual Results of Cadre Programs

The complementarity of the motives of health center and village officials produces some manifest short-term results. However, only over the longer term is it possible to evaluate how cadre-client relations have developed and whether the program is truly understood and accepted by the population. It is revealing in this regard to look at the results of our survey of cadre and noncadre respondents in three villages. Cadre programs had been in progress in each of these villages for at least two years. In each village, twenty-five cadres (an average 40 percent sample) and fifty noncadre household heads (an average 10 percent sample) were interviewed. In a fourth village, without a cadre program, another fifty noncadre household heads were interviewed as a control group.

The findings of the survey show clearly that many villagers were ignorant about the program. Four out of ten villagers did not even know that cadres were present in their village. Of the six out of ten villagers who did know, only two had any understanding of the essential elements of the programs (such as the fact that the cadres had received some training). Only two out of ten villagers felt that the cadres were chosen democratically by the inhabitants of the neighborhoods they were to serve. This finding is in agreement with the cadres' own responses to the question as to how they were selected: 6 percent said that they were chosen by villagers, 73 percent said that they were appointed by village officials, and 21 percent said that they had been recruited by health center staff or core cadres. These findings cast doubt on the official claim of popular participation in the design and execution of the program.

The survey yielded interesting information not only about the villagers' perceptions of cadres, but also about the characteristics of the cadres themselves. First, the cadres tended to be younger than noncadre household heads (although most of the cadres were household heads as well). There were few cadres in the influential older age groups. The small percentage of female cadres, only one out of six, also merits attention. This small percentage is unfortunate because female cadres can usually outperform male cadres in certain programs, such as baby weighing, because of their traditionally greater role in infant care.

Whether or not female cadres were given a chance to develop appeared to depend largely on the support of the village head's wife. The general influence of the village leadership on cadre selection is also reflected in the fact that 60 percent of the cadre sample occupied some public office (other than that of cadre), which compares with just 10 percent of the noncadre sample (see Table 2.1). In addition, the cadres tended to be better educated than noncadres, they more often possessed a secondary occupation in addition to their main occupation, and they had higher patterns of consumption.

Finally, the survey provided some data on the performance of the cadres. Cadre performance was operationalized and measured in terms of the number of households for which each cadre felt responsibility, the frequency of their contacts with these households, the extent of their supervision of medicine consumption, and the character of their response to cases of tuberculosis and malaria. Based on these indicators, 37 percent of the cadres surveyed engaged in little or no activity and 57 percent engaged in only intermittent activity and depended on the continued guidance of either clinic staff or village leaders, while just 6 percent were self-motivated and approached the standards of performance set forth in the training manuals. These findings are in accordance with the cadres' own perception of their training and work: only 7 percent of those surveyed admitted to having thoroughly understood the training, and only 31 percent stated an interest in helping their fellow villagers. The above measures of cadre performance are also supported by the villagers' own measures: while 32 percent of the villagers surveyed said that the cadres have had a significant impact on health care in the village, 42 percent said that their impact was incidental, and 26 percent said that there was no impact at all.

The authors concluded that a majority of the cadres studied were confused and insecure about their place in the health care delivery system. They hesitated to promote themselves as cadres and, when addressed as such, exhibited either embarrassment or even anger, cou-

Table 2.1. Association between Holding Public Office and Selection as a Cadre

| | | Holder of Public Office | |
		No	Yes
Selected as	No	134	16
a Cadre	Yes	30	45

N = 225 respondents in three villages
X^2 = 63.6
P < .001

pled with a disavowal of the status of cadre. The cadres explained this reaction in terms of their belief that the selection process was not democratic and the training was coercive. These are problematic characteristics, because in the indigenous system of heatlh care, no one can become a healer without explicit popular support. Because the cadres typically lacked this support, many of them considered themselves to be imposters. To understand more fully the sense in which this is true, and the problems that this poses for the government's cadre program, it is necessary to understand the indigenous system of illness and curing.

The System of Indigenous Medicine

It is illustrative of the general arrogance concerning rural health care that a well-known (and in itself very good) village health care handbook is entitled *Where There Is No Doctor* (Werner 1977). Of course, it is true that in many rural areas of the world there is no healer with an M.D. degree, but this does not always mean that there is no one who can give advice and support in the case of accident or illness. In Java there exists an elaborate, indigenous system of curing that is associated with the basic cosmology of the people, has illness categories of its own, and is carried out by a diverse and stratified range of healers. The introduction of the cadre concept would be facilitated by articulation to this system, and it will be inhibited by ignoring it, as is presently the case.

The Cosmology of Health in Java

The first thing that a medical anthropologist learns in the field is that people possess not a system of medicine but rather a religion or cosmology that deals with human vulnerability (cf. Glick 1967). Central to Javanese thought is this matter of vulnerability, the question of how someone achieves and prolongs the state of *slamet* (a feeling of inner peace, physical health, social harmony, and economic prosperity) and avoids the states of *nglamun, bingung,* and *ruwat* (conditions of aimlessness, uncertainty, and ill health). According to Javanese cosmology, a person should move through four *alam* or "worlds of being." Anyone who fails to do so correctly will enter into a fifth and undesirable world. The first world is the *alam kandungan* (womb world), in which the fetus grows to maturation. This world is extremely vulnerable and very liable to the influences of both good and evil spirits. It is also susceptible to influence by good or bad aspects of the parents' behavior. The second world is the *alam nyata* (real world), the tangible reality of life in which a person can act well or badly and is held responsible accordingly. The third world is the *alam kubur* (grave world), in which the deceased is judged on the quality of his or her past life and it is determined whether or not he or she may enter the fourth world, the *alam kelanggengan* (eternal world), mankind's origin and destination and the residence of the holy spirits. The fifth world is the *alam antara* (world in between), where the evil spirits and lost souls reside.

Folk Diagnosis

Javanese villagers make a broad distinction between *lara nemen* (serious illness) and *lara mriang* (simple illness).[4] Seriousness is measured in terms of whether or not cosmological concepts of guilt and punishment are involved. For example, someone who falls from a tree because the trunk was wet and slippery may suffer a major injury, but the resultant sickness is still considered "simple" because it is explained by stupidity and neglect and not by improper social or religious behavior. There is an associated difference between *lara nemen* and *lara mriang* with respect to the type of treatment deemed appropriate. It is believed that only indigenous healers can treat serious illness (cf. Lozoff, Kamath, and Feldman 1975), but that simple illness can be cured by self-therapy. There is extensive folk knowledge of these simple illnesses, the majority of which have only one defining symptom (a situation that often, in modern medical terms, distinguishes different stages in the course of one disease from separate diseases). When this knowledge fails, in the case of simple illness, an indigenous healer and/or the health center will be consulted.

The difference between the two types of illness, and also the two types of therapy, and the associated differences in cosmological explanation, can be illustrated by a description of the principal categories of *lara nemen*. The first type of serious illness is *kebendu* (damnation), which refers in general to physical deformities like a clubfoot or harelip that are directly visible at birth or shortly afterward and are attributed to parental misbehavior toward the holy spirits. Such offenses toward the "eternal world" are expressed in the fetus' misdevelopment in the "womb world."

The second category of serious illness is *sawan* (childhood disease), referring to the illnesses contracted by children during their youngest and most vulnerable years (typically under five years of age). Villagers recognize that young children fall ill easily, and they have the special phrase *dereng kemirab sawan* (not yet invulnerable [to] *sawan*) to express this vulnerability. They believe that such illnesses are caused by inadequate protection by the family during the transition of the infant from the "womb world" to the "real world." Every infant, they believe, enters the real world before it is fully ready to cope with it. The infant is *dereng Jawa* (not yet Javanese), or still ignorant, and must be taught as quickly as possible how to cope with life. Accordingly, parents and older siblings take pains to escort the infant to "adult" occasions such as a wedding, a shadow play, a funeral, the market, and so on. During these trips, they address long and serious explanations to the infant. During each such exposure to the real world with all its hazards, the parents carry out the *sawanan,* a special ritual to safeguard their infant. Depending upon the occasion to which the infant has been escorted, this ritual may take the form of applying to the infant's face some yellow powder given by a bride, kissing the *dalang* (maestro of a shadow play), or touching some earth from the site of the grave. If this prophylactic ritual is neglected, the infant will suffer *sawan penganten* (wedding illness), with symptoms like jaundice, associated with the yellow powder applied to the face of a Javanese bride; *sawan wayang* (shadow play illness), with symptoms of stiffness, like an inanimate puppet; or *sawan wangke* (corpse illness), with symptoms of paleness and lack of appetite. There are at least thirty different types of *sawan,* which include most serious childhood diseases as well as the consequences of some simple ones when they are neglected. Each type is associated with the specific social occasion to which the infant was introduced improperly, and the specific characteristics of each type of *sawan* are related to the specific characteristics of each such occasion. The explicit association of these illnesses with major social and cultural events signifies that, even if evil spirits are the proximate cause, the ultimate cause is inadequate enculturation or socialization by the parents.

The third category of serious illness is *kewalat* (curse), which refers to misfortune, unhappiness, or illness encountered by an older child or adolescent because of offense to his/her parents. Even after the immediate symptoms of this illness vanish, the state of *kewalat* continues until pardon is begged from, and granted by, the parents. In such cases, therefore, the indigenous healer focuses on mending family ties, regardless of whether the patient has already recovered or not.

The fourth category is *kesiku* (punishment), which refers to misfortune occasioned by an adult's violation of sociocultural norms. By this stage in life, a person is supposed to have internalized the norms that guide behavior toward both human society and the supernatural world. Any adult who nevertheless offends his parents, mishandles ritual possessions like a *keris,* or continually misbehaves toward his fellows, will be punished with *kesiku.* The punishment is administered by the good spirits from the "eternal world" but its effects are felt in the "real world." *Kesiku* carries connotations of setting the record straight. It gives satisfaction to the enemies of the recipient.

The fifth category of serious illness is *kesambet* (seizure), referring to vengeance wreaked on a human being by an evil spirit. Whereas the cause of *kesiku* is usually known to the acquaintances of the afflicted prson, causes of *kesambet* are surrounded with speculation. Perhaps the victim broke a promise to sacrifice the health of a child—not necessarily his own—in return for material wealth provided by an evil spirit; or perhaps the victim was disrespectful to a spot frequented by ghosts (such *anker* are scattered all over the countryside). In each case, it is human disturbance of the "world in between" that results in supernatural revenge in the real world.

The sixth category of illness, *kebelisen* (possession), refers to misfortune that is wrought at the spirits' own initiative. They seize the opportunity to take possession of the body when a person is spiritually weak. This can occur only when people are in a condition that deviates considerably from the state of *slamet* (personal, social, and ritual well-being).

The seventh and final category of serious illness includes *keguna-guna* and *kelebon*, both translated as "caught by black magic." Both consist of a pact or agreement between someone in the real world and the evil spirits in the world in-between, the intent of which is to influence or punish someone else in the real world. In many cases a black magic specialist acts as mediator. The victims of such magic experience sudden changes in bodily and psychic states.

Use of the foregoing supernatural explanations of illness depends upon the stage of a given illness and its comparison with any preceding stages (viz., indicating an improving or worsening condition). During the initial stages of an illness and/or when an illness shows signs of abating, it is likely to be identified as *lara mriang* (simple illness) and explained in terms of symptomatic criteria. However, when an illness worsens and enters a more advanced state, then it is identified as *lara nemen* (serious illness), and etiological, supernatural criteria become most important to its explanation. In this Javanese case, therefore, the academic debate as to whether etiology or symptomatology is most important in folk diagnosis appears to be irrelevant (cf. Foster 1976; Jordaan 1982), because the Javanese in effect move back and forth between these two frames of reference (viz., they move back and forth between serious and simple illness). This movement is perhaps most readily observed in the case of infant diseases where an initially and apparently "simple" illness such as diarrhea can become "serious" and even fatal in just a day or two (Rienks 1982).

This system of folk diagnosis is the equivalent—within the indigenous health care system—of the modern medical knowledge imparted through the cadre training. One crucial difference is that the latter is a new and strange body of knowledge known to no one aside from the cadres and the educated elite, whereas the former is known to patients as well as healers. Folk diagnosis proceeds in an atmosphere of mutual trust and consultation. The healer, the relatives of the patient, and/or the patient as well discuss the illness together until they agree on a diagnosis.

Folk Healers

Javanese villagers draw a distinction between *tiyang biasa* (ordinary people), *tiyang pinter* (clever ordinary people), and *tiyang saged* (capable people). (In informal conversation the low Javanese equivalents *wong biasa, wong pinter,* and *wong bisa,* respectively, are used.) There are several ways to become a capable person. In general this involves improvement of one's inner character *(batin)* until the limits of each individual's unique spiritual constitution *(dasar)* are reached. Such improvement is reflected in one's outer manners *(lahir)*. Abstinence, meditation, study, and careful behavior all contribute to this process of strengthening one's character and increase the chance that beneficial power will be granted by the spirits. Beneficial power may enter a person as a *pulung* (star), *wahyu* (ray of light), or *andaru* (fire-ball); and it opens the way to understanding and influencing the different worlds of being. A person can also be entered by destructive powers, as when a pact is made with evil spirits in order to harm one's fellow humans. Both types of power are central to folk treatment, whether this treatment is intended to help or hurt someone. When a villager evaluates an indigenous healer, the basic criteria are (1) the quality of the healer's inner character; (2) the quality of the healer's behavior; and (3) the depth of the healer's *ngelmu* (esoteric knowledge based on an understanding of the supernatural world). A crucial prerequisite to indigenous health care is that the *ngelmu* of both patient and healer should *cocok* (fit each other).

The authors investigated the range of indigenous healers by asking thirty-six key respondents in the village of Situsari (pop. 2400) "To whom do you turn if you need important advice or if you are in serious trouble?"[5] On an average, each respondent mentioned the names of six persons within the village and the names of four persons outside it (these latter referring mostly to inhabitants of neighboring villages, but also including some famous healers outside the subdistrict). Approximately fifty persons inside the village and sixty persons outside the village were mentioned at least once apiece. The respondents were asked to categorize each person mentioned (what type of healer is the person, in which problem area(s) is the person competent, and why is the person competent). On the basis of these categorizations, it was possible to construct a hierarchy of indigenous healers.

Tukang refers to the lowest layer of this hierarchy. In 95 percent of all cases the term refers to people who have mastered one or two techniques within a small area of competency but who do not possess beneficial or destructive power (hence they are "clever" but not "capable" people). For example, they know how to give massages or make traditional drugs, but they cannot recite the *mantra* (ritual spells) that would make these activities most efficacious. *Tukang* is also used as a derogatory term for persons of greater ability who are suspected of practicing black magic, such as the *tukang pencuri* (expert in theft).

The second category of indigenous healers and the largest category of "capable" persons are called *dukun*. They are paid advisers and healers with a medium level of competency who have mastered at least several of the major ritual skills such as *pijet* (massage), *petungan* (numerology), *jampi* (the reciting of magical formulas), and *tamba* (the fabrication of *jamu*, "traditional drugs"). A *dukun* may become mainly associated with one field of problems or sphere of activities, in which case he or she is then referred to as, for example, *dukun bayi* (birth expert), *dukun pre-wangan* (numerical expert), *dukun sunat* (circumcision expert), or *dukun penganten* (marriage expert). *Dukun* may also be categorized according to the way in which they acquired their skills. There are, for instance, *dukun kranjingan,* who act on behalf of an intruding good or evil spirit, and *dukun kebatinan,* who have acquired a strong inner character through abstinence, meditation, and the study of Javanese or Islamic texts.

The third category of indigenous healers is *kasepuhan,* nonpaid advisers whose level of knowledge and competency varies considerably. Some are just above the level of *tukang,* while others have more fame than *dukun.* Their common characteristic, in addition to declining payment, is that while they are often well-respected, this is only within a small geographical area and/or by certain categories of persons (e.g., the members of a particular occupation, religious orientation, political party, or village faction). They are seldom consulted by persons from outside their own villages. Also, when one is consulting them (e.g., on family problems, health care, agriculture, etc.), the atmosphere is more relaxed than when consulting a *dukun.*

The fourth and final category of indigenous healers is the *kamisepuh.* This is the most elite group. In the village of Situsari it includes just three of the twelve persons who were mentioned more than ten times apiece. Usually the *kamisepuh* are elderly villagers who are highly respected in a wide geographical area. They have mastered many ritual skills and can give advice on all sorts of matters. They have very strong inner characters and, since they are typically well-off economically, they do not care greatly about being financially recompensed for their services. However, if the patient can afford it, the *kamisepuh* will not decline payment (whereas *kasepuhan* will).

The placement of a given healer in one or another of the above categories is strictly the affair of the individual patient or client. One villager may regard a certain healer as a *kamisepuh* while another may regard the same healer as a *tukang* or even as an incompetent, common villager. From the client's point of view, this categorization depends entirely on his/her own personal relationship with the healer and/or the positive results of the latter's efforts. Hence, some of the authors' respondents vigorously disputed the categorizations made by other respondents, saying, for example, "That person is a fake"; "He used to be a good *dukun* but has misused his power"; "He no longer practices abstinence"; and so on. The fact that the status of healer is dependent upon and varies with public perceptions and opinions reflects the manner in which this status is acquired. The methods of becoming an indigenous healer are in principle open to all. They require constant personal reflection on one's behavior and experience and perceived competency in the counseling of one's fellow villagers. This is not easily attained. Indeed, it may be more difficult to become a good *dukun* than it is to become a good physician. In order to become a physician one needs only the intellectual and economic resources to attend a university; but to be regarded as a healer entails the rigorous development and management of one's character and behavior under public scrutiny. The way in which this status is acquired is also reflected in the way in which it is remunerated. Financial transactions with indigenous healers are regarded not as *bayaran* (payments), such as one makes to the physicians at the health center, but rather as *penetep,* tokens of respect and thanks for the use of the healer's powers. In exceptional cases, healers are honored with *slametan* (ceremonial feasts). Repeated assistance may result in establishment of the all-important relationship of *bapak anak buah* (father [and] fruitchild) between healer and client, wherein the client considers himself/herself to be the "fruit" or result of the healer's "plant" (experience, knowledge, and actions).

Summary, Conclusions, and Recommendations

It has not been our intention in this paper either to idealize the indigenous system of health care or to belittle the government's own approach to rural health care. Rather, we have tried to identify and analyze the differences between these two systems that appear to be of the greatest importance to the villagers themselves. It is this comparison that will ultimately determine whether governmental health care is accepted or rejected by the rural Javanese. It is in this knowledge that we present the following conclusions.

The government health service created the cadre program to fill a perceived need, to address a perceived, undertreated category of illness. It remains to assess how accurate this perception was and how closely it fits with the villagers' own perceptions of illness and healers. One immediately apparent discontinuity involves the conception of the illness category that is supposed to be the province of the cadres. From the standpoint of the rural health center, it is the biomedically most simple diseases; but from the villagers' point of view it may be the etiologically most complex cases of illness. There is no mutual comprehension of this distinction: the simple biomedical information in the cadre training manuals is no more comprehensible to the villagers than the villagers' concept of *sawan,* for example, is to the health center physicians. The physicians either are unaware of this difference in perspective or, if aware, do not take it seriously.

The cadre program has been troubled not only by differences in the perception of what illness should be treated by the cadres but also by differences in the perception of who should become cadres. A major difference is that, while the indigenous healers occupy informal roles, the cadre is a formal role. The cadre, as a member of the village council, holds an official public office, while the ranking of indigenous healers emerges in social interaction and may vary sharply from client to client and from event to event. This is the difference between what Jay (1969:239) calls personal rank and situational rank.[6] Situational ranking allows for a great deal of client control and involvement in health care. Such control and involvement are not possible in the cadre system, in which the rank of the healer is personal. Such personal ranks are relatively scarce in rural Java, and this too adds to the problems of the cadre system, since any newly introduced rank immediately becomes an object of contention.

Given these differences between indigenous health care and governmental health care, as well as the differences between the philosophy and the reality of the cadre program, it is understandable that many villagers are reluctant to accept the programs. Acceptance means giving up (at least in part) a health system they can control and understand for a system independent of and incomprehensible to them. It means giving up a health system in which they set the priorities for a system whose priorities are set by village leaders and health center staff. Since the villagers are understandably reluctant to make these sacrifices, it appears increasingly necessary for the government to alter its basic approach to primary health care and indigenous medicine.

The government's current view of indigenous medicine is reflected in the official terminology of the health care system. Thus, the government applies the term "primary health care" to the services offered by its rural clinics and their various extensions (viz., auxiliary posts, mobile units, and cadre programs). By implication, since only "zero health care" can be lower on the scale than "primary health care," there is no health care available below or beyond the lowest level of service of the government system. This perception is not only chauvinistic, but it involves a massive denial of reality, given that an estimated 76 percent of all disease cases never enter the government health centers and a substantial portion of these receive some kind of treatment within the indigenous system.[7] Instead of ignoring the indigenous system or expecting it to be easily replaced by the government one, therefore, the government should look at the former as an inevitable and also beneficial foundation for the latter.

The cadre program is an obvious starting point for an interface between the indigenous and government systems, assuming that the program can be redirected to this end. For example, the cadre training could and should be given to existing indigenous healers, most logically the *kasepuhan* and *dukun*. The training could be presented as merely one more type of *ngelmu* (knowledge), to be added to the several types of *ngelmu* (e.g., massage and numerology) that the indigenous healers already have mastered. The selection of indigenous healers as cadres would facilitate both the acceptance of the training, given that the healers are already experts in this realm of knowledge, and acceptance of the program as a whole, given that many healers are also formal village leaders (cf. Williams and Satoto 1979).

The foregoing suggestions need to be supported and informed—and doubtless supplemented and improved—by more and better anthropological research on both governmental and indigenous health care. Regarding the latter, research is particularly needed on (1) decision-making processes in poor families in the event of infant and childhood illness, (2) the relationship between the folk diagnosis of adult illnesses and the past social behavior of the patient, and (3) the role of the indigenous healer in both diagnosis and therapy. Regarding governmental health care, what is needed are not further, normative studies and commendations of existing programs, but rather critical, empirical evaluations of these programs and their potential for improving rural health care.

Notes

1. The research upon which this paper is based was carried out in the context of the HEDERA (Health Development in Rural Areas) project's study of cadre programs and family illness strategies in Central Java. The project, begun in 1978, is a joint effort of the Free University (Amsterdam) and Gadjah Mada

University (Yogyakarta), and is sponsored by NUFFIC (The Netherlands Universities Foundation for International Cooperation) and the Indonesian government. We are grateful to the government of Banjarnegara district for its support during the period of fieldwork and in particular to Arif Haliman, the director of the district medical service, and to the following physicians at local health centers: Ilyas Winoto, Yahya Wardoyo, Agus Suwandono, and Titien Januar. An earlier draft of this paper was read at the International Union of Anthropological and Ethnological Sciences' (IUAES) Intercongress in Amsterdam, 21–25 April 1981 and was published as *Primary and Indigenous Health Care in Rural Central Java: A Comparison of Process and Contents,* HEDERA Report no. 4 (Yogyakarta: Gadjah Mada University Medical Faculty, 1981), pp. 63–89. We are grateful to Benson A. Hausman and Michael R. Dove for comments and guidance at various stages during the writing of this paper. But we alone are responsible for the opinions and conclusions expressed here.

2. This calculation is based on averaging the size of both health expenditures and the national population over the five-year period (1979–1984), using the exchange rate of 700 rupiah to the dollar that prevailed as of March 1983.

3. Boutmy (1979:61–88) gives a general description of Banjarnegara's primary health care system, with useful summations of working papers written by the district health service. See also Haliman (1977).

4. These and all other Javanese illness terms are specific to the Banjarnegara area. The same terms may have different connotations elsewhere in Java (e.g., *lara mriang* specifically means "headache" in the environs of Yogyakarta).

5. Situsari is a pseudonym for a particular village where the authors worked in the Banjarnegara district.

6. In this we disagree with Geertz (1960), Koentjaraningrat (1979), Suparlan (1978), and Utrecht (1975), all of whom suggest that being a *dukun* is a dimension of personal rank.

7. The estimate that 76 percent of all disease cases are not treated in health centers is taken from the 1980 national health survey. This figure breaks down as follows: self-treatment, 35 percent; *dukun* (healer), 6 percent; hospital, 7 percent; and the private practices of doctors, nurses, and midwives, 24 percent, 13 percent, and 1 percent, respectively. The 24 percent that are treated in health center break down as follows: *Puskesmas* (Health Centers), 12 percent of all cases; *Balai Pengobatan* (Health Subcenters), 11 percent; *Balai Kesejahteraan Ibu dan Anak* (Mother and Child Clinics), 1 percent (Department of Health 1980:71). These figures differ considerably from the results obtained in the 1972 Serpong project. Among 1,243 disease cases studied, in 38 percent only a *dukun* was consulted; in 13 percent a *dukun* and a nurse were both consulted; and in just 3 percent a *dukun* and a doctor were both consulted (Lubis et al. 1974:19). While it is reasonable to infer that *dukun* play an important role in village healing strategies, therefore, without additional data it is impossible to say precisely in what percentage of all disease cases they are involved.

References Cited

Boutmy, Hudion L.
  1979   *Developing Health Care Delivery Systems in Indonesia.* HEDERA Report
          no. 1. Yogyakarta: Rural and Regional Studies Center, Gadjah
          Mada University.

Department of Health, Republic of Indonesia (BPPK)
  1980   *Survai Kesehatan Rumah Tangga 1980: Data Statistik* [Survey of house-
          hold health: statistical data]. Jakarta.

Foster, George M.
  1976   "Disease Etiologies in Non-Western Medical Systems." *American
          Anthropologist* 78:733–782.

Geertz, Clifford
  1960   *The Religion of Java.* Glencoe: Free Press.

Glick, Leonard B.
  1967   "Medicine as an Ethnographic Category: The Gimi of the New
          Guinea Highlands." *Ethnology* 6:31–56.

Government of Indonesia
  1979   *Rencana Pembangunan Lima Tahun Ketiga: 1979/80–1983/84* [Third
          five-year development plan]. 4 vols. Jakarta: Government of Indo-
          nesia.

Haliman, Arif
  1977   "Indonesia: Community Development through Primary Health
          Care—The Banjarnegara Experience." Read at the UNICEF con-
          ference on Primary Health Care, Hyderabad, India, October.

Hull, Terence H., and Jon E. Rohde
  1980   *Prospects for Rapid Decline of Mortality Rates in Java: A Study of Causes of
          Death and the Feasibility of Policy Interventions for Mortality Control.* 2d ed.
          Yogyakarta: Population Studies Center, GMU.

Iskandar, Poerwanta, A. S. Rienks, Soesartono, and Sunarsih
  1979   *Pengamatan Anthropologis tentang Pembentukan dan Pelaksanaan Program
          Kader* [Anthropological survey concerning the formation and imple-
          mentation of the cadre program]. HEDERA Report no. 2. Yogya-
          karta: Rural and Regional Studies Center, GMU.

Jay, Robert
  1969   *Javanese Villagers: Social Relations in Rural Modjokuto.* Cambridge,
          Mass.: M.I.T. Press.

Jordaan, Roy E.
  1982   *"Tombuwan* in the 'Dermatology' of Madurese Folk-Medicine."
          Bijdragen tot de Taal-, Land-, en Volkenkunde 138:9–29.

Koentjaraningrat
  1979   "Javanese Magic, Sorcery and Numerology." *Masyarakat Indonesia*
          6:37–52.

Lozoff, Betsy, K. R. Kamath, and R. A. Feldman
    1975   "Infection and Disease in South Indian Families: Beliefs about
            Childhood Diarrhea." *Human Organization* 34:353–358.

Lubis, Firman, et al.
    1974   Health Behaviour and Image of the Health Center in the Kecamatan
            Serpong. Jakarta/Leiden: Serpong Paper No. 12.

Rahardjo, A. S. Rienks, Slamet, and Soesartono
    1979   *Hasil Survei Sosiologis tentang Kader dan Klien* [Results of a sociological
            survey of cadres and clients]. HEDERA Report no. 3. Yogyakarta:
            Rural and Regional Studies Center, GMU.

Rienks, Adriaan S., and Poerwanta Iskandar
    1981   *Primary and Indigenous Health Care in Rural Central Java: A Comparison of
            Process and Contents.* HEDERA Report no. 4. Yogyakarta: Medical
            Faculty, GMU.

Rienks, Adriaan S.
    1982   "Pesti Siji Marga Sewu [One fate, one thousand causes]: Percep-
            tions of Infant and Childhood Illnesses and Mortality in a Javanese
            Village." Read at the Workshop on Infant and Child Mortality, held
            at the Demographic Institute of the Universitas Indonesia, Jakarta,
            13–14 December.

Subekti
    1978   "Pembangunan Kesehatan Masyarakat Desa sebagai Usaha ter-
            padu Pemerintah dan Masyarakat" [Rural health development as
            an integrated effort of government and people]. Paper prepared for
            the seminar Ikatan Ahli Kesehatan Masyarakat Indonesia, Kongres
            ke II, Surabaya, 11–13 December.

Suparlan, Parsudi
    1978   "The Javanese *Dukun.*" *Masyarakat Indonesia* 5:195–216.

Utrecht, Ernst
    1975   "The Javanese *Dukun* and His Role in Social Unrest." *Cultures et
            development* 7:319–335.

Werner, David
    1977   *Where There Is No Doctor: A Village Health Care Handbook.* Palo Alto,
            Calif.: The Hesperian Press.

Williams, Glen, and Satoto
    1979   "Kekuasaan dan Artinya bagi Orang Desa: Kasus LKD Sukodono"
            [Authority and meaning for village people: The case of the LKD
            Sukodono]. *Prisma* 8 (3): 16–31.

PART II: ECONOMICS

3. The "Wild Punan" of Borneo: A Matter of Economics

Carl L. Hoffman

Abstract

Widely dispersed throughout the island of Borneo are small groups of nomadic hunters and gatherers generally referred to as "Punan." Little known and only sketchily documented until recently, the Punan are often presumed to be the aboriginal, autochthonous people of the island, distinct and apart from the other Dayak groups. This paper suggests that the term "Punan" in fact refers to a diverse assortment of peoples deriving from sedentary agricultural groups and functioning as specialized collectors of forest products within large trade networks that involve not only Punan, but also sedentary Dayak, coastal Malays, and Chinese.

Introduction

Among the most interesting and confusing problems within the anthropology of insular Southeast Asia is that of the "Wild Punan" of Borneo. For well over one hundred years, these people have continued to fascinate and befuddle virtually all who have come into contact with them. Perhaps no other group of people in this portion of the world has been the object of so much intrigue and misinformation.

Not long after the earliest sustained contacts of Europeans with Dayak groups in Borneo's interior, reports began to circulate concerning strange groups of people, more primitive than the other Dayak tribes and apparently different from them in many respects. Unlike the other Dayak, these people, it was claimed, had no villages or fixed dwelling places of any kind. They moved constantly throughout the deep forest, sleeping in caves and rude shelters made simply of leaves and sticks. It was reported that they neither grew nor ate rice nor any other cultigen, that they subsisted—barely—by hunting game and gathering edible fruits and plants. The reports went on to describe a people who were extremely elusive and seldom seen by anyone, including other Dayak. Timid by nature and frightened of other people, they were said to sequester themselves in the dark world of the inner jungle, from which they rarely if ever dared to venture. These inordinately remote and primitive people, it was claimed, were even afraid of direct sunlight. In time it came to be known that people of this sort were to be found in many widely scattered areas throughout the island of Borneo, and that they were generally called (by others) "Punan." As stories about these jungle nomads began to spread, considerable interest arose in finding out just who these people were.

One of the first theories was formulated by the naturalist and adventurer Carl Bock. In the late 1870s he ventured into the forests of what is now the Muara Wahau district of East Kalimantan. He wrote: "I was intending to penetrate into the forest . . . and endeavour if possible to solve for myself the mystery of the Orang Poonan or Wild People of the Woods" (Bock 1882:69). Bock encountered a small handful of people, about seven individuals in all, with whom he spent a single afternoon. He emerged shortly thereafter to announce: "I believe these savages to be the true aborigines of Borneo. They live in utter wildness in the central forests of Borneo, almost entirely isolated from all communication with the rest of the world" (ibid.:75–76). This was similarly the verdict of the British civil servant and scientist Charles Hose, whose encounters with Punan in Sarawak led him to declare: "I have no doubt in my mind that this wandering race of people are aboriginals of the country" (Hose 1893:157).

Despite these and numerous other reports published during the decades to follow, some observers doubted that such people actually existed. The American anthropologist Fay-Cooper Cole (1945:99) stated in 1945: "It is certain that . . . these authorities and others did see people called 'punan,' but the writer is inclined to doubt their existence as a distinct people. In central Borneo any party gathering jungle products and making temporary camps is known as 'punan' or campers." Cole's doubts elicited this response the following year from Robert von Heine-Geldern (1946:61): "The merest outlines only are known of the nomadic and truly primitive Punan. . . . Recently, even doubts of the existence of the Punan as a distinct people have been expressed by Fay-Cooper Cole. . . . These doubts are wholly unfounded. The Punan have been seen, described, and photographed by numerous observers." Cole restated his position a year later, arguing (1947:340):

Despite the fact that people called Punan have been seen and reported by reliable parties I still am inclined to doubt their existence as a distinct people. . . . I went to Borneo looking for Punan. While in Central Borneo I sought in vain for any such people, but I did find that any group which was away from home gathering jungle products and living in temporary camps was known as Punan. I saw several such Punan groups but upon enquiry found they all related to fixed villages. Under the circumstances I believe that in Central Borneo the term has no other significance than our word "camper." It is possible that in Sarawak and elsewhere there may be truly nomadic Punan, but for the moment I think there is reasonable doubt that this is true.

The crux of the problem of understanding the Punan and their identity was enunciated more than thirty years ago by the late Tom Harrisson (1949:131), who observed: "We do not even know if the persons so termed really represent a culturally, a linguistically or physically related people, or whether they have several origins and are uniform only in a common habit of nomadism." After noting various theories concerning the origins of the Punan—for example, that they are the descendents of runaway slaves, or criminals, social misfits, and the like—Harrisson himself suggested (ibid.) that the Punan may have originated from whole villages of settled groups that had "gone bush in despair," as a consequence of military defeat at the hands of larger and stronger groups. The manner in which Punan have been thought to interact with neighboring settled groups, as well as their habit of periodically settling within agricultural longhouse communities, has led other observers, such as Hildred Geertz (1963:91), to suggest that Punan "probably represent only the poorest fragments of the latter groups, who are forced to inhabit uncultivable land."

In this paper I intend to present a very different analysis of the relations between Borneo's sedentary agriculturalists and the Punan, and to suggest that a radical revision of theories of Punan society is in order. Specifically, I will suggest that the Punan do not represent a single ethnic group at all, but rather that they are the forest-based "wings" of many of the different tribal groups of sedentary agriculturalists.

An Ethnographic Overview of the Punan

Between August 1980 and November 1981 I conducted a comprehensive ethnographic survey in Kalimantan on present and former nomadic hunters and gatherers, known generally to outsiders as "Punan" (Figs. 3.1–3.3). I visited and studied Punan groups in the subdistricts of Tanjung Palas, Peso, Malinau, and Kayan Hulu in the district of

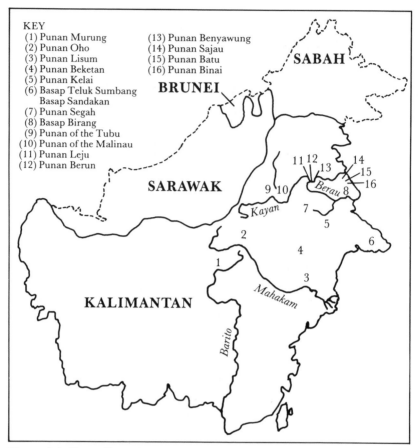

KEY
(1) Punan Murung
(2) Punan Oho
(3) Punan Lisum
(4) Punan Beketan
(5) Punan Kelai
(6) Basap Teluk Sumbang
     Basap Sandakan
(7) Punan Segah
(8) Basap Birang
(9) Punan of the Tubu
(10) Punan of the Malinau
(11) Punan Leju
(12) Punan Berun
(13) Punan Benyawung
(14) Punan Sajau
(15) Punan Batu
(16) Punan Binai

Figure 3.1 Nomadic and Formerly Nomadic Groups Studied

Bulungan; the subdistrict of Kelai in the district of Berau; and the sub-district of Tabang in the district of Kutai—all in the province of East Kalimantan—as well as the subdistrict of Sumber Barito in the district of Barito Utara, in the province of Central Kalimantan. I also visited and studied nomadic groups known generally as "Basap" in the subdistricts of Gunung Tabur and Talisayan in Berau district and met briefly with representatives of formerly nomadic Basap in the subdistrict of Sangkulirang in Kutai district.

Settlement Pattern

While profound differences and variation were found to exist among the many scattered groups known as Punan, it is still possible to make certain generalizations with respect to the Punan lifestyle. To begin with,

Figure 3.2 Major Cities and Towns in the Area of Study

nomadic Punan groups are invariably smaller than those of other Dayak peoples, rarely exceeding one hundred. The exigencies of nomadism, coupled with the limited carrying capacity of the natural environment under their system of exploitation, constrain the formation and maintenance of larger groupings. Villages of settled Punan are substantially larger, their greater numbers facilitated by agriculture and by the accretions of non-Punan who settle in as families or marry in as individuals.

Under normal circumstances, a still nomadic Punan tribe rarely if ever lives together in one place as a single group. The usual settlement pattern involves a small residential grouping of two or three nuclear families, related by blood or marriage, living together in a temporary encampment in the forest. Each of these nuclear families may have several coresident dependents—aged widows, visitors, and the like. Each

Figure 3.3 Major Rivers in the Area of Study

encampment is usually no more than an hour's walk from at least one
other similar encampment of two or three families, and often several
such residential groups may be found within the radius of a day's walk
from any single encampment.

Some Punan groups who are presently settled report that in former
times they had temporary base camps, from which nuclear families
fanned out in different directions for weeks at a time. In effect, however,
the settlement pattern appears to have been the same. The "base
camps" were usually little more than storage places for rattan, damar,
and other jungle produce. Only a few individuals were to be found there
at any given time, the majority of the group being scattered among
encampments such as those described above.

These residential groups are by nature unstable units, subject to constant fission and fusion as individuals or whole families break away from one encampment to join another some distance away. People leave one encampment to join another due to quarrels and disputes, as well as the desire to find better hunting and gathering opportunities in other parts of the forest. Marriages and divorces similarly cause people to move from one local group to another.

There are and have been, however, alternative modes of settlement. Punan of the upper Malinau and Tubu rivers areas in Malinau subdistrict, for example, tend to reside semipermanently in larger band aggregates. The men go out sporadically in groups of two or three to hunt and gather jungle produce for several days at a time, while the women gather food or tend small gardens close to home. On the other hand, the Punan Batu and Punan Binai of the upper Sajau River in Tanjung Palas subdistrict still spend most of the year wandering about the deep forest in single nuclear family units.

Economy and Material Culture

Like hunters and gatherers elsewhere in the world, the nomadic Punan groups of Kalimantan make use of a wide range of animal resources. Simply stated, Punan will eat any and every animal, with the exception of certain species of birds that are of religious significance. Punan share with settled Dayaks an extreme fondness for wild pigs *(Sus barbatus)*, which is the food of preference for every Punan group I encountered. Two species of wild deer are also greatly favored *(Muntiacus muntjak* and *Cervus unicolor)*, as is, to a lesser extent, the mouse deer *(Tragulus javanicus* or *Tragulus napu)*. Punan will also hunt and eat such animals as monkeys and snakes, but only as a last resort in the prolonged absence of pigs and deer.

As with some other Dayak, the primary hunting weapon of all Punan groups is the *sumpit* (blowpipe)—a long pole of ironwood *(Eusideroxylon zwageri)* with a hole bored through its length and a metal knifeblade lashed to one end with rattan. The blowpipe darts are generally made entirely of wood, although one group was seen making dart tips from discarded tin cans. The manufacture of poison for the darts varies somewhat from one region to another. It is usually extracted from particular species of jungle plants, which are ground, pounded, and boiled together. In addition to the blowpipes, Punan also make liberal use of spears. These are simply knife blades lashed with rattan to the ends of crudely hewn sticks. The bow and arrow is unknown, and the ownership and use of firearms is prohibited by the Indonesian government.

Not unlike other Dayak peoples, all Punan groups employ dogs in the

hunting of wild pigs. Punan dogs are generally considered to have superior hunting abilities and are avidly sought by settled Dayak tribes.
Kenyah of the Apo Kayan region (Kayan Hulu subdistrict), for example, point proudly to dogs that they say are descended from a dog given
to them by Punan. Dogs are not, however, used to hunt monkeys,
which are generally taken with blowpipes when they appear in groups to
drink at a riverbank. Nor are they often employed in the hunting of
deer, which most Punan groups prefer to hunt at night.

The nomadic Punan lifestyle is as much a riverine adaptation as it is a
forest adaptation, and all Punan are as skillful at fishing as they are at
hunting. Fish are caught with cast nets, fixed nets, dams, and weirs, as
well as with spears. The hook-and-line method is rarely employed.
Some groups in addition use various plant poisons. When introduced
into small streams and rivers, these stupify the fish to the point where
they can easily be taken by hand. This method is often carried out as a
communal operation, involving an entire Punan village.

The gathering of wild foods substantially supplements the produce of
hunting and fishing in the diets of all nomadic Punan groups. Punan
avail themselves of a wide variety of edible fruits and vegetables, as well
as honey. Wild sago (*Metroxylon* spp.), the traditional Punan staple, is
now rarely eaten. I observed its use only among Punan groups of the
upper Tubu River area in the Malinau subdistrict. Nomadic Punan are
much more likely to practice a half-hearted and tenuous form of horticulture in poorly tended, widely scattered plots. These Punan also regularly trade their jungle produce for rice, to which they have now grown
accustomed. The situation is quite different for the settled Punan. Their
swiddens and gardens are quite comparable with those of the other
Dayak tribes. Indeed, Kenyah at the village of Long Nawang in the
Apo Kayan informed me that the nearby settled Punan Oho have
become better farmers than they are themselves.

As might be expected, the material technology of nomadic Punan is
sparse. Dwellings are little more than shelter against the rain, fashioned
from wooden poles, leaves, and bamboo and held together with strips of
rattan. There are neither walls nor internal partitions. Among most
Punan groups, these dwellings are square and built on piles several feet
off the ground. Among some groups, however, much smaller, rectangu-
lar dwellings—more like lean-tos than huts—are built on the ground,
with the bamboo floor no more than a couple of inches above the soil.
The houses of settled Punan, constructed of wooden boards and occasionally featuring corrugated tin roofs, are not appreciably different
from those of other Dayak, except for those houses of Punan groups
only recently settled. Dwellings of newly settled Punan are often a sort
of transitional hybrid between the traditional forest shelters and the
sturdier village houses.

The contents of a nomadic Punan hut, comprising the family's household goods and personal possessions, are easily enumerated. A spear, a blowpipe, a bamboo container full of wooden darts, a small gourd container for the dart heads, one or two bush-swords in wooden sheaths, a few pots and pans, several rattan baskets, and a couple of woven rattan mats comprise the normal complement of articles. These, along with clothes, necklaces, bracelets, and the like are typically the sum total of a family's material possessions. The material possessions of settled, village-dwelling Punan are generally more numerous and elaborate, entailing, in addition to those items noted above, drinking glasses and dishware, as well as wristwatches, cassette players and shortwave radios, and occasionally outboard gasoline motors for the long, narrow, locally made canoes that many settled Punan families possess. The clothing and jewelry of settled Punan are similarly more abundant and more costly.

Political Structure

A nomadic Punan tribe is a relatively egalitarian grouping: there are no fixed ranks, classes, or castes of any kind. Each Punan encampment normally has a senior male who is generally acknowledged as the head of the group. He has no real power but is rather *primus inter pares.* He functions as headman only during instances of decision making, when his role is to advise and suggest a course of action. Final decisions are arrived at through consensus, the headman having neither power nor authority to impose his will upon others. Moreover, even when a consensus has been reached, no one is obliged to abide by it. Each family always has the alternative of leaving the encampment and joining another one.

Political organization beyond the level of the residential group is so diffuse as to be almost nonexistent. A nomadic Punan tribe is an extremely amorphous unit, with vague boundaries and fluid composition. Indeed, it is reasonable to ask whether a bunch of widely scattered nuclear families, in only sporadic contact with one another and spread out haphazardly over miles of dense jungle, is really a "tribe" at all. Punan families conceive of themselves as belonging to a larger group on the basis of common kinship, a common dialect, and the use of a common, loosely bounded territory, usually at the headwaters of the river that gives the group its name (e.g., "Punan Berun," "Punan Benyawung," "Punan Leju," etc.). These three factors operate on people separated by miles of jungle and difficult terrain to produce a sort of loosely worn ethnicity or "consciousness of kind." However, this sense of ethnicity is not associated with much in the way of political organization beyond the residential group. A tribe of nomadic Punan almost never acts in concert. Indeed, it rarely even gathers together in one place. Effective "tribal leadership" does not exist, nor are there any other overarching social institutions that embrace the group as a whole.

Leadership and politics among settled, village-dwelling Punan are somewhat different (although, again, there is no supravillage organization that links two or more villages inhabited by members of the same Punan tribe). Having more or less entered the mainstream of Indonesian society, settled Punan conform to the general pattern of provincial political organization. Each village has a *kepala kampung* (village headman), who is a salaried government official. The village headman is more powerful than the headman of a nomadic Punan settlement for two reasons, the first being that he is supported by the full weight of local government. The second reason arises out of the special circumstances of a settled, agricultural—as opposed to a nomadic—adaptation. A village-dwelling farmer, possessing a house, a swidden, and a garden, feels more tightly bound to his community than does a jungle nomad to his temporary encampment. While a nomadic Punan has always the option of deserting his present encampment for another, the settled villager is tied to his house, his fields, and his perennial crops. The headman of a settled village is thus a more effective force with respect to its inhabitants than is the headman of an impermanent jungle encampment. This is not to say that the village headman has the power or the authority to arbitrarily make decisions and impose them on his village, for he definitely does not. Decisions concerning such matters as land use, allocation of government funds, dispute settlement, and indemnity payments for social offenses are arrived at through consensus among all male heads of families, meeting in the house of the village head. Once a decision has been reached in a village, however, the members of the village are more obliged to abide by it than are jungle nomads with respect to decisions made at their encampments.

Social Structure

Kinship within all Punan groups—both nomadic and settled—is reckoned bilaterally, usually with a slight patrifocal emphasis. There are no descent groups of any form whatsoever, as lineality is completely irrelevant. Indeed, most Punan are unable to remember their ancestors back beyond two generations. A Punan "tribe," structurally speaking, is essentially nothing more than a loose network of overlapping, ego-focused personal kindreds.

The overwhelming majority of Punan groups prohibit marriage between first cousins, and many of these frown upon second cousin marriage as well. Yet among a few groups, such as the Punan Batu of the upper Sajau River, first cousin marriage is the preferential form, referred to as "good marriage." First cousin marriage is preferred, they say, because it keeps people close to their families.

As with some other Dayak groups, marriage among Punan groups is usually contracted through payment of brideprice, varying in amount from group to group and region to region. Nomadic Punan groups may be expected to pay no more than a couple of bush-swords or blowpipes, while among others the payment of brass gongs and large porcelain jars is *de rigeur.* Money and such modern goods as outboard motors enter into the brideprice among many settled Punan groups living close to upriver towns, such as the Punan living near Kota Malinau in Bulungan district and those living near Kota Tabang in Kutai district. Among these groups the brideprice, which is paid in a combination of cash and goods over a period of several years, may reach as much as 300,000 rupiah (equal to US$479 at exchange rates prevailing in mid-1981). At the other end of the spectrum are such groups as the Punan Kelai of the Berau region, the Punan Berun of the middle Kayan River area, and the aforementioned Punan Batu, who all marry without any payment of brideprice.

Punan groups, both nomadic and settled, exhibit no fixed pattern of postmarital residence in marriages involving two encampments or villages. Nomadic Punan will encamp wherever they have kin relations through blood or marriage; and the villages of settled Punan usually contain an equal number of in-marrying males and females. Among all Punan groups it is the desire of newly wedded couples to obtain their own dwelling place immediately after marriage. Among nomadic Punan this desire is easily enough realized as the newlyweds build their own shelter in whatever encampment they choose to call home. Among settled Punan, however, there is usually a brief period of waiting in which the couple resides in the house of either the boy's or girl's parents, or at the house of some other relation, until they are able to build a house of their own. The couple is normally settled in their own house by the time their first child is born.

The families of nomadic Punan are usually smaller than those of either settled Punan or other Dayak peoples. There are, on the average, about three children per family among nomadic Punan, while settled Punan families average around five children. Family planning may be a factor in the family size of the former. Many Punan groups claim to have traditionally had effective methods of birth control. Punan groups of the upper Malinau and Tubu rivers areas, for example, speak of having used a certain type of rare grass found deep in the forest. According to accounts I was given about this grass, it was cooked and consumed in very small quantities with other vegetables, drunk with water or coffee, or simply eaten alone. It had only to be consumed once, by both husband and wife, to prevent further pregnancies throughout the entire life of the couple. This grass is rarely used today, most Punan now preferring to obtain conventional oral contraceptives at the local family planning office in Kota Malinau. "With the pill," as I was told, "you can always change your mind and have children," while the effects of the traditional grass remedy were said to be irreversible.

People dwelling in the coastal cities and larger upriver towns of Kalimantan, many of whom have never actually seen a Punan, enjoy relating the story of how nomadic Punan women, about to give birth while their band is on the march, simply drop behind, give birth alone, and then run with their newborn children to rejoin the band, usually within the space of an hour after the birth. I related this story to every Punan group I visited, and they invariably reacted with astonishment and laughter, especially the women. They called this story variously "nonsense," "craziness," or simply "lies." I was told that Punan women generally give birth with the aid and assistance of at least one other woman, and that usually at least one full week passes thereafter before the mother is up and around.

Throughout the early years of its life, the Punan child is the object of constant attention and affection. From the moment it awakens until the moment it falls asleep, the small toddler is held, caressed, cuddled, and petted. It is never spanked, rarely if ever spoken sharply to or disciplined in any other way. Its life is characterized by almost total indulgence. This idyllic state of affairs ends abruptly at the birth of the family's next child, at which time the parents shift almost all their attention and affection to their newborn. By the time a child is about five years old, it is already being given its share of small responsibilities, such as caring for its younger sibling(s), performing light chores, and running short errands. As the child grows older it is gradually made to learn through observation and imitation the full range of day-to-day activities appropriate to its gender. While there are in actuality no rigid boundaries between men's activities and women's activities in Punan society, girls tend to concentrate upon learning such activities as cooking, mat weaving, food gathering, and infant care, while boys tend to learn hunting, fishing, and such work as the clearing and burning of swiddens. By the time a Punan child reaches middle or late adolescence, he or she has only to marry and produce a child in order to become a socially recognized "adult."

Belief System

Approaches to sickness and methods of therapy vary somewhat from one Punan group to another. Most of the Punan groups I studied possess a traditional pharmacopeia, consisting of preparations made from various forest plants, which are mixed with water in various ways and then drunk. Many groups have shamans, who cure illnesses through trance and spirit possession. A small handful of Punan groups have neither shamans nor traditional medicines of any kind. The principal approach to therapy among these peoples involves simply sitting by the campfire to keep warm. This was previously the case among the Punan Lisum of the upper Belayan River area in the Tabang subdistrict. The majority of these people, however, are now freshly settled into a large village near Kota Tabang and have recently adopted the custom of shamanism, which they consider to be commensurate with their development and modernization. These and other Punan groups living near towns also buy patent medicines or, when seriously ill, go to the local government health care center.

The overwhelming majority of nomadic Punan groups have a common approach to the death of one of their members. The deceased is at once buried directly in the ground, after which the entire residential group immediately abandons the encampment. They do this, they say, out of fear of the deceased's *hantu* (ghost). This pattern was also noted by such earlier writers as Harrisson (1949) and Needham (1972) among Punan groups of Sarawak. My own inquiries, however, unearthed some notable exceptions to this general pattern. Punan groups of the upper Malinau and Tubu rivers areas, for example, are part of a larger culture complex that includes the settled Merap and Tebilun peoples, who customarily (formerly) practiced secondary burial. Among all of these tribes, including the Punan groups noted, a newly deceased individual was first interred in a wooden chest, which was then placed inside a rudimentary shelter in a tree. The body lay in state for one year, after which the bones were retrieved, washed, placed in a porcelain jar, and then reinterred in a finer "house" built atop a tree. Each of the two tree burials was accompanied by a ceremony—a small one for the primary burial, a larger and more elaborate one for the secondary burial.

I also observed exceptional treatment of the dead among the Punan Murung of the upper Barito River in Central Kalimantan, who are part of a larger culture complex that includes the Ot Danum and Siang tribes. All of these groups bury their dead only once, and always in a wooden chest placed in the ground. However, custom dictates that every death be elaborately commemorated with a major feast involving animal sacrifice, sponsored by the nearest relatives of the deceased. Ideally, this feast is held soon after the burial, but the attendant high costs often delay its staging for months or, in some cases, years after the actual death. While the feast commemorates the death of an individual, the feast is itself commemorated by the construction of a wooden memorial, of a size and form commensurate with the elaborateness of the feast. Families sacrificing at least ten pigs for their funerary feasts are allowed to erect within the village wooden memorial posts, normally around twenty feet in height, with simple ornamentation on top. A family sacrificing a water buffalo, however, is permitted to erect a wooden statue with carved anthropomorphic designs.

The traditional religion of the Punan groups appears to be a sort of abridged or "portable" version of that practiced by settled Dayak peoples. This religion is based on bird augury (cf. Freeman 1960; Sandin 1980). Each Punan group possesses a small pantheon of certain birds that are believed to communicate with human beings, through the medium of their flight and calls. A Punan entering the deep forest to hunt game or seek jungle products watches and listens for advice. A certain bird flying overhead toward the left is a bad sign, informing him that the path he is taking is either devoid of game or fraught with danger. The bird flying overhead toward the right, however, indicates that the presently trod path is safe and will lead the man toward game or the jungle produce he is seeking. The mental equation of left with "bad sign" and right with "good sign" is a deeply embedded notion shared by all the Punan groups I studied.

The bird's call is just as important as the direction of its flight. Most of the spirit birds within any Punan group's pantheon can issue two (or more) variant calls, one of which is described as a "refined" or "good" call and one as a "coarse" or "bad" call. Good calls are interpreted as auspicious indications of imminent success; bad calls are warnings of impending danger or failure. The plethora of calls heard in the forest from the various spirit birds bear a variety of messages for those who know how to interpret them. One call tells a man to halt for a day or two and make camp at his present location. Another tells him that pigs will be plentiful if he veers off toward the left. Still another call may warn him of danger at the spot where he is resting, while another predicts a chance meeting with a friend. Certain calls indicate a crisis back at camp and direct the hunter to return at once. Among the aforementioned Punan Murung, a certain bird singing in the middle of the night informs its hearer that a close relation has just died. An elderly Punan Beketan from the upper Tuboq River in the Tabang subdistrict related to me the manner in which one of his ancestors became a legendary hunter of wild rhinoceros. The man, I was told, was guided in his quest for rhino horns by a succession of helpful spirit birds. Their calls led him through the forest by many twists and turns, eventually enabling him to kill a grand total of twenty rhinoceros—all of them tracked and taken with the birds' unflagging assistance.

As the Punan explain it, the calls and flight signs of their spirit birds are simply a matter of friends advising friends. Punan regard these birds with fondness and respect: most groups will not hunt or harm their spirit birds under any circumstances. Punan Beketan say that the birds that speak to them are more than mere messengers. Some are capable of issuing calls that render their hearers immune to danger and invincible against enemies. While many Punan have at present become nominally either Christians or Muslims, most still retain varying degrees of belief in the spirit birds. They see no inherent conflict in this. As an old Punan Lisum explained it to me one day: "Since God cannot speak directly to human beings, he appoints the birds as his assistants to communicate with people."

Analysis of the Origins and Function of Punan Society

Anthropologists working in Kalimantan and Sarawak have had difficulty making sense of the Punan for one fundamental reason: they have insisted upon seeing these people as being somehow outside and apart from the general pattern of Borneo's traditional tribal life. A closer and more detailed examination of the situation reveals that this view is not shared by the island's groups who, to a great extent, depend upon the scattered and diverse forest specialists known generally as "Punan." I suggest that the key to understanding the Punan is to be found in a study of the broader economic framework of traditional Borneo life.

Relations with Sedentary Agriculturalists

First, it is noteworthy that groups known as "Punan" are present almost everywhere in Kalimantan, Sarawak, and Sabah. The individual Punan groups, however, do not wander freely across the length and breadth of the island. Rather, each group stays within a fairly circumscribed area and always within reasonable distance of one or more settled village groups to whom the Punan group is well known. The local Punan group is never a mystery to its settled neighbors. Individual members of the Punan group are known to the settled villagers by name, and the latter often refer to the former as "our siblings." In addition, any one Punan group is almost always closer in language and customs to the neighboring settled peoples than it is to other Punan groups in other regions.

Thus, in the Peso district of the middle Kayan River I heard Kayan Malaran people refer to the Punan Berun as "our younger siblings." In the Apo Kayan I was told by Kenyah Lepo Tau that they and the nearby Punan Oho are both descended from one common ancestor. A similar story was told to me in the Berau area by Punan Kelai and their settled neighbors, the Segai. In the Malinau district I was informed by both Tebiluns and Meraps that the local Punan groups are "the same as us—same people," a judgment concurred in by every Punan group I visited there. A similar statement was made to me by Ot Danum of the upper Barito River concerning the nearby Punan Murung.

Such ties do not exist between Punan groups in different regions, however. Here one is struck by the wide and considerable differences in language, as well as in customs relating to virtually everything, including such "baseline" activities as hunting and patterns of movement. Moreover, it is significant that the Punan of any one region rarely have contact with the Punan of other regions. Indeed, they are often ignorant of the very existence of Punan groups in adjacent subdistricts. I shall never forget the look of total amazement on the face of a Punan Berun of the Peso subdistrict when I told him I had recently been with the Punan Sajau of the neighboring Tanjung Palas subdistrict. "Are there Punan over there?" he asked me, quite bewildered. The Punan Oho of the Apo Kayan insisted that I describe the customs and way of life of the Punan Berun, shaking their heads in astonishment as I did so. In Malinau, a densely populated area (for Kalimantan) where Punan groups are also numerous, the Punan expressed an almost arrogant lack of interest in the Punan groups I had met in other areas, feeling no sense of kinship with them whatsoever.

The Bornean Trade in Forest Products

The question that thus emerges—one that is perhaps a central issue in the ethnography of Borneo as a whole—is: Who are the Punan and what are they doing there? The best way to answer this question is to first direct our attention away from the Punan and toward the various groups of village-dwelling, swidden horticulturalists, and in particular toward the role of trade in their lives.

Down to the present day, when traveling through the Dayak areas of Kalimantan, one still notices the many bronze gongs and huge ceramic jars so beloved by these people. One sees these in profusion, particularly in the houses of village headmen and other individuals of rank. Whether in the huge, central longhouse apartments of headmen in the Apo Kayan or in the large, ornate single-family residences of headmen elsewhere, gongs and jars are prominently displayed. The extreme social importance of these brass gongs and ceramic jars has been duly noted and described throughout the literature on Borneo societies over the last one hundred years. Here I will just reemphasize that these gongs and jars are not items of local manufacture. The Dayak obtain them in trade with outsiders. These Dayak people attest to the fact that *dari jaman nenek moyang dulu* (from the time of the ancestors long ago) they have been trading with *orang luar* (people from outside), from downriver. Most often these outsiders have been coastal Malays and, more recently, Buginese. It is from these traders, the Dayaks say, that they have received their precious gongs and jars.

It is also from these traders that the Dayak have obtained other trade goods—such as salt. While a few Dayak groups, such as the Kelabits and Lun Daya, have been fortunate enough to have their own nearby sources of salt, most groups elsewhere have depended upon trade for this essential commodity. This has also been the case for metal. While such peoples as the Kenyah of the Apo Kayan were able in former times to mine and work their own metal, most Dayak groups have had to rely on trade to obtain metal for their weapons and agricultural tools. For most settled Dayak groups, trade has also been the source for such items as cloth, tobacco, and, in recent years, currency. Indeed, throughout the areas of Kalimantan that I visited, trade was the major, if not only, source of cash income for settled Dayak groups.

Thus, trading relationships with downriver and coastal Malays and Buginese have served as the principal means by which most Dayak groups have obtained not only heirloom property such as gongs and jars, but also a variety of essential commodities. It is important to note that these Malay and Buginese traders have merely been the middle-men within a much broader trading network, the ultimate sources of which have always been Chinese.

It is difficult to say with any certainty when the Chinese first arrived in Borneo. There is little doubt, however, that their presence on the island has been long and constant. Heine-Geldern (1945:147) writes:

> Taking all into account, one may come to the conclusion that direct Chinese influence in Indonesia goes back at least to the early Han period, that is at the very latest to the 1st century B.C. However, the ornamental designs of the Dayaks tribes of Borneo and of the Ngada of Flores are so clearly related to Chinese designs of the late Chou period that one can hardly avoid the inference that Chinese contacts started as early as the beginning of the third century B.C., and probably earlier.

Other authorities, notably Wang (1958), Wheatley (1959), and Wolters (1967), have suggested somewhat later dates. Regardless of the divergence of opinion among these and other authorities concerning when the Chinese first appeared in Borneo, there is nonetheless a general agreement on why the Chinese came. The motive was trade.

The Chinese have chiefly been interested in the trade of certain natural products found within Borneo's primary forest.

Damar Readied for Transport Downriver

Rattan Readied for Transportation

1. Aloes wood, called *kayu gharu* throughout Borneo, is the pathologically transformed portion of several different species of trees of the genus *Aquilaria*. When burned, this wood gives off a rather pungent fragrance, and it has been used as incense by Chinese, Indians, and Arabs.

2. Edible birds' nests, called *sarang burung,* are made of a gelatinous, translucent, beige-colored substance secreted through the saliva of a small swift *(Collocalia nidifica)*. Another type, regarded as quite inferior, consists of smaller quantities of this substance mixed with moss and other impurities. It is made by a related species of swift *(Collocalia linchii)*. All nests are found deep within caves, attached to the upper sections of the walls close to the roof. Long valued by Chinese for the preparation of various culinary dishes, they are said to have medicinal uses as well.

3. Bezoar stones, generally referred to as *guliga* throughout central and eastern Kalimantan, have been used for medicinal purposes not only by Chinese, but also by Indians, Persians, and Arabs. In most countries the term refers to the hardened concretions occasionally found in the internal organs of certain animals, especially ruminants. Two special and very valuable types of bezoars are found in Borneo, however. One, the more common, is the *batu monyet* (monkey stone). These are found, I was told, in the gallbladders of only three varieties of monkey, and in perhaps only one out of every hundred cases. These monkey stones range in size from a pea to a lima bean, very occasionally attaining the size of a small chicken's egg. They are inordinately valuable to traders, and the larger the stone the higher the value. Even more valuable, however, is the second type of bezoar found in Borneo, called *batu landak* (porcupine stone). These concretions form around external wounds in Bornean porcupines (which include *Trichys lipura, Hystrix brachyura,* and *Thecurus crassispinis*), and they are extremely rare. I was informed that only one out of "hundreds" of porcupines carries such a concretion, and that porcupines themselves are encountered only occasionally—most often at night. Porcupine stones are always very small and extremely light in weight; they fetch fantastic prices at all times. These two bezoars from Borneo, monkey stones and porcupine stones, have been highly valued for centuries by the Chinese as medicinals. Both varieties have been, and continue to be, the raw sources of an extensive array of pharmaceutical remedies for everything from stomachache to asthma.

4. Horns of the Bornean rhinoceros *(Didermocerus sumatrensis),* called *tanduk badak,* also have been thought for centuries to possess enormous curative properties. As such they have been pounded, pum-

meled, and ground up into a wide variety of Chinese medicines, in particular aphrodisiacs and treatments for impotence.

5. Resins (damar) are collected from certain trees and used chiefly as adhesives and caulking putty. Such putty dries quickly, becomes rock hard, and is very durable. In former days, before the introduction of the now common kerosene lamp, hardened chunks of damar were widely used for making torches. A small piece, supported by three sticks tied together at one end and set upright, gives off a rather faint, smoky light but can burn for more than an hour.

6. Rattan, referring to several species of climbing plants, is utilized throughout Borneo for everything from basket making to house building and is used for furniture elsewhere in Asia and the rest of the world.

7. Gutta-percha, a resinous latex obtained from the sap of certain trees of the genus *Palaquim,* has traditionally been used by Chinese as an adhesive and as waterproof caulking for sailing vessels. Less frequently, it was also used medicinally.

8. Camphor is obtained in Borneo from the tree *Dryobalanops aromatica,* where it is found in hardened, crystalline form. Camphor has long been used to make medicines, incense, and embalming fluids.

9. Beeswax has traditionally been used by Chinese in the making of base substances for a variety of ointments and medicines for external use.

10. The most recent addition to this list is a nut, of roughly the same size and shape as an avocado, known in Kalimantan as *buah tengkawang* (the illipe nut). This nut grows both wild (in primary forest areas) and planted, and is produced by several species of *Shorea.* The Chinese, and coastal Malay peoples as well, value these nuts as a source of cooking oil.

Excluding perhaps the illipe nut, the forest products catalogued above have been in demand for centuries by Chinese, as well as Indians, Arabs, and Persians (Wolters 1967). It has been these items— many of them serving as basic ingredients in the Chinese pharmacopeia —that have attracted Chinese to Borneo since perhaps the earliest days of their maritime trading. It has been demand for these items that has led the Chinese to exchange not only gongs and jars but also basic trade goods with the native peoples of Borneo's interior.

The Dilemma of Trade and the Dualistic Solution

For most of the native peoples of Borneo—sedentary, village-dwelling, swidden agriculturalists—this important trading activity has involved one noteworthy problem. All the forest product items noted above are found chiefly, if not exclusively, within large tracts of primary forest. These sedentary agriculturalists, on the other hand, live outside of and considerable distances away from the primary forest. More often than not, their villages are surrounded by gardens and swiddens, and these in turn are surrounded by broad expanses of secondary forest. Primary forest is usually found only at the outer boundaries of a village's lands, and this may give way to another stretch of secondary forest belonging to some adjoining village. Many of these sedentary peoples would thus be forced to travel great distances from their villages to gather forest products in quantities sufficient for trade. The undertaking of such long-distance journeys involves an expenditure of time that these sedentary agriculturalists cannot often afford. The travel to distant primary forest areas, and the seeking, collecting, assembling, and transporting of the forest products would necessarily divert time from the annual cycle of activities associated with swidden agriculture. In addition, it would require a potentially dangerous diversion of manpower from the ever-present requirements of village defense—thus entailing not only economic costs but security costs as well.

The dilemma faced by the native agricultural peoples of Borneo is now clear. On the one hand, they need and want the goods and commodities offered by the traders in exchange for primary forest products; but on the other hand, they are often unable to expend the time and effort needed to collect these products in quantities sufficient for trade. This last point is worthy of some emphasis. Almost all settled agricultural people in Borneo today can and do gather forest products to some extent. Often they gather rattan if nothing else. But with regard to the other forest products traditionally in demand by traders, the essential question is whether they can collect sufficient quantities of products from the primary forest to exchange for significant returns in salt, metal, cloth, tobacco, and so on. It is my belief that most sedentary agriculturalists can do no more than hazard an occasional excursion to the deep forest.

This ecological-economic dilemma is the key to the origins of the Punan. I suggest that it was precisely this inability of sedentary agricultural groups to adequately exploit two distinct ecological niches— namely, tropical forest horticulture and tropical forest hunting and gathering—that led to the evolution of the separate hunting and gathering culture that is found in Borneo today. That is, this ecological-economic dilemma was resolved through just the sort of adjustment one would expect of human groups adapting to their environment: in many parts of Borneo, and at many times in history, the autochthonous peoples specialized. Having done that, they came to present the ethnographic picture that greeted the anthropologists who came to Borneo in the nineteenth and twentieth centuries: a sedentary, village-dwelling agricultural group interacting culturally and economically with an affiliated group of nomadic hunters and gatherers, these latter known to the former as *orang punan* (upriver people).[2]

This ecological specialization at the group level has resulted in a distinctive pattern of economic interaction that has persisted to the present day. Each Punan group trades products from the primary forest with a nearby village of sedentary agriculturalists with whom it shares a historical tradition of alliance and cultural affiliation. These products commonly include damar, rattan, aloes wood, birds' nests, bezoar stones and, in former times, rhinoceros horns. In exchange the Punan receive such items as salt, tobacco, cloth, and the long iron bush-swords in wooden sheaths known variously as *parang* or *mandau*. Rarely, the Punan might also receive such status goods as gongs and jars. Nowadays some groups receive money as well.

The goods and commodities that each sedentary agricultural group gives to its affiliated Punan group are themselves the result of trading relationships carried on between the former and non-Dayak traders. After receiving forest products from the Punan, the settled Dayak villagers subsequently trade them downriver for salt, tobacco, cloth and clothing, metal, household implements, gongs, jars, and nowadays also money. The downriver traders are primarily from coastal Malay ethnic groups, including Orang Bulungan, Orang Berau, Orang Kutai, and Orang Banjar, although Buginese from Sulawesi have also long been conspicuous participants. In recent decades, many Dayak groups have also traded directly with small-scale Chinese shopkeepers operating out of downriver market towns. Whoever the downriver trader may be, however, his role in the trade network is essentially to assemble the forest products for eventual transport and sale to larger-scale, coastal, Chinese exporters.

Until quite recently the various settled Dayak groups have acted as shrewd middlemen in keeping the Punan and downriver traders away from each other, thus guarding against the sort of direct trade that is only now beginning to occur on the island. The settled groups have always known that direct exchange between the Punan and the traders would render their mediating role redundant. Even now, for example, the Merap people of the village of Langap in Malinau subdistrict refuse to tell their Punan neighbors just how large a profit they make from selling birds' nests to the Chinese. Despite their role as middlemen, however, I found that the settled peoples have scarcely greater knowledge than their Punan neighbors concerning the uses to which the Chinese put forest products. Up to the moment I myself told them, none of the settled Dayak that I met had any idea, for example, that "monkey stones" and "porcupine stones" are made into Chinese medicines, that aloes wood is used as incense, or that the birds' nests are used to make soup. Nor was anyone aware that rattan is exported to foreign countries in the form of expensive furniture.

We can now address the original question of who these Punan are and what they mean in terms of Borneo ethnography as a whole. It seems indisputable that the Punan share a common origin with the settled groups and that they diverged when some people, in different places and at different times, opted to specialize in the nomadic gathering of primary forest resources, while others opted to specialize in the sedentary, swidden cultivation of the forest itself. The lifestyle of the Punan, it bears emphasizing, is based on the gathering of forest products; it is not based on hunting. The historic demand for these forest products is the reason why the Punan—or more precisely the distinctive Punan way of life—came into existence.

Alternate Theories and the Empirical Evidence

This conclusion contradicts the generally held opinion that the Punan must live deep in the forest because they subsist by hunting deep forest game. This has been the opinion of the three generations of anthropologists who have studied the various non-Punan Dayak groups. It is also the opinion of the local people in coastal towns (most of whom have never actually come face to face with a Punan). In such places as Tarakan, Tanjung Selor, Tanjung Redeb, Samarinda, and Tenggarong I was often told: *Orang Punan hidup hanya untuk makan. Mereka cuma tahu berburu babi jauh dalam hutan* (The Punan live only to eat. All they know about is hunting pigs deep in the forest).

This long-held view of the Punan is flawed not because it associates them with the deep forest—for they are a true forest people—but because it explains this association in terms of hunting. This explanation, in turn, is based on a false association of large game populations with the deep forest. In fact, pigs, deer, and other game animals are often more plentiful in downriver areas and near towns than they are in the deepest recesses of the jungle. Indeed, downriver Dayak living in or near such towns as Malinau, Long Bia, Long Peso, and Tabang often told me that they have all they can do to keep pigs from devouring the crops in their gardens at night. Both monkeys and deer can be seen along the riverbanks no more than five kilometers outside any of the towns mentioned above. Thus, even if hunting was the principal economic activity of the Punan (which it is not), its pursuit would not require their residence in the deep forest. On the other hand, the gath-

ering of the earlier mentioned forest products, most of which are found
in quantity (or only found at all) in primary forest, does require their
residence there. And all Punan groups that I studied or heard of do
engage in a major way in the gathering of these products. Moreover, all
of these groups insisted that they had been so engaged since the time of
their earliest remembered ancestors.

This analysis of the Punan not only explains why they live in the forest, it also explains why they live—or more accurately, why the Punan
culture is found in its purest form—in forests nearer to Borneo's coasts
than to its remotest interior. It is the popularly held assumption among
those unfamiliar with the interior regions of Kalimantan that the farther
one journeys away from the coast and into the interior, the more "primitive" the Punan will be. In fact, the reverse is true. The most
modernized and assimilated Punan groups of East Kalimantan are
those dwelling in the remote Apo Kayan and upper Mahakam River
areas. These peoples are settled in "proper" villages, have excellent
gardens and swiddens, wear factory-made clothing, possess numerous
modern appliances, and are virtually indistinguishable from other sedentary Dayak agriculturalists. As one moves eastward and coastward,
however, one encounters the more traditional, seminomadic Punan
groups of the Tubu River in the Malinau subdistrict, the middle Kayan
River area in Peso subdistrict, and the Segah and Kelai rivers areas in
the Berau district. This increasing traditionalism culminates as one
arrives near the coast and encounters the truly nomadic Punan Batu of
the upper Sajau River in the subdistrict of Tanjung Palas and segments
of this same ethnic group on the upper Birang River in the subdistrict of
Gunung Tabur, who are called "Basap" rather than "Punan." These
latter groups live in small lean-tos made of sticks and leaves, wear loincloths—sometimes made from tree bark—and are so close to the coast
that helicopters from ARCO's oil installations on the coast fly over
them several times a day.

Based on the analysis presented in this paper, it is clear that the
Punan appear increasingly more traditional or "primitive" closer to the
coast, because the closer they are to the coast, the more they are
influenced by the demand for forest products by coastal traders. Conversely, Punan groups that live farther from the coast and are less accessible to coastal traders have both the opportunity and the need to diver-
sify their economy, thus joining the general present-day movement
toward modernization that is in evidence among all of the other Dayak
peoples of the interior. The aforementioned Punan Basap living within
a ten-minute helicopter ride from the coast, in contrast, have had neither the opportunity nor the need to change. These people, who in former days gathered birds' nests for the Sultan of Berau at Tanjung

Redeb and today do so at the behest of coastal traders, continue to maintain a way of life that strikes the outside observer as primitive in the extreme. The "primitiveness" of these people, as well as that of other Punan groups living relatively near the coastal areas, lies in the eyes of the beholder. They are not "primitive"; in fact, they are simply *more specialized* in the activity that traditionally has distinguished them from other Dayak, namely, the gathering and trading of forest products.

Summary, Conclusions, and Recommendations

I began this analysis with the observation that individual Punan groups have greater contact with proximate, sedentary agriculturalists than they do with one another. These contacts largely involve the important trade in forest products, in which the sedentary Dayak have long played an important role as middlemen. There are ecological and economic constraints on the simultaneous pursuit of forest-gathering and sedentary agriculture, which has led in Borneo to the evolution of a dualistic society of Punan and settled Dayak; each specialized in the exploitation of one of these niches, and each benefiting from the other's specialization through close economic ties. This interpretation of the Punan explains both the prominence of the Punan-Dayak ties and the lack of Punan-Punan ties. It also explains why the Punan are found more often in virgin forest areas along Borneo's coastline, where trading activity is most intense, than in Borneo's remote interior, where trading activity is minimal.

Based on this analysis, then, Punan society must be viewed as a particular adaptation to a particular social and physical environment. It is an adaptation that people have opted into, and probably out of as well, throughout the long course of Borneo's history. My thesis here, that the contemporary Punan are, in effect, commercial hunters and gatherers who share common historical origins with sedentary agriculturalists, should not be taken, therefore, to imply that the Punan are "backward" or "retrograde." The Punan did not "lapse" or "fail" at agriculture, rather they specialized at forest-gathering. This specialization developed and has persisted in Borneo for one fundamental reason: the exploitation of two distinct ecological niches by two distinct societies— forest nomads and village-dwelling agriculturalists—has been a far more efficient and productive arrangement than the simultaneous exploitation of two niches by one thinly spread group.

In their specialized adaptation toward gathering forest products, the Punan—however unknowingly—have performed a vital economic service for the region as a whole. First, they have enabled the far more numerous sedentary groups to profit from the trade in forest products while still engaged in full-time, year-round subsistence agriculture. Second, they have assured the coastal traders and exporters with a more or less constant flow of forest products. And finally, there have been benefits to the world at large, where the demand for certain of these products (e.g., rattan) is large and growing. These benefits—and the possibility of further enhancing them—should be the focus of developmental efforts involving the Punan.

The overwhelming majority of the tribal peoples that I encountered in Kalimantan want very much to be brought into the mainstream of national growth and development. They want a better and easier way of life for themselves and, especially, their children. The Punan are no exception. Over and over again in the course of my research, I heard the statement *Kami mau maju* (We want [to] progress) expressed with a fervent and poignant sincerity. Their sentiments can perhaps best be understood by noting a comment made to me by a young Punan Murung man of the upper Barito River: *Baiknya kalau anak saya nanti ikut sekolah. Saya tidak mau dia jadi bodoh seperti saya sekarang* (It would be best for my child to go to school. I don't want him to become stupid like I am now). The Punan are no less eager than other Dayak peoples in their wish to inaugurate a new period of growth and development in their respective areas. Of most importance, they have not only the desire but also the ability to participate in such development. Indeed, the rudiments of their potential economic contribution already exist.

Over thirty years ago, the development experts Buchanan and Ellis (1955) noted the importance of labor specialization and trade in the early phases of economic development in England, Western Europe, and Japan. Specialization and trade, they argued, were important prime movers in each of these areas during the nineteenth century. They wrote (407):

> A predominantly agricultural economy with numerous local village markets that are largely self-sufficient and have few trade relationships with one another or with the world abroad offers little scope for entrepreneurship and little likelihood of generating innovations from within. Furthermore, it has few channels through which innovations might filter in from the outside. Consequently, its value patterns tend to be impermeable and its institutional structure unvarying. Such was the situation of many now developed countries a century or more ago, and such is the position of many underdeveloped areas today.

This analysis of development strongly suggests that there is an alternative to the present policy of inducing the Punan to settle in downriver villages and take up full-time, year-round agriculture. The alternative and perhaps more productive approach would involve building and improving upon what Punan groups already do. Rather than introducing new activities, that is, it might be far better to simply develop the activities that the Punan have traditionally engaged in.

I have stated in this paper that the Punan of Kalimantan are above all else commercial hunters and gatherers, collecting a small inventory of forest products for trade. While some of these forest products—notably aloes wood and gallstones from monkeys—are of minimal commercial value on the present-day world market, others—like rattan and edible birds' nests—are the objects of increasing, worldwide demand. The demand for rattan is already huge. Peluso (1983:95) has calculated that "rattan generates more foreign exchange for Indonesia than any other forest product except logs," and that export from Indonesia rose at least 200 percent in the ten-year period from 1968 to 1977. Forty-nine percent of this rattan, she notes (ibid.), comes from Kalimantan, and most of this from East Kalimantan Province. In addition to being the foremost area for the collection of wild rattan, East Kalimantan Province is also—and this is probably no coincidence, if the thesis of this paper is correct—that part of Indonesian Borneo where the overwhelming majority of Punan groups are situated. They gather rattan for trade, and—according to their own accounts—have always done so. The Punan are also the primary, if not only, full-time collectors of edible birds' nests in the parts of Kalimantan that I studied. In addition to rattan and birds' nests, the present importance of illipe nuts also bears mention. In the nineteenth century, Europeans began to use these nuts commercially in the manufacture of tallow, candles, and lubricating oil for industrial machinery. Today illipe nuts are in commercial demand for use in making cooking oil and, more notably, for use as the base substance in the manufacture of high-priced European cosmetics. In 1968, the only year for which I have figures, the export of processed illipe nuts reached upwards of US$5 million (Alexander 1973:47). The nuts are collected in quantity by Punan of the upper Barito River in Central Kalimantan, who trade them in their raw form to merchants from Teluk Jolo, Puruk Cahu, and Muara Teweh. Finally, mention should also be made of gutta-percha. This naturally occurring latex, similar to rubber but more resinous, is presently used for a variety of purposes, most notably as electrical insulation and in dentistry. While gutta-percha is not an object of major collection efforts by Punan groups at present, it could easily be made one in the future.

At a time when Indonesia is emphasizing the rapid development of nonpetroleum exports, the traditional trading and collection activities of the Punan of Kalimantan clearly merit governmental attention and support. As I have attempted to show, the Punan are already making a significant contribution to the export sector, and the potential exists to greatly increase this contribution and at the same time increase capital formation at the local level. Developing this potential would involve no more than minor organizational shifts and initial capital inputs to increase the productivity of what the Punan already do. One initial step might involve the use of appropriate incentives to redirect Punan attention away from forest products of relatively low value in the present world market, such as aloes wood and bezoar stones, and concentrate it on products with greater present value, such as rattan. A second step might involve developing the Punan capacity to process forest products themselves, instead of trading them in raw form as they have always done. Not only would this greatly alleviate the common problem of the spoilage during transport to downriver market areas, it would increase the collectors' share of the eventual export price. Punan groups could demand much higher prices for processed rattan, birds' nests, and illipe nuts than they can expect for these products when traded in raw, bulk form. Finally, it may be possible for the Punan to deal directly with downriver and coastal merchant-traders, circumventing the traditional settled Dayak middlemen. Such direct dealing is already occurring in many areas of Kalimantan, as a result of improvements in transportation and communication; it perhaps could be facilitated by the government, and would lead to far better trade terms for the Punan than they have at present.

The fostering of direct trading relationships between Punan and traders might have an important and far-reaching impact on provincial development, through its stimulation of entrepreneurship. Buchanan and Ellis (1955) have analyzed the importance of the entrepreneur in local development, noting that it is he who promotes the expansion of trade and commerce, becomes the initial source of innovations, fosters the spirit of change in rural areas, creates incentives for production, acts as a conduit for new ideas from outside the region, and establishes trading and commercial contacts in other regions and overseas. The beginnings of such an entrepreneurial spirit are already in evidence among the merchant-trader class in Kalimantan. What is still needed is a transition from the present pattern of sporadic ad hoc trading to a pattern of trading based on long-term commercial goals. What is needed is a change from the habit of making ad hoc trading forays upriver for quick profits that are immediately consumed to a strategy based on the advantages of long-term tenure, capital formation, and reinvestment. This shift in perspective is already becoming apparent in some areas of Kalimantan, and it deserves to be encouraged. This encouragement entails —as it is also entailed by—acknowledging the crucial role of the Punan in this broader trading network, taking the obvious steps to increase the productivity of this role, and ensuring that the returns to the Punan are commensurate with their contributions.

Notes

1. Research for this project was made possible through the support of the United States National Institutes of Health (Grant No. 5F31MH07995–03), and through the cooperation of the Indonesian Institute of Science (LIPI). A full monograph-length treatment of the economic, sociological, and historical issues touched upon in this paper is in preparation.

The author gratefully acknowledges the assistance of Adrianna Kulczycky in preparing the maps used to illustrate the text.

2. Concerning the word "Punan," Tom Harrisson stated: "It is essential to recognize that Punan is only a descriptive, imposed term, very probably based on a word found in many inland dialects, 'Punan' = upriver or headwaters of a river" (Harrisson 1949:130).

References Cited

Alexander, Garth
    1973   *The Invisible China.* New York: Macmillan

Bock, Carl
    1882   *The Headhunters of Borneo: A Narrative of Travel up the Mahakkam and down the Barito.* London: Sampson Low, Marston, Searle & Rivington.

Buchanan, Norman S., and Howard S. Ellis
    1955   *Approaches to Economic Development.* New York: The Twentieth Century Fund.

Cole, Fay-Cooper
    1945   *The Peoples of Malaysia.* Princeton, N.J.: Van Nostrand.

    1947   "Concerning the Punan of Borneo." *American Anthropologist* 49:340.

Freeman, D. J.
    1960   "Iban Augury." In *The Birds of Borneo,* edited by B. E. Smythies, pp. 73–98. Edinburgh: Oliver & Boyd.

Geertz, Hildred
    1963   "Indonesian Cultures and Communities." In *Indonesia,* edited by R. T. McVey, pp. 14–96. New Haven: Human Relations Area File Press.

Harrisson, Tom
    1949   "Notes on Some Nomadic Punans." *Sarawak Museum Journal* 5:130–146.

Heine-Geldern, Robert von
  1945   *Prehistoric Research in the Netherlands Indies.* New York: Southeast Asia
          Institute.

  1946   "Research on Southeast Asia: Problems and Suggestions." *American
          Anthropologist* 48:149–175.

Hose, Charles
  1893   "The Natives of Borneo." *Journal of the Royal Anthropological Institute*
          23:156–172.

Needham, Rodney
  1972   "Penan." In *Ethnic Groups of Insular Southeast Asia,* vol. 1, edited by
          Frank LeBar, pp. 176–180. New Haven: Human Relations Area
          File Press.

Peluso, Nancy
  1983   "Networking in the Commons: A Tragedy for Rattan?" *Indonesia*
          35:95–108.

Sandin, Benedict
  1980   *Iban Adat and Augury.* Penang: Penerbit Universiti Sains Malaysia.

Wang Gungwu
  1958   "The Nanhai Trade: A Study of the Early History of Chinese Trade
          in the South China Sea." *Journal of the Malayan Branch of the Royal
          Asiatic Society* 31 (2): 1–133.

Wheatley, Paul
  1959   "Geographical Notes on Some Commodities Involved in Sung Mar-
          itime Trade." *Journal of the Malayan Branch of the Royal Asiatic Society* 32
          (2): 5–140.

Wolters, O. W.
  1967   *Early Indonesian Commerce: A Study of the Origins of Srivijaya.* Ithaca,
          N.Y.: Cornell University Press.

4. Traditional Land Use and Government Policy in Bima, East Sumbawa

JEFFREY D. BREWER

Abstract

The five governments that ruled Bima between 1925 and 1975 made major changes in the laws affecting agricultural land use. These changes had two goals: eliminating shifting cultivation and ending village influence over land use. A detailed study of two villages shows that government land policies did succeed in reducing village control over land and inducing the adoption of more intensive farming methods, but they also increased inequities in landholdings and failed to end shifting cultivation. This study suggests that these unexpected and undesirable consequences were due to the policy makers' failure to consult the farmers themselves.

Introduction

This study traces the history of government intervention in land use in Bima over a fifty-year period and describes some of its consequences in two Bimanese farming villages. Government actions were not motivated by farming concerns nor were the farmers consulted. It is not surprising, then, that government intervention did not fully succeed in its aims, nor that some of its consequences have been less than desirable. This history offers some lessons for future land-use planning.[1]

Background

Bima is the proper name for the eastern half of Sumbawa Island in Nusa Tenggara Barat. Bima's topography is very broken; steep mountains are present everywhere, and river valleys are narrow and short. Bima's climate has two distinct seasons, a rainy season from November to March and a dry season during the rest of the year. The population consists primarily of speakers of Bimanese and related dialects, most of whom are farmers living in nucleated villages. Bima's main port, government center, and trade center is the town of Kota Bima.[2]

During the twentieth century, Bima has been controlled by several different overlords and has had several different forms of government (Amin 1971). Until 1905 Bima was an independent sultanate, although the Dutch had controlled Bima's trade and foreign policy since the seventeenth century. The colonial period proper began in 1905 when the Netherlands East Indies government assumed direct rule. Two other colonial powers followed. The Japanese military ruled Bima between 1942 and 1945, and the Dutch puppet state of Negara Indonesia Timor controlled Bima between 1945 and 1950. Each of these colonial powers retained the traditional Bimanese sultanate under a policy of indirect rule. Colonial rule ended with the unification of Indonesia in 1950. The sultanate ended in the same year, with the death of the last sultan, but the *swapraja* (autonomous) government that followed closely resembled it. In 1958 Bima became a *kabupaten* (district) within the newly created province of Nusa Tenggara Barat.

Rasa and Sila, the two villages studied, are farming villages.[3] Although similar in size and in some other respects, they differ greatly in land resources and access to markets. Rasa is located in a small river valley about ten kilometers from Kota Bima (Fig. 4.1). The village economy is based primarily on the farming of the irrigable bottom lands in the valley. Rasa has easy access to the market in Kota Bima, and Rasa farmers have long been accustomed to growing cash crops.

Sila, on the other hand, lies on top of a mountain ridge some eighteen kilometers from Kota Bima and eight kilometers by trail from Rasa (Fig. 4.2). Irrigable bottom land is scarce in Sila's mountain location, hence Sila farmers are largely dependent upon dry farming, in particular upon swidden farming. In addition, Sila's access to markets is restricted because of distance and rough mountain trails, so Sila farmers produce crops only for their own subsistence. Because of these differences, the effects of government land policies on the two villages have not been entirely the same.

During the twentieth century both Rasa and Sila, as well as the rest of Bima, experienced a population explosion. Both villages have had annual growth rates of about 2.5 percent. Rasa's 1925 population was only about 250 persons, but it reached approximately 475 in 1950 and 882 in 1976. Sila's 1925 population was about 270; it reached approximately 500 in 1950 and 925 in 1976. Although this paper is a study of

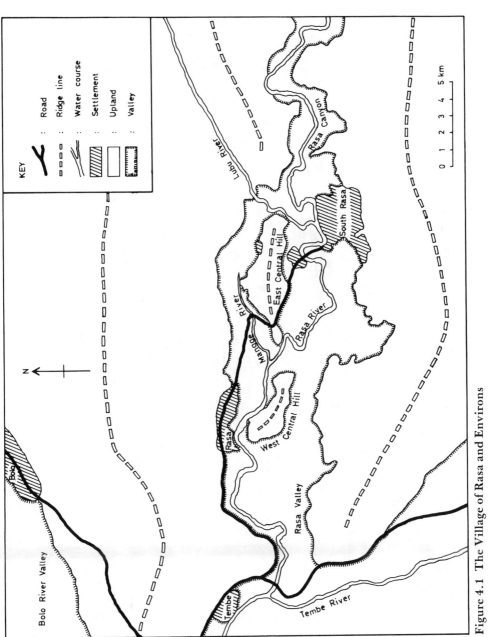

Figure 4.1 The Village of Rasa and Environs

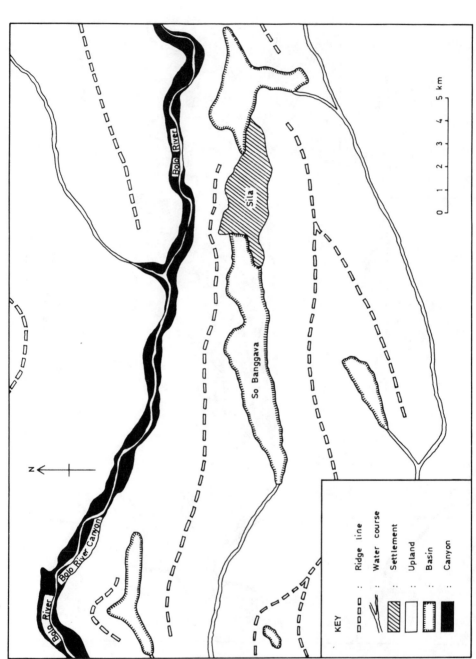

Figure 4.2 The Village of Sila and Environs

the motives and consequences of government intervention in land use, the effects of this rapid population growth must also be considered.

The Precolonial Period

Although the Dutch assumed power in Bima in 1905, changes were made very slowly. It was not until the 1920s that the Dutch began reforming governmental structure and law. Hence, the precolonial land control system persisted until about 1925.

Under this precolonial system, each village had final jurisdiction over all land use within a well-defined village territory. Village decisions on land use, including both policy decisions and the settling of disputes, were made by a body of men called the *doumtuatua* (old, old persons or elders). Two basic principles governed the assignment of rights to land: use of a particular plot of farm land established the right to reuse that plot; and any village member had a residual right to use any village land not under cultivation. The first principle meant that individual village members normally held exclusive rights of use to wet rice fields and other continuously cultivated land. A landholder could transfer his use rights to another village member with or without compensation. Unless challenged before the village elders, such transfers took place unhindered.

For swidden land, however, the situation was quite different. A swidden is typically fallowed for a number of years after each cropping. This break in cultivation makes it possible for persons other than the last cultivator to later reuse the same plot. As a result, more than one person would come to hold rights to the same plot. This fragmentation of rights, despite plentiful land for swiddens, led to a high number of disputes over the use of particular plots. This was exacerbated by the preferred pattern wherein multiple households would make their swiddens in a large block of contiguous plots, to minimize crop losses to swidden pests. This block pattern severely limited a farmer's choice of swidden plots, making disputes all the more likely. All such disputes were settled by the village elders, most commonly by awarding use of the plot to that farmer who had used the plot most frequently in the past. All village members had access to some swidden land somewhere, however, because of the recognized residual rights to uncultivated land and because the village elders viewed it as their responsibility to ensure the welfare of all villagers.[4]

Although it is an important feature of Islamic law, inheritance of land was not recognized by Bimanese *adat* (custom). Instead, land transfers between generations were accomplished by gift. Rights to permanently

Rasa River Valley, Showing Rasa Village and Environs

Puddling a Wet-Rice Field in Rasa Village

cultivated land were given to heirs either at marriage or later, when the parents wished to retire from farming. If a landholder died before distributing his land, the village elders acted in his place. Swidden use rights were transferred indirectly. A man with rights to a particular plot would allow his heir to use that plot, which thereby established rights for the heir.

This pattern of land use and control extended to all land in the village jurisdictional area except land belonging to the Bima government. The government owned wet rice land in a number of villages, including Rasa, which it used to compensate its own high-level officials. Lower level officials, such as the village headman, were compensated with land under the control of the village elders. The Sultan also personally owned land in some village areas; this land was worked for him by villagers (Jasper 1908:105–108).

Toward the end of the precolonial period, Rasa residents concentrated their agricultural activities on irrigated rice fields and orchards on the valley floor. The irrigated fields were planted with rice during the rainy season and with mung beans or maize during the dry season. Rice and maize were both subsistence crops, but the mung beans and fruit from the orchards were sold in Kota Bima. With a population of only 250, and with about forty hectares of wet rice land, including perhaps twenty hectares of government land plus another twenty hectares of orchard, Rasa residents had no land problems. During the same period, Sila residents had approximately fifteen hectares of wet rice land, most of which was irrigated solely by rainfall. This land produced only one rice crop per year and no maize or mung beans. Sila's 270 residents needed to cut another twelve to sixteen hectares of swidden to provide sufficient rice, maize, and other subsistence crops.[5]

The Colonial Period: 1925–1950

Under the Agrarian Land Law of 1870, the Netherlands East Indies government classified all land not under permanent cultivation as inalienable state property (Geertz 1963:83–84). This land was often made available to Europeans for plantations or other uses. In 1925 a team of surveyors mapped all of the permanently cultivated farmland in Bima, including that in Rasa and Sila, to determine the limits of state versus private land. Because it was not permanently cultivated, all swidden land was classed as state property, and its further use for swiddens was prohibited. The Dutch never made a serious attempt to enforce this prohibition, however, perhaps because no great interest was shown by Europeans in establishing plantations in the area. Only one plantation was created in Bima under the colonial regime.

Some state land, mostly on mountain peaks, was designated as forest preserves. These preserves were closed to all farming, and the colonial regime expended considerable effort to enforce this ban. Thus the colonial government, which viewed Sila swidden farmers as a threat to a forest preserve established on the mountain peaks just above Sila, decided to meet this threat by extending the preserve to include Sila's own territory. In or about 1927 the government ordered all Sila residents to move to a designated site in the lowlands. Some households obeyed the order, but most chose to remain in Sila, seeking to prove that they were not a threat to the forest preserve by developing their permanent field agriculture. During the 1930s, Sila residents increased their acreage of wet rice fields more than 30 percent. Moreover, they developed a new dry land farming technology, involving the planting of cassava on plowed land, which also represented a type of permanent field farming. By 1939, Sila farmers had developed about eight hectares of this cassava garden land. Previously, cassava had been a crop of very little importance. Swidden farming probably decreased during this period but never ceased entirely. By 1939, government pressure for resettlement had ended and all households had returned to Sila.[6]

The ban on the use of state land, however rarely enforced, remained in effect throughout the colonial period. During this period, swidden farmers were in constant jeopardy of jail or fines. (One Sila farmer reported being fined in 1948.) However, population growth caused many villages to expand their swidden areas. By 1950, Sila farmers were planting some twenty-five hectares of swidden each year in addition to twenty hectares of wet rice fields and six hectares of cassava gardens.

New markets for Rasa crops opened up after the Dutch constructed a vehicular road into Rasa in the 1930s. This road was later improved by the Japanese.[7] After World War II, the development of transportation facilities for shipping soybeans to Java opened a new large-scale market to Rasa farmers. In addition, population growth in Kota Bima led to an expansion in the market for rice and the inception of a market for fresh vegetables. Presented with these opportunities, the Rasa farmers replaced mung beans with soybeans and increased their planting of rice at the expense of maize. New land was brought under cultivation, and much of the less productive orchard land was converted to wet rice fields. By 1950, Rasa farmers were farming about sixty hectares of wet rice land (thirty-nine of which belonged to the government) and about ten hectares of orchard. In addition, to take advantage of market opportunities and to alleviate a growing land shortage, they were also cutting perhaps five hectares of swiddens for rice and soybeans each year.[8]

The Dutch were responsible for a second measure that also influenced land use. According to European theory at the time, modern governments should be supported by taxes rather than by service. Taxes are a more flexible source of revenue, and taxation policies provide a means of influencing the activities of the populace. Accordingly, the Dutch colonial administrators introduced a tax on farm land to provide a secure government income and to provide accurate information on land use. In 1939 and 1940, teams of surveyors mapped the permanently cultivated farm land in Bima and registered its holders. The first land taxes were collected in 1941.

Problems arose immediately and worsened over the years. Tax collection was delegated to village headmen, but headmen lacked the power to coerce payment from their fellow villagers. In addition, landholders rarely bothered to inform the tax authority of land transfers. It was left solely to the headmen to reconcile tax assessments with the facts of land-holdership. As a result, the government did not collect all of the taxes due, nor did the tax records accurately reflect the current facts of land use. On the other hand, land taxation did affect the control of land within the villages. The *surat putih* (white letter), the proof of tax registration, quickly became the only sure proof of rights to farmland, thus weakening the village elders' authority over land. As a result, it became increasingly difficult for the elders to adjust land rights to suit village needs. Although both Rasa and Sila were surveyed at the same time, Sila elders retained their authority much longer because this survey did not affect swidden land, which was more abundant in Sila.

Postcolonial Modernization: 1950–1960

Independence turned the Bimanese government over to men whose primary concern was modernization. In 1953, in pursuit of this aim, the government ordered the consolidation of the 401 recognized *kampung* (villages) in Bima into 143 new municipal units called *desa*. In each municipality, the former village officials were replaced with a smaller number of municipal officials headed by a *kepala desa* (municipal head). Rasa was combined with a nearby village called South Rasa into the municipality of Desa Rasa, while Sila was combined with three other villages to form Desa Bolo. This consolidation weakened the authority of the village elders still further. Although most Bimanese still viewed the village as the basic governmental unit (cf. Goethals 1961), much of the authority formerly exercised by the village elders passed to the formally recognized municipal officials.

The new government officials in Kota Bima felt, like the Dutch before them, that swidden farming was destructive and backward, and in 1953 they announced that the ban on swidden farming on state land would be enforced. They announced at the same time that state land— other than forest preserves—brought under permanent cultivation could be surveyed and registered by the tax authority upon petition by the municipal head. Such land was called *tanah pembukaan baru* (newly opened land).

To Sila villagers, the ban on swidden farming represented a genuine threat to their livelihood. They responded, as they had twenty-five years earlier, by expanding the area under permanent cultivation. Between 1954 and 1960, wet rice fields increased in area by 20 percent while cassava gardens tripled to some twenty-five hectares. The first official survey of newly opened land, in 1958, registered approximately twenty-five hectares of land that had formerly been under swiddens. Most of this land had been improved, although some bore only a poten- tial for more intensive cultivation. Nonetheless, most of the claims to state land were approved by the village elders. These increases in per- manently cultivated land were not sufficient to eliminate all need for swiddens, however. Swidden farming continued, to the accompaniment of occasional fines and the threat of jail.

In contrast to Sila villagers, Rasa villagers viewed the offer to survey and register state land as an opportunity rather than a threat. As noted earlier, Rasa farmers had already begun planting soybeans in swiddens and had discovered that soybeans could be replanted several times in plowed dry land.[9] With this use in mind, they prepared state land for plowing and then had it surveyed and registered. About thirty hectares of dry land were surveyed and registered in two surveys in 1954 and 1958. Since few Rasa farmers had prior claims to this land, the village elders played no part in the process.

Land Control after Passage of the Basic Agrarian Law

The passage of the national Basic Agrarian Law (*Undang-undang Pokok Agraria,* or UUPA) in 1960 drastically changed the legal basis for land control in Bima. One purpose of this law was to rid Indonesia of the col- onialistic and paternalistic biases of the Agrarian Land Law of 1870 (Boedi Harsono 1975). It attempts to do this by prescribing private ownership of land, to ensure that the man who farms the land also owns it. To prevent abuse, local governments are allowed to limit the size of landholdings. UUPA also recognizes that in some parts of Indonesia, local *adat* law is still strong. In such areas, land control is to be based on *adat* for an indefinite transition period. Another basic feature of UUPA is repudiation of the colonial concept of state lands. UUPA provides only that land may be set aside for specific national purposes. Under this provision, the forest preserves in Bima have been declared national lands and placed under the care of the forestry service.

Because of the already weakened village authority over land, the government in Bima concluded that local *adat* law could not serve as the basis for land control. In 1960, therefore, the Bimanese government instructed the tax authority to survey and register private ownership of all state land as quickly as possible. Swidden lands were included since, following the abolition of the state land concept, there was no longer a legal basis for the prohibition of swidden farming. At the same time, a land title registry was established and it was ordered that land titles be registered upon the transfer of all parcels of land. No longer was tax registration alone to be considered proof of ownership.

Land surveys were carried out in Sila in 1962, 1964, and 1972. Together with the surveys of newly opened lands, these surveys registered the ownership of approximately 85 percent of the 440 hectares of arable land within Sila's jurisdictional area. An additional 120 hectares of land, which had formerly lain within the jurisdictional area of Sila, was registered by the residents of several proximate villages. These latter claims to Sila land were approved by the municipal head, while the claims made by the Sila residents themselves were approved by their own village elders.

In Rasa's jurisdictional area, surveys were carried out in 1962 and 1972. Including the surveys of newly opened lands, these surveys registered about 31 hectares, or 23 percent of the 132 hectares of arable land in Rasa's traditional jurisdictional area. Another 95 hectares of dry land located in the traditional jurisdictional areas of other villages (including Sila) were also registered to Rasa residents. Since the majority of residents in both villages believe that the product of these surveys, the tax registration letter, is equivalent to legal title, few of them have bothered to register land titles per se.

The conversion of Sila swidden land to private ownership has significantly altered the means of acquiring swidden land. In the past, claims were adjusted by the village elders and plot sizes were modified as needed. Today the village elders no longer have authority over land claims, and plot sizes have been fixed by the surveys. Now, after the locations of the multihousehold swidden blocks are chosen each year, those farmers who do not own land in the chosen areas—usually about half of all the Sila farmers—must make individual rental or borrowing arrangements. To ensure that all have access to swidden land, Sila villagers today recognize the principle that one is obligated to help one's kinsmen obtain swidden land. Thus, farmers who own land in the selected areas feel obligated to share that land with close kinsmen who do not. Sharing reduces the size of each plot, however. Sila swidden plots currently average .31 hectare, although Sila farmers consider .5 hectare to be the optimal size. Those who do not manage to share a kinsman's land must rent land instead.

The land reform program has also had an impact on the government land. With the creation of the province of Nusa Tenggara Barat in 1958, all government officials other than municipal officials were placed on salaries and the land formerly used to compensate these officials was rented out by the government to individuals. (It was then felt that UUPA enjoined the sale of this government land to private parties.) Most of the renters were wealthy men from Kota Bima who had the political connections to obtain leases. They sublet most of this land in small parcels to local farmers at a substantial profit.

Then in 1961, all of Bima's government land was divided up by a land reform committee: 49 percent (1,923 ha) was allocated for direct sale to individual farmers; 32 percent (1,234 ha) was retained as compensation for municipal officials; 10 percent (389 ha) was assigned to the Bima government to distribute as it saw fit; 7 percent (284 ha) was granted to the *Yayasan Islam,* an organization that had taken over many of the religious functions formerly performed by the sultanate government; and 2 percent (62 ha) was assigned to the government agricultural and fishery services. The land to be sold directly to private parties was first offered, at low prices and on easy terms, to whoever was already renting it. Most of it was snapped up, therefore, by well-off and well-connected residents of Kota Bima.

Of the thirty-nine hectares of government land in Rasa's jurisdictional area in 1960, twenty-three were reserved as compensation for municipal officials, and slightly over one hectare was given to the *Yayasan Islam.* Of the remaining fifteen hectares, only three passed directly to Rasa farmers, the remainder going to wealthy outsiders. Since that time another four hectares have been acquired by the few Rasa farmers able to raise large amounts of cash. (The prices paid for the land far exceed the original prices set by the land reform committee, even after accounting for inflation.) The very small amount of government land in Sila's jurisdictional area was retained as compensation for the municipal head.

The Bima government decided to use the land assigned to it in 1961 by the land reform committee to compensate farmers whose land was appropriated for expansions of village residential areas. As in all land surveys prior to 1960 (when the Basic Agrarian Law was passed), application for this type of land exchange had to be made through the municipal head. The municipal head of Bolo from 1953 to 1967, a man from Sila, arranged in 1962, 1967, and 1972 for land exchanges in which about seven hectares of relatively worthless dry land around Sila village was exchanged for an equal amount of wet rice land outside the village. The Sila residential area more than doubled in size through these transactions and today is far larger than needed. Although several Sila residents benefited from these exchanges, the one who benefited most was the municipal head himself. He obtained two hectares of good quality wet rice land not far from Sila. Because of these exchanges and because he allowed Sila land to pass to outsiders, this municipal head was voted out of office in 1967. The municipal head of Rasa during the same period was a man from South Rasa (the other village in the municipality in addition to Rasa itself). Although one exchange for about one hectare of Rasa land was made in 1967, the largest share of exchange land went to villagers from South Rasa. Again the main beneficiaries were the municipal head and his kinsmen. As in Bolo, this municipal head was voted out of office in 1967.

Since the passage and implementation of the Basic Agrarian Law, wealth disparities have increased in both villages. In Rasa, although the average wet rice land holding is only .36 hectare, five households each own more than two hectares. In Sila, the former municipal head and some of his kinsmen and cronies each own more than four times the average holdings of every kind of land. In the precolonial situation, such wealth disparities were prevented by the residual rights of all villagers to fallowed land and by the power of the village elders to award land rights to needy villagers.

In addition to these changes brought about by the Basic Agrarian Law, other changes have been brought about by population growth. Today, the residents of both Rasa and Sila are experiencing a shortage of land. More than half of all Rasa households now find it necessary to plant dry land to supplement their wet rice crops. Land use also has intensified. Most orchard land has been converted to more productive wet rice land; only four hectares of orchard remain in Rasa's jurisdictional area. In 1974, Rasa farmers went from planting two rice crops to three crops annually on their wet rice land. In spite of this population/land pressure, however, there is less hardship in Rasa than in some other villages, because per capita income is above average. Some Rasa residents who have lost out in the struggle for land within their own village area have been able to buy or otherwise obtain control of land in other villages.

Sila villagers are not as well off. Because they are much poorer than Rasa villagers, they have not been able to purchase wet rice land in other villages. As a result, the villagers of Sila are now obliged to cut some fifty hectares of swidden every year. Because of pressure from population growth and the sale of land to wealthier villages, they are obliged to cut most of these swiddens after inadequate fallow periods: the average fallow is just four years, far below the seven years considered adequate by Sila farmers. This results, in turn, in low yields and a poor diet: the average Sila resident eats only eighty-seven kilograms of husked rice annually, which is well below average for Bima as a whole. This situation causes Sila farmers to cast longing eyes on the untouched forest preserve nearby. In 1972, several Sila farmers were fined for cutting swiddens there.

Conclusion

Through four major changes in government and two major changes in land laws, government actions in Bima have persistently addressed two objectives: eliminating swidden farming and ending village control over land.[10] Neither of these goals was based on the farmers' own concerns and, more importantly, both were based on mistaken assessments of local conditions.

Opposition to swidden farming has been based on the fear that swidden cultivation contributes to forest fires and slope erosion. In fact, the monsoon forest of Bima is quite difficult to burn. Swidden farmers in Bima rarely achieve good burns even after cutting and drying the brush well beforehand. Also, many studies (e.g., Geertz 1963:15–28) have shown that swidden farming is destructive of soils only when fallow periods become too short. At the time of the original ban on swiddening by the colonial authorities, land was plentiful and swidden farming was clearly nondestructive. Today, however, rising population levels and diminishing fallow periods have made swidden farming a major cause of erosion. The runoff from swidden land during the rainy season contributes to serious flooding, which endangers wet rice fields further downstream.

An effective government response to the erosion problem has not been developed. Government officials regularly exhort farmers not to cut swiddens, but they have no legal power to prohibit swidden farming. The government does have the power to prohibit swidden farming in the forest preserves, and officials are quick to track down and prosecute any violators. The basic problem, however, is not one of law enforcement. The problem is that swidden agriculture is the only way to farm the steep, rocky slopes that cover much of Bima, given the agricultural technology available to Bimanese farmers. What is needed is an alternative means of support for residents of those villages that, like Sila, must depend upon swiddens. In recognition of this fact, the government distributed candlenut *(Aleurites moluccana)* seed to the villages in

1975, with directions to plant some in every swidden. The hope was that candlenut cultivation might eventually replace swidden farming. This effort was shortsighted, however, in that there is no wholesale market for candlenuts in Bima at present, nor is one likely to develop. More importantly, isolated swidden villages like Sila lack the transportation facilities to make large-scale cash farming economic. The government's effort was also too small and poorly organized. Each municipality received only one sack of seeds, with some villages—including Rasa—receiving a few seeds and others—including Sila—receiving none at all.

The second major objective of government land actions in Bima, namely, to end village control over land and to convert it to private ownership, has had varying motives depending upon the government in power. During the colonial era, the motive was to provide government income through a stable source of taxes and to use the tax records to keep track of land use. The Dutch clearly misunderstood the real basis of land control, however, and this misunderstanding resulted in major difficulties in tax collection and recording of land-use data.[11] Following independence, the motive to interfere with village land control was a perceived need to break the power of village elders, who were viewed as hidebound conservatives opposed to modernization. Private ownership was also viewed as an incentive to agricultural development. In fact, the rapid adoption of new crops in Rasa and the development of new agricultural technologies in Sila, before the authority of the village elders began to be undercut, show that this authority posed no obstacle to change. Subsequent passage of the Basic Agrarian Law was motivated by the belief that private ownership is the surest way of obtaining social justice. As the histories of both Rasa and Sila show, however, the conversion of land to private ownership resulted in greater disparities in wealth and in a loss of village land to outsiders with greater economic resources.

Throughout this fifty-year period, the actions of the Bima government toward land use have been marked by misunderstandings of local land use and control. Never were farmers consulted or their concerns taken into account. Instead, each group of government officials adopted the attitudes of their predecessors, which derived originally from Dutch colonial concepts. It is not surprising, therefore, that government land policy has persistently failed to achieve its goals. Despite the various measures enacted against it, swidden farming has actually increased, not decreased, over the period in question. Nor is there any evidence that modernization and agricultural development have been facilitated by ending village control over land. There is evidence, however, that social justice and the general welfare of farmers have suffered as a direct result of these various attempts at land control and reform. The lesson of this history is that greater care must be taken to match land reform efforts to local conditions and the needs of farmers rather than to abstract theories, and this is best achieved by consulting the farmers before implementing the reforms.

Notes

1. The data for this study were derived from interviews conducted in Bima in 1975 and 1976 and from tax records kindly made available by the District Development Fund (IPD). The research was supported by grant no. MH57325 from the National Institute of Mental Health of the United States, and was conducted under the auspices of the Indonesian Institute of Science (LIPI). For more information on Bima, see Brewer (1979).

2. In 1975, the official administrative center was the village of Raba some four kilometers from Kota Bima. However, most government offices were then in the process of moving to new buildings on the outskirts of Kota Bima.

3. For more information on the two villages, see Brewer (1979).

4. See Goethals (1961) for a detailed description of this type of land tenure system.

5. The cultivated land figures for both Rasa and Sila are my own estimates. They are based on a reconstruction of the original 1925 survey maps from the 1939 expanded maps. The figure for government land is also my own estimate.

6. The government was more forceful and successful in moving the village of Kuta, situated on the next ridge north of Sila. By 1930, Kuta residents had all moved to a site some three kilometers down the ridge from their original site. They also abandoned some eight hectares of wet rice land. Today the old village site is part of the forest preserve.

7. The Japanese had the road improved because they interned the sultan in the village of South Rasa just up the valley from Rasa. South Rasa was considered safe from Allied bombings.

8. These figures are based on reconstructed tax records. They show a sizable increase in the area of government wet rice land since 1925. It is probable that the government simply ordered the enlargement of its land as part of the villagers' labor obligations. But, as I said in note 5, the 1925 figure is in any case my own estimate.

9. Soybeans, like other legumes, fix nitrogen and thus help fertilize the soil. Bimanese farmers, however, attribute the continued fertility of dry land planted in soybeans to the attendant plowing.

10. Although the authority of village elders over land no longer exists in Rasa, some such authority still remains in Sila. In 1975, when an unusually large number of cassava gardens were left fallow, the municipal official in charge of Sila threatened publicly to convene the elders in order to redistribute the land for the season. In fact, nothing was done, but no Sila resident voiced an opinion that such an action would have been improper.

11. In a private interview in 1976, a high provincial official characterized Bima as a difficult place to collect taxes. Land taxes in particular always fall short of goals.

References Cited

Ahmad Amin
　1971　*Sedjarah Bima* [History of Bima]. Bima: Kantor Kebudajaan, Kabupaten Bima.

Boedi Harsono
　1975　*Hukum Agraria Indonesia* [Indonesian agricultural laws]. 4th ed. Jakarta: Djambatan.

Brewer, J. D.
　1979　"Agricultural Knowledge and Cultural Practice in Two Indonesian Villages." Ph.D. dissertation, University of California, Los Angeles. Ann Arbor: University Microfilms.

Geertz, C.
　1963.　*Agricultural Involution.* Berkeley and Los Angeles: University of California Press.

Goethals, P.
　1961　*Aspects of Local Government in a Sumbawan Village.* Monograph Series. Ithaca, N.Y.: Modern Indonesia Project, Cornell University.

Jasper, J. E.
　1908　"Het Eiland Soembawa en Zijn Bevolking." *Tijdschrift voor het Binnenlandsch Bestuur* 34:60–147.

PART III: ECOLOGY

5. The Ecology of Intoxication among the Kantu' of West Kalimantan

MICHAEL R. DOVE

Abstract

The focus of this study is the traumatic consumption of alcohol on ceremonial occasions among the tribal Kantu' of West Kalimantan. This pattern of ceremonial drinking can be explained in terms of socioeconomic integration. The integration of Kantu' society is problematic because their agricultural technology and environment place a high value on small, dispersed, semiautonomous socioeconomic units at the same time as they necessitate the regular exchange of grain and labor among these units. By facilitating such exchanges on a regional basis, ceremonial drinking helps to redress the disjunctions inherent in this swidden society. The criticism that this pattern of drinking receives from government officials is, therefore, misplaced.

Introduction

The Kantu' of West Kalimantan engage in a pattern of alcohol consumption, in the context of ceremonial feasting, that is marked by apparent coercion and physical trauma. On the basis of data gathered during two years' research among the Kantu', it is suggested here that the physical trauma experienced during drinking has a behavioral rather than physiological explanation, that the Kantu' conception of the relations between friends and strangers is central to this explanation, and that the ritual enactment of this trauma helps to regulate socioeconomic ties among the units of Kantu' society.[1]

The approach to alcohol use taken here follows the shift in cross-cultural studies of drinking over the past twenty-five years, from a focus on the effects of alcohol on the individual to a focus on its effects on the social system (MacAndrews and Garfinkel 1962; MacAndrews and Edgerton 1969; Marshall 1979a; Kennedy 1984). This shift was stimulated by increasing evidence that the effects of alcohol on humans vary less as a result of physiology than as a result of culture. As Mandelbaum (1979:17) wrote:

> When a man lifts a cup, it is not only the kind of drink that is in it, the amount he is likely to take, and the circumstances under which he will do the drinking that are specified in advance for him, but also whether the contents of the cup will cheer or stupefy, whether they will induce affection or aggression, guilt or unalloyed pleasure.

Accordingly, scholars such as Marshall (1979a) have attempted to study not the physiological effects of ethanol (the active ingredient in alcohol), but what society thinks about these effects. If the effects of ethanol are indeed determined (at least in part) by social norms and values, then an understanding of the latter is a prerequisite to understanding the former (Mandelbaum 1979:26). At the same time, an understanding of drinking behavior may provide unique insights into the dynamics of the society as a whole (ibid. 14). Marshall (1979a:132) concluded that his study of "ethos and ethanol" on Truk illuminated not only drunken comportment on the island, but also the "emotional tone" and even world view of Trukese society.

The function that I attribute to Kantu' drinking in this study, namely socioeconomic integration, is a familiar one in cross-cultural studies of alcohol use (Doughty 1979; Hutchinson 1979; Kennedy 1984; Lemert 1954; Madsen and Madsen 1979; Mangin 1957). As Leacock (1979:90) notes, social integration is one of the two functions most commonly attributed to the use of alcohol (the second being the reduction of anxiety). Socioeconomic integration is also a familiar topic in studies of swidden agriculture. The special constraints that swidden technology place on settlement size, for example, have been studied by Frake (1955), Carneiro (1960), Rappaport (1968), and Ellen (1973), notable among many others.[2] More recently, Marxist scholars have added a new perspective to such studies. Friedman (1975), for example, views these constraints as disjunctions inherent in the structure of swidden societies, the need to reconcile which determines much of their social and economic history. In my own approach, in the analysis to follow, I will wed the systemic focus of the Marxists to a more positivistic, cultural materialist perspective.

My analysis will proceed with (1) a sketch of Kantu' society and environment, (2) a description of Kantu' drinking and the roles of host and guest therein, (3) a presentation of the hypothesis that the function of this behavior is integration, (4) an analysis of the pressures for and against integration in Kantu' society, and (5) an analysis of how the ceremonial drinking system actually works to reconcile these pressures.

Kantu' Society and Environment

The Kantu' live along the Kapuas River and its eastern and western tributaries in West Kalimantan, Indonesia (Fig. 5.1). Between August 1974 and June 1976, I conducted research among one subgroup, the Melaban Kantu'. At that time, some 659 members of this subgroup occupied five longhouses and one village of detached dwellings along the banks of the Empanang River (a western, secondary tributary of the Kapuas). Peoples closely related to the Kantu' occupy the Ketunggau River system to the southeast. Within the Empanang valley itself there are, in addition to the Kantu' settlements, several dozen longhouses of Iban—a large, distinct ethnic group that occupies much of Sarawak in addition to these border areas of West Kalimantan. The Kantu' and Iban both belong to a broader "Ibanic" complex of peoples, whose historic homeland was in this same Kapuas River valley (cf. King 1979:23–28). The present-day Iban of Sarawak migrated out of this valley and into Sarawak, beginning in the sixteenth century (Sandin 1967). Beginning at the end of the nineteenth century, as a result of population/land pressure in Sarawak, some Iban began to migrate back across the border into their original homeland in Kalimantan; and it is from these migrants that the contemporary Iban of the Empanang valley are descended.

The economy of the Kantu' includes both subsistence and market-oriented activities. The latter, carried out chiefly to obtain salt, tobacco, cloth, and kerosene, includes working as day laborers (in one another's fields or, for brief periods, in the commercial plantations of Sarawak); cultivating pepper; and, especially, tapping rubber. Subsistence activities include hunting, fishing, gathering, and raising pigs and fowl. However, the most important aspect of the subsistence economy— indeed, of their economy as a whole—is the swidden cultivation of dry rice and a variety of other crops.[3] The swidden system is the focus of Kantu' society: their settlement pattern, social structure, concepts of property, and ceremonial life all are intimately related to the unique imperatives of this system of agriculture.

Kantu' Drinking

The consumption of alcohol in ceremonial contexts is widespread among the upland, tribal peoples of Southeast Asia. It is mentioned (although not studied in depth) in most of the classic ethnographies from the region (e.g., Condominas 1977:passim; Izikowitz 1951:161, 302). This includes the ethnographic accounts of the Dayak peoples of

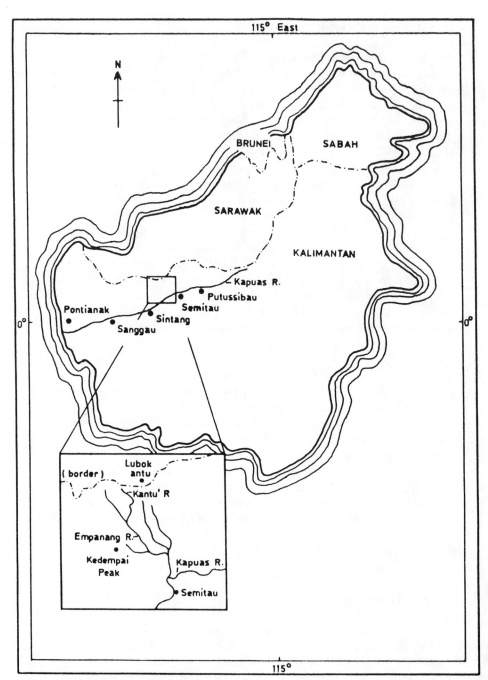

Figure 5.1 Kalimantan and the Research Site

Borneo, especially of the Iban (e.g., Lumholtz 1920:27). Ceremonial drinking is now in decline among many of the Christianized Dayak groups, such as the Kayan (Whittier 1973), but it continues unabated among the Ibanic groups such as the Kantu', living on either side of the Sarawak-Kalimantan border.

General

The Kantu' drink home-brewed liquor as well as trade *arak.* Most of the home brew is what Burkill (1935:1634) defines as "rice wine," namely the liquid drawn from a mash of fermented glutinous rice. The Kantu' call this *ai' utai* (water of the things), the "things" being the animals (pigs and chickens) that—along with the rice wine itself—make up the typical ritual offering. The first step in wine making consists of drying and husking the glutinous rice, which is then put into old Chinese jars along with water and a special package of herbs and yeasts to initiate fermentation.[4] After the fermentation has been completed, which usually takes about ten days, the mash is packed into special baskets, which in turn are placed in a special press (made from a partially split log) used to extract the liquid from it. This liquid has the color and consistency of milk. When brewed by women (who have charge of this matter) with the appropriate secular knowledge and ritual power, it tastes sweet; when brewed by less well-endowed women (who are in the majority), it tastes acidic and sour. This liquid, whatever its taste, is ready for consumption. Sometimes, however, it is further processed in primitive but effective stills to produce what Burkill (ibid.) defines as "rice spirits" or "arak"; the Kantu' also call it *arak,* as well as *ai' utai salai* (smoked water of the things). To this potent liquor, the Kantu' usually add black peppers *(Piper nigrum)* and chili peppers *(Capsicum frutescens).* Rarely, a similar liquor is distilled from Job's tears *(Coix lachryma-jobi)* or cassava *(Manihot esculenta),* instead of the usual base of glutinous rice mash. The trade *arak* (of varying manufacture) that the Kantu' also consume resembles their own distilled spirits in appearance and taste, if not ingredients. After being separated from the mash, rice wine is returned to the ceramic jars in which it was brewed. At the time of drinking, the wine is transferred to small tin teapots or plastic jerrycans, from which it is more readily served into the cups, glasses, or bowls from which it is drunk. Distilled spirits are stored in quart bottles, from which they are served into cups or glasses.

All Kantu' drinking is social as opposed to solitary, and all of it takes place within a ritual (or ritual cum juridical) as opposed to secular context (cf. Condominas 1977:18). The libation and consumption of alcohol is a necessary aspect of any communication between the Kantu' and

A Woman Giving Rice Wine to Men as They Carry the Harvest into the Longhouse

Intoxicated Men Singing and Dancing in the Longhouse Gallery

their gods or spirits. The basic forms of communication consist of agricultural ceremonies to safeguard the health of the swidden crops, shamanistic ceremonies to safeguard the health of individual Kantu', and prophylactic ceremonies to avert divined threats to the health of the community as a whole.

During these ceremonies, sometimes staged in the swidden or swidden house of a single household, but most often staged in the central, multihousehold longhouse, drinking typically extends over one afternoon or evening. Less frequently, during the feasts marking the end of the swidden year or the celebration of a major life crisis (viz., the ear-piercing or first hair-cutting of a juvenile, or the death of an adult), drinking may extend over three days and three nights or more. The periodicity of alcohol consumption is a function of the periodicity of these ceremonies: with an average of slightly less than one ceremony per week throughout the year, Kantu' drinking follows a pattern of total abstinence interrupted by brief intervals of heavy consumption and extreme intoxication. This characteristic was observed (across the border in Sarawak) in the mid-nineteenth century by St. John (1862 I:220), who wrote: "It must not be supposed, however, that the Dayaks are habitual drinkers; on the contrary, except at their feasts, they are a very sober people."

Participation in the consumption of alcohol varies somewhat according to age and gender. There is near total participation among juvenile, adult, and elderly males. There is lesser participation among females, both adolescents and adults (cf. St. John 1862 I: 66–67, 220); and there is little if any among children. Both women and children have a role other than that of drinker to play on these occasions, however. They (especially the young maidens) serve the liquor to the circles of seated men, and they care for those men who drink so much as to become delirious.

The Role of the Host

Whenever there is drinking, there is a clear division of the participants into hosts and guests. The host is the household or longhouse for whose benefit the ceremony is being performed and that is paying its costs (viz., food, drink, and possibly shaman's fees). The guests are those members of other households or longhouses who attend the ceremony. In the case of intralonghouse ceremonies held in the longhouse itself (as opposed to the swidden or swidden house of one of its members), all of the longhouse's constituent households are expected to attend, and they all expect to be welcomed, so no invitations are issued. In the case of interlonghouse ceremonies, however, attendance is by formal invitation. The members of a longhouse that does not receive such an invitation will not, indeed cannot, attend. Such invitations are issued from and received by the longhouse as a whole, following discussion in informal longhouse moots, attended by the longhouse's adult males. The acceptance of an invitation from another longhouse obliges the acceptor, at some later time, to invite the donor to a similar ceremony. The Kantu' call this reciprocation *malas utang* (to repay a debt). Each longhouse participates in a number of such ongoing, reciprocal, feasting relationships with other longhouses.

The distinction between host and guest is manifested not only in the provisioning and the location of the ceremony, but also in drinking roles. It is the role of the host to provide liquor, and it is the role of the guest to consume it. In small intralonghouse ceremonies, the host household presents the guests from other households with cups or glasses of liquor, which the latter must raise to their lips and drain in an unbroken series of swallows. In the largest interlonghouse ceremonies, the host longhouse may present the guests from another longhouse with a large basin of liquor, which the latter must drain en masse. The role of the host is always to encourage the guests to consume as much liquor as possible. To this end, the hosts employ a number of different stratagems.

The most subtle of these stratagems involves verbal sparring. For example, the host may ask a diffident guest if he likes the liquor with which he has been presented. If the guest replies in the affirmative, the host will purposefully misconstrue this as a request for more, which he will immediately press upon the hapless guest. If, on the other hand, the guest replies in the negative, implying that he does not like the host's liquor, the host will misconstrue this as a personal insult, which can only be effaced by payment of a *hukum* (fine). The fine of course consists in a specified amount of liquor that the guest has to consume. Finally, if the wary guest gives the host neither a positive nor a negative answer, but says that he is not sure, this also will be misconstrued as grounds for pressing more liquor upon the guest, to "help him make up his mind."

Less subtle stratagems employed by the hosts involve exciting or embarrassing the guest into drinking. Faced with a reluctant guest, for example, the hosts will surround him and chant bawdy verse to the accompaniment of rhythmic hand-clapping and foot-stamping until the guest has drained the cup or glass placed before him.[5] The least subtle stratagem employed by the host is brute force. Angered by a guest's demurrals, a host may drag or carry him to a jar of rice wine and demand that he drink. It is not unusual for a host to force open a guest's mouth, fill it with wine or *arak,* and then induce it down with a timely punch to the stomach. The ultimate form of suasion, in the largest ceremonies, is monetary. The host *ngengkah* (pays) the guests, with currency, for *tolong kami ngirop* (helping us to drink).

The eagerness of the host for the guest to drink stands in marked contrast to the latter's own reluctance. Guests typically try to refuse any liquor offered to them, particularly after the first cup or glass (cf. St. John 1862 II:118). It is difficult for a reluctant guest to outwit a determined host, however. As indicated above, protestations of not liking or not wanting the liquor are usually not efficacious. A reluctant guest may say that he is ill or, with the recent introduction of antibiotics into the region, he may say that he has just taken some pills—the inadvisability of mixing these with alcohol having already acquired the status of folk knowledge (cf. Doughty 1979:72). Such pleas also are rarely effective: they usually are greeted derisively as the feeble excuses that they in fact often are. Facing a not-to-be-denied host, a particularly hard pressed guest may request or be volunteered the assistance of another guest in consuming the given amount of liquor that has been set before him.

In addition to these efforts—however futile—to avoid the drink itself, the guests usually make a variety of efforts to avoid the perceived effects of drink. These include chewing, before drinking, various roots and herbs (called *ntambah ntau' mabok* [medicine to prevent intoxication]) that are reputed to inhibit the effects of alcohol on the drinker. These efforts also include, after drinking, removal of the alcohol from the stomach by vomiting. The Kantu' affirm that this always makes them feel better, and they speak of vomiting as, indeed, a way to feel better. Thus, people will ask of someone who is obviously feeling the effects of his drinking, "Has he not vomited yet?"

Even the relief of vomiting is short-lived, however. When a guest vomits and starts to recover, this is taken by his host as an indication that he can be plied with more drink. Guests are commonly forced to drink within minutes of vomiting. The ultimate and only truly efficacious recourse of the harried guest is flight—to another part of the longhouse if attending a ceremony in his own longhouse or out of the longhouse into the forest if attending a ceremony at another longhouse. Surreptitious or even open flight is institutionalized as a way of departing from Kantu' ceremonies (cf. Doughty 1979:77).

The cost of the drink that the host so avidly pushes upon his guests is not shared by them, nor are any of the other costs of the ceremony (except in the singular case of Kantu' attendance at Iban ceremonies, to be discussed later). The cost of the liquor is a function of the amount of glutinous rice that is used to prepare the wine mash or (in the case of an insufficiency of glutinous rice) the amount of nonglutinous rice that is traded for commercial *arak*. In an average year (not marked by the staging of a major life crisis ceremony), the average Kantu' household devotes the equivalent of approximately 370 kilograms of unmilled rice to ceremonial consumption.[6] Approximately one-third of this represents the cost of drink alone.[7]

The host does not necessarily take these ceremonial costs from an agricultural "surplus." It is not uncommon for a household to use grain to brew wine or buy *arak,* even though this will lead to (or exacerbate) a shortage of grain for daily consumption before the next harvest.[8] For example, in each of two years, 1975 and 1976, eight of the households in the Kantu' longhouse of Tikul Batu hosted large postharvest ceremonies to which other longhouses were invited (Table 5.1). These households each devoted, on average, the equivalent of 93 kilograms of unmilled rice to each ceremony, despite the fact that three of them did not have sufficient grain (counting the grain from the recent harvest, as well as any grain in storage) to meet their own consumption needs for the coming year.[9]

All of the resources consumed in ceremonies could be used instead for subsistence consumption or traded for goods that can be so used. This includes the glutinous rice from which the liquor usually is made. It is a highly esteemed food, whether cooked in mixture with the staple non-glutinous rice or cooked separately as sweet patties or rolls. Some of this food value may be retained when glutinous rice is made into a mash and then into wine, but it is lost (to the guests as well as host) in the vomiting that accompanies most drinking. The solid residue that remains after pressing out the wine is not considered fit for human consumption and is simply fed to the pigs.[10] Since the feeding of pigs is not otherwise problematic, and given the general inefficiency of converting vegetable foods into protein, this contribution to the pig diet cannot significantly offset the loss to the human diet. The Kantu' recognize that these cere-

Table 5.1. Sufficiency of Grain and Hosting of Ceremonies at Tikul Batu

	Number of households with grain insufficiency	Number of households with grain sufficiency
Number of households hosting large post-harvest ceremonies in 1975	3	5
Number of households hosting large post-harvest ceremonies in 1976	3	5

monial costs can be burdensome, especially for households already short of grain for subsistence, but they believe that this burden is more than offset by the good relations that are thereby established not only with their fellow Kantu', but also—and principally—with the spirit world.

The principal stated motive in staging any ceremony is to maintain or redress relations with the *antu* (spirits), which include the benign deities of the earth and sky as well as the malign spirits that appear in the guise of jungle creatures (cf. Jensen 1974:94–95). This is achieved, the Kantu' believe, by providing food and—especially—liquor to the spirits. During each ceremony, the host formally presents a small amount of liquor to the spirits—calling them, and then addressing and supplicating them while pouring a libation onto the ground. Additional liquor is presented to the spirits informally and indirectly. According to Kantu' belief, the spirits share in any liquor that is drunk by the human participants in the ceremony.

The spirits express their gratitude for this liquor, the Kantu' believe, by ensuring the welfare of the host who provided it—in particular, the welfare of his swiddens. This belief provides explicit justification for the expenditure of scarce resources on ceremonial feasting. For example, the Kantu' say that the expenditure of a given amount of resources on a ceremony will result in a rise in their favor with the spirits that, in turn, will result in an increase in their subsequent swidden harvest that is sure to surpass the initial expenditure.

The host of a ceremonial feast endeavors to please not only his spirit guests, but his human guests as well. In particular, the host tries to meet the latter's expectation for a "good" feast, which is measured by the amount of drinking and vomiting that take place. If the host fails to meet these expectations, the guests will publicly disparage the feast, saying *Nadai isi' ti mutah din* (There was no one who vomited there). The Kantu' say that this is a *malu besai* (major embarrassment) for the host, whose disappointed guests may thereafter refuse to attend any more of his feasts. To avoid this, the host will devote to his feast whatever resources are necessary, even if—as noted earlier—the resources of the host household or longhouse are not sufficient for its own daily subsistence.

The Kantu' justify these expenditures on the human guests at a feast —just as they justify the expenditures on the spirit guests—in terms of the resultant benefits that they expect to flow from the guests to the host. The medium for this flow of benefits is the rice wine itself. The Kantu' believe that rice wine is *celap* (ritually cool), and that it therefore attracts *tuah* (luck or fortune).[11] If two people drink from a single cup of rice wine, the Kantu' believe that some of the luck of the first will pass

into the cup and can then be imbibed by the second.[12] The Kantu'
guard against unwelcome appropriations of their luck in this manner—
which they call *ngami' tuah* (taking of luck)—by ensuring that no one else
surreptitiously finishes a cup of wine from which they have started to
drink. Hence the cultural norm of draining all cups or glasses of liquor
in a continuous series of swallows, without removing it from one's lips.
This circumspection is relaxed between host and guest, however, the
latter of whom is indeed obliged to share some of his luck with the former. Hence the host always drinks after the guest (cf. Condominas
1977:56), either from the same cup or from a refill of the same cup,
either of which is considered to produce some transfer of luck from the
first drinker to the second. An explicit illustration of these principles
occurs during the ceremony *Begela' jari* (blessing of the hands).

If a Kantu' has experienced a series of poor harvests (or other misfor-
tunes), he will conclude that his hands are ritually *angat* (hot) and
unlucky, and he will stage this ceremony to make them *celap* (cool) and
lucky. Those members of his longhouse believed to have the most luck
(in agriculture as well as in other endeavors) will be invited to the ceremony and asked to drink from—but not drain—a cup of rice wine. As
they drink, a fishhook will be dangled in their cup, with the avowed
purpose of *ngait* (hooking) some of the drinkers' luck for the host, who
will subsequently drain the cup. This act, in which the drinkers freely
participate, is called *bedua' tuah* (dividing the luck); it contrasts to the
previously mentioned *ngami' tuah* (taking the luck), against which
drinkers guard themselves.

The Role of the Guest

The role of the host is to provide food and drink to his guests, in
exchange for which he expects to receive their luck (and, in the case of
spirit guests, support). Similarly, it is the role of the guest to consume
the host's food and drink and provide him with this luck (and support).
The cost to the host is the expenditure of large quantities of food and
drink; the cost to the guest is the physical trauma produced by the consumption of this food and—especially—drink.

Some rice wine is sweet, but most of it is sour and disagreeable to
consume. Moreover, when it is consumed in quantity during major
ceremonies, whether sweet or sour it produces extreme intoxication.
This intoxication is accompanied by nausea and vomiting, often terminating in delirious seizures (cf. Condominas 1977: 173, 335; St. John
1862 I:66). When a man shows signs of slipping into delirium, the
women and children—who attend the drinkers for this reason—pin him

to the floor and administer to him (cf. St. John 1862 I:67). Treatment consists of pounding the drinker on his back to make him vomit, kneading the skin between his shoulder blades to make him feel better, and immobilizing him to keep him from doing any harm to himself or others.[13] Delirium and incapacitation usually end within a few hours of when drinking ends. One aftereffect that may linger on for a day or two, however, is a painful inflammation of the vocal chords that is produced by repeated vomiting of the acidic wine (and also the acidic foods, such as eggplant [*Solanum melongena* L.], that are customarily eaten with it). While this inflammation persists, the drinkers usually cannot speak.

This loss of speech, like all the other physical trauma associated with drinking, is unwelcome to the Kantu'. They refer to the state of intoxication itself as *mabok,* the same term they use to describe the physical state of someone who has been poisoned. Similarly, the term they use to refer to the state of drunken delirium, *luput,* is also used to refer to the loss of consciousness brought on by the bite of a poisonous snake or insect.

This antipathy toward the effects of drink notwithstanding, guests are hard put to moderate their drinking. While it is appropriate for a host to show anger toward a guest who does not want to drink, for example, it is not appropriate for the guest in this situation to show anger toward the host. Similarly, while a host can use force on his guests to get them to drink, it is unheard of for a guest to counter with force of his own. The guest can meet his host's anger and force with nothing more than sheepish good humor and, ultimately, compliance with his demands.

The ultimate compliance of the guest and predominance of the host is assured by the ill consequences that are thought to follow any refusal of drink. For the guest, such a refusal is thought to result in bad dreams (which are viewed as portents of misfortune). The Kantu' explain such dreams by saying *Antu iya ka' ngirop* (His spirits wanted to drink [with him]), and when they were deprived of the opportunity, they sent the bad dreams as punishment. For the host, any guest's refusal to drink is thought to hurt—or, minimally, to not help—the chances for a good crop in his current swiddens. Thus, the host can beseech a reluctant guest to drink by saying *Awak kami bolay maioh padi* (So that we will get a lot of rice). Once the host says this, any further resistance on the part of the guest is impossible, since it would then appear to be unfriendly if not, indeed, malicious. This moral imperative was perceived (if not understood) by Rajah Brooke (as quoted in Roth 1896 I:256), who wrote "It seems, in fact, to be a sin to be sober, and a virtue to be drunk."

The Role of Host vs. Guest

The difference between the roles of host and guest is well illustrated in two minor variants on the normal pattern of drinking. In the first variant, which is restricted to large ceremonies, the drinkers sit in a circle around a jar of rice wine and an empty *arak* bottle. The wine is doled out by spinning the bottle. After each spin, the person at whom it points —namely, the "loser"—must drink a cup (cf. Singer 1979:315–316). The second variant involves a Chinese card game that the Kantu' like to play during quiet moments in small ceremonies. They bet on each hand, and it is their custom for the winners to use their winnings to buy liquor for the group (cf. Doughty 1979:74). In both cases, therefore, the winners provide the drink and the losers drink it: the winners are the hosts and the losers the guests. This association between winner and host on the one hand and between loser and guest on the other again demonstrates the agreeable benefits of the former role and the disagreeable costs of the latter.

These examples of drinking and gaming demonstrate why people assume the role of guest in the face of these disagreeable costs. They assume it because they know that it is a temporary role: as in the games just described, one who is now the guest/loser can the next turn be the host/winner. More accurately, people assume this role because they know that they must sometimes play guests if they are ever to play hosts. That is, in the regional exchange system, just as in the games of chance, participation is predicated upon willingness to periodically play the role of guest as well as the role of host.

Kantu' Drinking and Integration

The peculiar drinking behavior of the Kantu', involving marked physical trauma, cannot be attributed to some peculiar feature of Kantu' physiology, because this traumatic reaction to alcohol is not shared by the other Malay peoples to whom the Kantu' are racially related. Neither can the trauma be attributed to some peculiarity of the drink itself, because of one historical fact. Within the past twenty years, trade *arak* has been introduced into the system of ceremonial drinking, which was previously based solely on indigenous rice wine (and spirits). This trade liquor is of entirely different origins and manufacture from the indigenous liquor, yet it is used by the Kantu' in the same manner as the latter and—of most importance—its consumption is associated with the same trauma. With physiological explanations of this trauma, whether in terms of drinker or drink, thus ruled out, an explanation must be sought in Kantu' culture.

One aspect of Kantu' culture that throws light on the way they deal with drink is the way they deal with food. The sharing of food, according to Kantu' customary law, is restricted to members of the same household. Except during a ceremony or a multihousehold swidden work party (in which part of the compensation given to the workers is a meal), two or more households never eat together or otherwise share foodstuffs. Sharing is proscribed even when one household has a surplus of food and another household has a deficit—as is frequently the case. The variation in and unpredictability of the local environment results in great interhousehold variation in swidden success and hence in the availability of foodstuffs. The households of the longhouse Tikul Batu harvested sufficient grain in 1975 and 1976 to meet an average of 96 percent of subsistence needs for the year (which average 2,820 kilograms of unhusked rice per household), but the standard deviation from this figure among the households was fully 49 percent (yielding a coefficient of variation of 51).

Given that households do not share their food and that there is perennial variation among them in the availability of foodstuffs, the act of consuming food is associated with some interhousehold tension. This is reflected in the custom for each household to eat in the privacy of its own longhouse apartment, in as brief a time as possible (five to ten minutes being the norm). If the household's eating can be seen, heard, or even inferred by a nonmember of the household, it is placed in a vulnerable position because, while no one from outside the household should ask to join in eating, there is no proper way to refuse such a request should it be made. This tension results in verbal sparring during mealtime in the longhouse, with people in one apartment calling out to those in a nearby apartment and asking what their *ngkayu* (relish) is. (The relish that is eaten with the rice staple is the highlight of the meal.) The latter must be quick with a reply such as *Nama ngkayu kami? Nadai isi' ngkayu* (What relish of ours? There is no relish). If they instead gave the name of their relish, they would become losers in this verbal sparring, because to tell someone about a desirable foodstuff and not invite them to share it represents a near violation of social norms.[14]

There is tension over food consumption not only within the longhouse but also between longhouses. It is the Kantu' custom for travelers to seek bed and board in whatever longhouse they happen to be near when night falls. The norms of tribal hospitality make it impossible to refuse such requests. However, especially during the lean times just prior to each year's harvest, board may be granted with some reluctance. It also may be received with some trepidation. There is a widespread fear among the Kantu' of being poisoned when eating in other longhouses, especially ones very distant from one's own or belonging to other tribes or subtribes. All Kantu' can cite cases of illness or even death that were supposedly caused by poisoned food consumed in another longhouse. Because of the implicit fear of such poisoning, important visitors to a longhouse are not fed until after the longhouse's own inhabitants have eaten in their presence and (presumably) failed to evince any symptoms of poisoning.

These characteristics of food consumption all contrast sharply with the characteristics of alcohol consumption. Whereas food is consumed within the household, alcohol is always consumed by multihousehold groups. Whereas food is consumed quickly and in the privacy of the household apartment, alcohol is consumed slowly and publicly in the longhouse gallery (Fig. 5.2). (Even during ceremonial feasts, in which the guests are given drink in the longhouse gallery, they are given food in the private apartments of individual longhouse families.) Whereas food is often given to a guest with reluctance or even resentment on the part of the host, alcohol is always given with decided eagerness. Similarly, whereas the guest will ask for food and receives it gladly, he will never ask for alcohol and receives it with reluctance. Finally, whereas the guest may fear that his host's food will make him ill (viz., poisoned), he knows and acquiesces in the certainty that his host's drink will make him ill.

The one similarity between the giving of food and the giving of drink is that both place the guest in a vulnerable position with respect to the host. Just as the host can use food to work harm against his guest, so too it is possible for him to use liquor. This possibility is dramatized during every *belian* (curing ceremony). The purpose of these curing ceremonies is to kill or drive away the malign spirits that cause illness. This is accomplished by preparing offerings—foremost among which is liquor—and then summoning the offending spirit to the longhouse. According to the Kantu', when the spirit arrives at the longhouse and sees the liquor prepared for it, it will squat down to drink. As it does so, it will momentarily lay its blowpipe (the weapon of malign spirits) across its knees, thus becoming vulnerable to attack by the shaman. This vulnerability is heightened when the spirit imbibes the liquor set out for it. The shaman also drinks during the ceremony, but the drink does not affect his capacity for combat. One of the characteristics that distinguishes shamans from ordinary people is their ability to drink—in their capacity as shamans—without becoming intoxicated. The ability to maintain sobriety is thus associated with invulnerability (while intoxication is associated with vulnerability) and with the manipulation of a

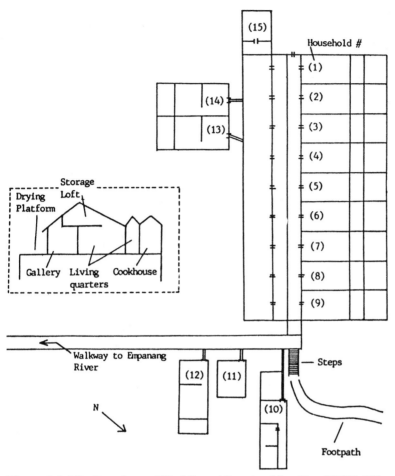

Figure 5.2 The Longhouse Tikul Batu (*Reproduced from Dove [1985b:12]*)

drinking relationship to one-sided advantage. The shaman-spirit relationship is exceptional in this regard, however. No element of manipulation is present in any other drinking relationship. And when shamans
attend ceremonies as ordinary guests, they drink and get drunk just like
the rest of the guests.

Although guests are potentially vulnerable when receiving food or
drink, hosts never take advantage of this vulnerability when serving
drink, only when serving food (at least according to Kantu' belief). It is
unheard of for a host to take advantage of a guest's intoxication or delirium to harm him. Thus, intoxication is freely engaged in without fear—
or threat—of personal jeopardy. Since it is associated with potential vul-

nerability, however, this experience and expression of intoxication on the part of the guest is a demonstration of faith in the good intentions of the host; and the host's failure to take advantage of this intoxication is a demonstration that this faith is not misplaced. Accordingly, submission to intoxication serves to make people who are (or have become) distant or estranged from the host less distant and less estranged. This is seen most clearly in the special drinking rite called *ngalu* (welcoming).

Ngalu involves the formal presentation of liquor to special categories of people who are visiting or returning to the longhouse, prior to their actual entrance into the longhouse. In its most elaborate form, the person being welcomed must pass a gauntlet of host women lining the path or walkway leading up to the longhouse, stopping and receiving a drink from each one in turn. Persons accorded this treatment arrive at the longhouse in a very intoxicated state, if indeed they arrive (under their own power) at all. The sorts of people who are welcomed to the longhouse in this manner include: (1) men returning to the longhouse after engaging in mock headhunting (in connection with mortuary rites); (2) workers who have heard an ill omen while carrying the harvest back to the longhouse from an outlying swidden; (3) shamans returning to the longhouse after performing a ceremony somewhere in the longhouse territory; and (4) guests from another longhouse coming to attend a ceremonial feast. The common element in each of these cases is that the arriving people bear with them some contagion (from death, spirits, or simply a group of people not one's own) that is thought to be inimical to the welfare of the longhouse but that is rendered harmless through contact with liquor. As stated earlier, rice wine is thought to have a "cool" quality that can neutralize the "hot" qualities of death, malign spirits, or strangers.

The function of ceremonial drinking in bringing estranged people together is reflected not only in the sorts of people who are given drink, but also in the sorts of people who give it. As just noted, it is the longhouse's females who serve the liquor during *ngalu*. In most ceremonial drinking, indeed, it is women—in particular young maidens—who serve the liquor to guests. These maidens represent potential sleeping companions and wives for the male guests, whether the ceremony is intralonghouse or interlonghouse (about half of all marriages are longhouse endogamous, half longhouse exogamous). The offering and consumption of liquor is in fact a traditional element in the courtship between a household's or longhouse's maidens and visiting youths.[15] Thus, the role of maidens in forging social ties among different households and longhouses, by virtue of their role in ceremonial drinking, enhances as well as reflects the integrative character of this drinking.

This integrative character is made clearest in the ceremonial drinking that follows the adjudication of disputes. It is the Kantu' custom for the winning party to a dispute to use a portion of his settlement (and/or for the tribal elder who adjudicated the dispute to use a portion of his fee) to purchase *arak,* which is then drunk by all the parties to the dispute. The Kantu' explain this practice as follows: *Kami ngirop arak awak bedamai laya', awak bado' pedih ati agi'* (We drink arak to settle the quarrel, so that hearts cease to be troubled anymore). This represents an exception among cross-cultural studies of drinking, in which alcohol is less often reported to be a means for allaying conflict than a source of conflict itself. Nevertheless, it is not a source of conflict among the Kantu'. Despite the inebriation and even delirium that accompany Kantu' drinking, despite the apparent tension between host and guests, the incidence of interpersonal violence (the violence of forced drinking aside), illicit sexual relations, and other disintegrative acts is extremely low. Moreover, when such acts do occur, they are not excused because of the drink: rather, they are punished according to tribal law, just as they would be if they had been committed when sober.[16] The Kantu' attitude is summed up in this remark by one young man: *Aku nadai peduli urang ti madah asa ia ngirop, asa mabuk, ia nadai ingat agi'* (I do not believe someone who says that if he drinks, if he gets drunk, he no longer remembers [how to behave]). Thus, Kantu' drinking fosters integration not by permitting people to temporarily engage in disintegrative social behavior, but by permitting and/or obliging them to engage, publicly, in behavior that both reflects and reaffirms integration.

Kantu' Integration

In the early studies of the integrative function of drinking, the association between drinking and integration was explained but the importance of this integration to society was not. In recent studies such as Kennedy's (1984) among the Tarahumara of Mexico, the particular historical, ecological, and political factors that make integration problematic for a given society—hence the role of drinking—are properly given equal weight. In the same vein, I will here discuss several factors that make integration both difficult for but necessary to Kantu' society. This exercise can be contrasted to much Marxist scholarship, in which the tensions or disjunctions of society are taken as a starting point for other investigations as opposed to being a subject of analysis themselves. Friedman (1974:466) has written, for example, "Structural marxism, unlike vulgar materialism, begins with the *assumption* [emphasis added] of disjunction between structures in order to establish the true relation-

ships that unite them as well as the internal laws of the separate structures which cause the contradictions of the larger whole."

The Problem of Integration

One of the major tensions in Kantu' society is between the need for
socioeconomic integration and the difficulty of achieving it, both of
which are functions of the Kantu' mode of production, namely swidden
cultivation of the tropical rain forest. (These tensions are also a function
of the particular social structure and social history associated with this
mode of production, namely a tribal society organized according to
principles of bilateral kinship.) This form of agriculture, which is economically attractive so long as adequate land is available (Dove 1985a),
favors the dispersal rather than concentration of population. The
Kantu' live in widely separated longhouses, which house from ten to
thirty households (between fifty and two hundred inhabitants). During
half the year, the inhabitants of each longhouse further disperse to single-family swidden houses, scattered over a longhouse territory that
may range in area from five to fifteen square kilometers (Dove 1985b:
chap. 11). Consonant with this scattering of the population, each household functions as an independent unit of production and consumption,
reflecting a fierce individualism and egalitarianism in the Kantu' character (cf. Freeman 1981). There is differentiation but no stratification
or discrimination among the Kantu' on the basis of age, gender, or
material wealth, nor are there any indigenous castes, classes, or ranks.[17]

Another character trait associated with the Kantu' mode of production is a highly competitive spirit. As noted earlier, the nature of the
environment and of their system for exploiting it result in chronic
interhousehold variation in agricultural success. This manifest variation, and the absence often of any obvious reason for it, gives rise to
envy on the part of those who fare worse in a given year and fears of
resentment and sorcery on the part of those who fare better. This com-
petitiveness extends not only to agricultural outputs, but to agricultural
inputs as well—in particular labor, which is the scarcest resource in an
extensive agricultural society such as this (Dove 1984). The value of
labor is reflected in the cultural ideal of maintaining large households,
based on the natolocal residence of children after marriage. Given an
ambilocal postmarital residence rule, the competition over labor is
expressed in efforts by both the groom's and the bride's households to
have the newly married couple reside with them. This competition is
particularly marked in the case of interlonghouse marriages, when the
out-marrying person is lost not just to his or her household, but to the
longhouse as a whole. In such cases, the longhouse that wins the compe-

tition exults in its victory and publicly gloats over the defeat of the other longhouse involved.

The Need for Integration—Utilization of Labor

These competitive and individualistic traits notwithstanding, there are great pressures for cooperation and integration in Kantu' society. These pressures derive from the fact that neither the individual, nor the household, nor even the longhouse is a completely viable unit. As Hose and McDougall (1912 II:194–195) wrote early this century in their study of tribal Bornean societies:

> The attachment of each individual to his community is also greatly strengthened by the fact that it is hardly possible for him to leave it, even if he would. For he could not hope to maintain himself alone, or as the head of an isolated family, against the hostile forces, natural and human, that would threaten him. . . .

In contemporary times, the forces that militate against survival by a single individual, household, or longhouse involve difficulties, first, in fully utilizing agricultural labor.

The utilization of labor is problematic during three stages of the nine-stage swidden cycle, namely planting, weeding, and harvesting. (The entire cycle consists in selecting the site; slashing, felling, and burning the forest; planting in the ashes; weeding, guarding, and harvesting the crop; and then carrying in the harvest [Dove 1985b].) Planting is a problem because it must be carried out quickly and in coordination with as many other households as possible, in order to achieve a short and intense harvest season. This maximizes the dispersion of pests and hence minimizes overall crop losses to predation. Weeding is a problem because it cannot begin until six to seven weeks after the swidden burn, before which the weeds are too short to be grasped in the hand. Once the weeds are long enough to be weeded, however, they must be removed within eight to nine weeks or the development of the rice plants will be permanently retarded. Finally, harvesting is a problem because it has to be completed quickly, in order to minimize losses both to pests and to lodging (the breaking of stalks of overripe plants by wind or rain) and shattering (the breaking of overripe grains from their panicles by wind or rain); the magnitude of both varies directly with the length of time that the mature crop remains in the field, unharvested.

Because the pressures on labor are greatest during planting, weeding, and harvesting, they place a cap on how much land can be farmed. There is no point in selecting, slashing, felling, and burning more land than can be planted, weeded, and harvested. During the less pressured stages of the swidden cycle, consequently, labor is not fully utilized. In short, while labor is scarce during certain stages of the cycle, it is in surplus during others. As a result of this imbalance between available labor and available work, there are potentially one hundred to two hundred days each year on which the average household cannot utilize its available labor in its own swiddens (Dove 1983, 1984).

The Kantu' redress this imbalance through interhousehold exchanges of labor, especially during the high pressure swidden stages. Because of variation among different households (especially those from different longhouses) in the timing of swidden activities, it is usually possible for the members of a household having a slack period to find work in the swiddens of another household that is having a busy period, to be reciprocated during the next busy period in their own swiddens.[18] By means of such exchanges, the household wastes less labor during its slack periods and, by translating this savings into labor debts among other households, it can put more labor into its swiddens during its busy periods. As a result of this increased labor input during the high pressure stages of its swidden cycle, the household can proportionately increase the use of its own labor during the less pressured stages, thereby raising the cap on the amount of land that it can farm.[19]

The Need for Integration—Returns on Labor

Interhousehold cooperation is vital not only to increasing the utilization of labor but also to guaranteeing the returns on it. The Kantu' swidden economy is distinguished by great uncertainty of returns, largely due to the character of the local environment. Two characteristics of this environment are particularly relevant here. The first is spatial diversity, referring to the unequal distribution across the Kantu' territory of different forest and soil types, concentrations of swidden pests, drainage patterns, and so on. The second relevant characteristic is temporal variation, referring to the unpredictable occurrence of drought, flooding, or outbreaks of predation. Because each of these factors can be a critical determinant of swidden success or failure, this diversity and variation greatly complicate Kantu' swidden strategies. They make it impossible for a given household to select the one swidden strategy that will cover all contingencies and guarantee success. As a result, there is considerable fluctuation from one year to the next in the swidden fortunes of even the most experienced and astute households. No household has a monopoly on either success or failure: when the fourteen households of the longhouse Tikul Batu are ranked according to the success of their swidden harvests (measured as a percentage of their subsistence needs for one year) in both 1975 and 1976, and then the two years' rankings are compared, no correlation at all is found (viz., $r_s = .05$).[20] There is similar fluctuation in the swidden fortunes of the longhouse as a whole vis-à-vis other longhouses. For example, in 1974 the overall harvest of the longhouse Tikul Batu was one of the worst in the Empanang valley, but its 1975 harvest was one of the best, and its 1976 harvest was about average.

While there is no guarantee that a given household or longhouse will succeed with its swiddens in a given year, there is a near guarantee that some households and longhouses will be successful. Because each longhouse—and each household within the longhouse—pursues its own idiosyncratic swidden strategy, swidden failures are no more uniformly shared than are swidden successes. When some or even most swiddens fail, someone's swiddens somewhere are sure to succeed, as is evident from the data on harvest successes versus failures within the longhouse Tikul Batu during the years 1974–1976 (Table 5.2). Moreover, while swidden successes in fact tend to be less common than swidden failures (cf. Freeman 1970:266; Grijpstra 1976:102), their magnitude tends to be greater. For example, among the six households whose harvests surpassed sufficiency at Tikul Batu in 1975, the average surplus equaled 37 percent of sufficiency, whereas among the eight households whose harvests fell short of sufficiency that year, the average shortfall equaled just 21 percent of sufficiency. As a result, the total harvests of all households tend to exceed the total needs of all households. In the year just cited (1975), the grain needs of all fourteen households amounted to less than 47,000 kilograms, but their summed harvests amounted to more than 48,500 kilograms. The same pattern prevails at the level of the longhouse: even when one or more of the longhouses experience an overall harvest shortfall, the total harvests of all of the longhouses in the valley are still likely to exceed their total requirements.

The problem of periodic shortfalls at the level of the household, therefore, represents a problem not of shortfalls but only of unequal distribu-

**Table 5.2. Harvest Successes and Failures
at Tikul Batu**

	1974	1975	1976
Number of households with harvests surpassing sufficiency	3	6	5
Number of households with harvests falling short of sufficiency	11	8	11

tion at the level of the longhouse or region. At this latter level, a number of mechanisms operate to achieve a more equal distribution. During harvest time, for example, households with good crops usually hire laborers from households with poor crops, paying them either a fixed amount of grain per day or a percentage of the grain that they reap. In addition, households with good crops sometimes allow less fortunate households to join in the harvest, keeping all that they reap as a loan to be paid back the following year. Finally, households with good crops may allow less fortunate households to carry out the final gleaning of their fields, keeping all that they find as a gift. Because of these several possibilities for sharing in the fortune of a household with a good crop, such households are usually inundated by their less fortunate brethren, coming from both near and far—a pattern that has been reported from throughout Borneo (e.g., Freeman 1970:271–272).

The incidence of such interhousehold distributions, which are supported by strong social norms, is quite high. Of the eleven households whose 1974 harvests fell short of sufficiency (Table 5.2), every one obtained grain from other households through one or more of the mechanisms just described before the 1975 harvest; and of the eight households whose 1975 harvests fell short, six obtained grain from other households before the 1976 harvest.[21] The amounts of grain involved in these distributions can amount to significant portions of the surpluses and shortfalls of the donor and recipient households, respectively. For example, after the 1975 harvest at Tikul Batu, six households held a grain surplus totaling 7,080 kilograms and eight households faced a grain shortfall totaling 5,100 kilograms. During the subsequent year, the former distributed over 40 percent of their surplus to the latter in the form of wage payments alone, which made up more than one-half of the latter's total shortfalls.

Two opposing principles determine how prospective recipients select donor households: the desirability of proximate households and the availability of distant ones. Other things being equal, a household in need of grain will prefer to obtain it from a household with which it has close kin ties and whose swiddens are also close to its own—meaning another household in the same longhouse or (although somewhat less likely) in a nearby longhouse. Closer kin ties are easier to presume upon; and the shorter the physical distance involved, the shorter the time that must be spent not only in traveling to the donor's swidden, but also in carrying back whatever grain is obtained (an exceedingly arduous task). While close donors are preferable, however, they are also few in number and likely to have shared the ill fortune of the prospective recipient. Contrarily, the further afield the needy household looks, the greater the potential number of donors, because population increases geometrically with distance. (The total population living within a ten-kilometer radius of any given household will be [*cet. par.*] four times as large as the total population living within a five-kilometer radius.)[22] Also, the further afield the needy household looks, the greater the likelihood of finding households that did not share its ill fortune. This is due to increases not only in the number of households, but also in the amount of microenvironmental variation. The further afield the needy household looks, the greater the likelihood it will encounter microenvironments other than the one that was responsible for its own agricultural misfortune.

The respective importance in donor selection of these two principles —the desirability of proximate donors and the availability of distant ones—varies according to the magnitude of the prospective recipient's agricultural failure. Following most harvest failures, which are of limited severity and affect only a small number of households or longhouses, needy households can usually find donors to whom they are close both physically and in terms of kinship. Periodically, however, a harvest failure occurs of such severity and extent that all proximate households are affected, forcing the needy to seek donors among less proximate households. Just such a harvest failure occurred in 1974 at Tikul Batu, when the households of this and all proximate longhouses almost uniformly experienced a very bad harvest (said to be the worst in ten years). The eight of Tikul Batu's fourteen households that were most severely affected—they did not even harvest sufficient rice for the following year's seed—sought assistance from households in four other longhouses at distances of one hour's to one day's travel from Tikul Batu. Because harvest failures of this magnitude occur relatively infrequently—and the greater the magnitude, the greater the infrequency— distant households are asked for assistance relatively infrequently as well. The incidence of requests and offers of assistance between households, therefore, varies inversely with the distance between them.

Discussion

The periodic necessity of interhousehold cooperation, whether due to uncertain harvest returns or difficulties in labor utilization, is in conflict with the basic Kantu' values of individualism and competition. My thesis is that this conflict is resolved and this cooperation is achieved in part through the ceremonial consumption of alcohol.[23] The generally "integrative" effect of drinking was discussed earlier. It remains to show how the system of ceremonial drinking ensures that the households and longhouses that are integrated are those that can, in fact, be of the greatest assistance to one another.

The Initiation and Termination of Ceremonial Relationships

Ceremonial relationships between households (viz., within the same longhouse) are relatively informal, but not so the ceremonial relationships between different longhouses. Such relationships can be initiated only by the extension from one longhouse to another of a formal invitation to a ceremony. Acceptance of this invitation sets the relationship in motion, because the host longhouse can expect to be subsequently invited to one of the guest longhouse's own ceremonies, and so on. A return invitation must be extended to any longhouse whose last invitation was accepted. The cycle can be stopped only by refusing an invitation. Assume that longhouse A invites longhouse B to a ceremony, and the latter declines the invitation by not attending (an invitation cannot simply be refused out of hand). Longhouse B is obliged to reciprocate longhouse A's extended if unutilized invitation by inviting the latter to one of its own ceremonies. However, because longhouse B declined A's invitation, social face will oblige longhouse A similarly to decline B's (by similarly not attending). In the next round of ceremonies, longhouse A would not extend another invitation to longhouse B. This would be permissible, given A's rejection of B's last invitation, and the ceremonial relationship between the two longhouses would end.

Decisions to initiate or terminate ceremonial relationships are based on information or messages contained in the ceremonies themselves. The most obvious such message involves the amount of liquor served. Guests measure this amount against one standard: either it is more than they can drink, so that they all drink to the point of vomiting; or it is less, and no one vomits. As noted earlier, the latter is cause for terminating a ceremonial relationship with the longhouse responsible, while the former is cause for maintaining or initiating one. A second important message that is conveyed during ceremonies involves the number of guests that attend. If attendance at ceremonies reveals a growing disparity in size between two ceremonial partners, the smaller of the two may decide to dissolve the relationship. A former ceremonial relationship between the Kantu' longhouse Tikul Batu and the Iban longhouse Empakan was dissolved for just this reason in the early 1970s. The people of Tikul Batu decided that the population of Empakan, which had grown to more than twice their own size, had become too much for them to handle during ceremonial feasts. A third message is conveyed by the incidence of the ceremonies. In extremes of material, social, or spiritual depression, a longhouse (or individual household) may forgo a ceremony that is normally held. Conversely, an unusually well-off or assertive longhouse (or household) may stage a rare, costly, or dangerous ceremony, such as the *gawa' motong bo'* (feast of hair-cutting), which marks a child's passage into adolescence, or the *gawa' bediri'* (standing up feast), which was traditionally staged upon the taking of a trophy head. Either case—the forgoing of usual ceremonies or the staging of unusual ones—may induce other longhouses to terminate or initiate, respectively, ceremonial relationships with the longhouse or household involved.

Each of these ceremonial messages, whether involving the amount of liquor, the number of guests, or the incidence of the ceremonies, is explicitly interpreted by the Kantu' as an indicator of the host's ability to provide for his guests, relative to the latter's ability to provide for him. On a less explicit but more important level, I suggest, these messages are interpreted as indicators of the host's relative ability to exchange grain and labor with his guests. This suggestion draws upon Rappaport's (1979:121) analysis of liturgical indicators, about which he writes: "Liturgical orders differ in what conditions prevailing in the external world their performance, or reports of their performance, may signify, but intrinsic to all rituals is indication of some aspects of the contemporary social, psychic, or physical state of the performers and, possibly, of aspects of their environmental relations as well."

Among the Tsembaga Maring, whom Rappaport studied, dancing at another group's feast is indexically related to fighting on their side in battle (ibid. 181). Among the Kantu', I suggest that there is a similar indexical relationship between attending another household's or longhouse's ceremonies and exchanging labor and grain with them.

Ceremonial Partners

The initiation and termination of ceremonial relationships in accordance with the ceremonial messages just described tend to favor ceremonial relationships in which the partners have the same capacity to drink and to provide drink. It tends to favor, that is, ceremonial relationships between like partners. This is consonant with the basic purpose of the regional system of grain and labor exchanges, which is to resolve not a problem of economic injustice, but rather a problem of economic uncertainty. Its purpose is not to distribute the wealth of the rich to the poor, but rather to distribute the wealth of the temporarily lucky to the temporarily unlucky.[24] This distribution takes place in the expectation that the exchange of the unlucky's labor for the lucky's grain will be reversed when (not if) their respective swidden fortunes are reversed. This reciprocity is most easily guaranteed if the partners in these exchanges—and, hence, in the ceremonial relationships—have labor forces of similar size.

The groups that drink together are not only the ones best suited to exchanging grain and labor with one another, they are in fact the ones that do so. When the longhouses nearby to Tikul Batu are ranked in terms of the amount of labor that they contributed to Tikul Batu in exchange (mostly) for grain during 1976 as well as the number of Tikul Batu ceremonies that they attended that year, a Spearman's rank order correlation coefficient of .76 (significant beyond the .05 level) is obtained (Table 5.3). That is, the longhouses that participate in the most grain-labor exchanges with Tikul Batu tend also to be the ones that attend the greatest number of ceremonies at Tikul Batu, and the reverse is also true.

Participation in both grain-labor exchanges and ceremonies tends to further vary according to proximity. Looking again at the pattern of exchanges and ceremonies involving the longhouse Tikul Batu in 1976, most exchanges and ceremonies involve households within the long-house (Table 5.4). Most of the remaining exchanges and ceremonies involve households from longhouses less than a ninety-minute walk away. The incidence of exchanges and ceremonies involving more distant longhouses is minor. This covariation between grain-labor exchanges and ceremonial attendance is consistent with the thesis of this paper: ceremonial attendance supports participation in these exchanges, and so as the latter increase or decrease in frequency—as a function of proximity—so too does this attendance.

The relationships that are most distant and least frequently invoked are not necessarily the least important. As noted earlier, most harvest

Table 5.3. Participation in Grain-Labor Exchanges and Ceremonies at Tikul Batu by Other Longhouses in 1976

Longhouse or village name	Number of man-days of wage labor contributed to Tikul Batu[b]	Number of ceremonies attended at Tikul Batu[c]
Kantu' Lalang	78	6
Tikul Batu Ili'	64	4
Kampung Baru (a)	21	3
Entipan (a)	12	0
Nanga Suhaid (a)	12	0
Jelemuk	9	0
Telutuk	8	2
Nanga Entipan (a)	4	0

[a]Villages of detached dwellings as opposed to longhouses.
[b]Total days of wage labor performed by the households of each longhouse or village for the households of Tikul Batu.
[c]Number of ceremonies held at Tikul Batu to which the longhouse or village was formally invited and that it attended.

Table 5.4. Role of Proximity in Grain-Labor Exchanges and Ceremonies at Tikul Batu in 1976

Location of participants	Exchanges[a] (%)	Ceremonies[b] (%)
Intralonghouse	50	73
Interlonghouse		
< 90 minutes distance[c]	41	27
> 90 minutes distance[c]	9	0[d]
Totals	100	100

[a]Exchanges of grain (mostly) for swidden labor.
[b]Ceremonies, sponsored by one or more of the households at Tikul Batu, at which liquor was provided to guests.
[c]Walking times between longhouses.
[d]At the time of this study, it had been three years since such a distant longhouse was formally invited to a ceremony at Tikul Batu.

shortfalls are remedied through participation in grain-labor exchanges with the preferred proximate households and longhouses, but the occasional serious and widespread shortfall forces its victims to seek donors farther afield. The fact that these distant relationships are invoked in times of greatest need, therefore, imbues them with a special importance. This importance is reflected in the fact that the ceremonies that forge and maintain these distant relationships are, while less frequent than other ceremonies, larger and more elaborate.

The thesis that the ceremonial drinking of the Kantu' has an integrative function illuminates not only which households and longhouses drink together, but also which members of each household or longhouse do most of the drinking. Men, as noted earlier, drink much more than women do. Mandelbaum (1979:17) wrote that "drinking is more often considered appropriate for those who grapple with the external environment than for those whose task it is to carry on and maintain a society's internal activities"—and it is so among the Kantu'. The gender that principally drinks, the male, is also the one that is normatively associated with interhousehold and, especially, interlonghouse relations. In contrast, the gender that drinks least, the female, is normatively associated with intrahousehold relations.[25] The relevance of this distinction is seen not only in the fact that men do most of the drinking, but also in where they do it: almost all drinking is done in the open gallery of the longhouse (Fig. 5.2). This is also where the Kantu' hold all of their interhousehold and interlonghouse meetings, which are attended usually only by adult males. The Kantu' see this part of the longhouse, accordingly, as public and male. In contrast, the family life of the individual households, in which the women play a dominant role, takes place largely within the individual walled *bilek* (apartments). This space, accordingly, is seen as private and female.[26] Drinking is not done within the longhouse apartments because it is concerned with public as opposed to private matters. It is not done much by women, for the same reason.

The integrative function of drinking is also seen in which males drink the most. While all adult males are supposed to participate in ceremonial drinking, the fullest participation is expected from the elder males, especially men of influence such as shamans and headmen. Such men cannot stoop to the limited means available to minimize or terminate their drinking. They cannot, for example, flee a ceremony, as the younger men commonly do. Anything less than direct acceptance of all liquor offered them evinces a casual attitude toward their host's welfare that is inconsistent with their position. Thus, this case belies Mandelbaum's (1979:27) assertion that the upholders of political scripture usually drink the least, and it belies it because in Kantu' society, drinking itself helps to uphold this scripture, a principal goal of which is the socioeconomic integration of politically discrete communities. This suggestion that participation in ceremonial drinking is in effect a political responsibility is reflected in St. John's (1862 I:66) mid-nineteenth century observation on Iban drinking in Sarawak: ". . . their drink having the appearance and the thickness of curds, in which they mix pepper and other ingredients. It has a sickening effect on them, and they swallow it more *as a duty* [emphasis added] than because they relish it."

Finally, the integrative function of drinking is seen in which men deviate from its norms. The most striking deviation among the members of the longhouse Tikul Batu involves a man called Bingun.[27] He and the other members of his household infrequently attend the ceremonies of other households and longhouses; and when he does attend, he comports himself in a distinctive manner. He was the only guest ever observed to pour his own drink and then consume it without pressure from the host. On one such occasion, he explained his action by saying *Awak jampa' mabuk* (So that I am quickly drunk). Thus, he completely reversed the normal roles of the reluctant guest and the aggressive host.

This role reversal is explained by Bingun's unusual economic fortunes. He is known throughout the Empanang valley as an unusually hard-working farmer. (It was said of him, for example, that if he had to urinate while felling a tree, he would urinate on the tree that he was felling, rather than pause to step back a few feet.) This industry is reflected in the fact that he and his household clear an average of twice as much forest per year for swiddens as the other households in Tikul Batu. The large amount of land that they farm is associated with proportionately large harvests, which to some extent insulate this particular household from the economic uncertainty (earlier described) that plagues the typical Kantu' household. Prior to both the 1975 and 1976 harvests, for example, Bingun's household had sufficient grain in storage to meet its needs for almost twenty months (compared with an average of just one month's supply among the other households in the longhouse). Even if one of these harvests had been a total failure, therefore, Bingun's household would not have needed help from anyone else.[28] The unusual economic security of this household gives a distinctive cast to its relations with other households. It does participate in grain-labor exchanges with others, but always in the role of grain-giver and labor-taker. This basic asymmetry is reflected in Bingun's unusual drinking behavior. Because he never has to assume the subservient role of asking another household for its grain in exchange for his labor, so does he never assume the role of the passive guest. Because he is always the giver of grain, so does he always, in effect, act as a host, even when attending someone else's ceremony.

A second example of asymmetrical relations occurs during intertribal drinking between the Kantu' and the neighboring Iban. When a Kantu' longhouse is invited to an Iban longhouse for an important ceremony, the Kantu' are not paid to drink, as is the custom when they attend the ceremonies of other Kantu'. Rather, on such occasions the Kantu' guests are asked to pay their Iban hosts, which is the Iban custom. When these erstwhile Iban hosts attend a ceremony hosted by the Kantu', however, they tend to follow the Kantu' custom of asking for (or expecting) payment from their hosts. No matter who is host and who is guest, therefore, the Kantu' pay the Iban.

This ceremonial imbalance is explained by the existence of a basic political and economic imbalance between the Kantu' and Iban. In the course of their return migrations from Sarawak back into Kalimantan at the end of the nineteenth century, the Iban drove most of the Kantu' population out of the border region. This is reflected today in the seven-to-one ratio of Iban to Kantu' in the Empanang valley. Given residual tensions from the years of intertribal warfare, this population differential places the Kantu' in a politically defensive position vis-à-vis the Iban. It also places the Kantu' in a disadvantageous position within the regional system of grain-labor exchanges: given their fewer numbers, they need integration with the Iban more than the Iban need it with them. Just as in the case of Bingun's household, therefore, an imbalance within the regional exchange system is reflected in an imbalance within the ceremonial system that supports it.

The Evolution of the Ceremonial System

The thesis that ceremonial drinking plays an integrative role in the economic system of the Kantu' is supported by data on historical changes in both systems. The most important change in the economic system, in this regard, was the introduction of Para rubber trees *(Hevea brasiliensis)* to the Kantu' region in the first quarter of this century. Today, most Kantu' households have producing rubber trees, which they tap during slack periods in the swidden cycle. They trade the raw latex for consumer goods (e.g., tobacco, salt, and cloth) or, following shortfalls in the swidden harvest, for rice. Rubber tapping has become one of the most important and dependable ways of dealing with such shortfalls. With its development, the individual household has become less vulnerable to harvest shortfalls and to the environmental uncertainties that cause them. This reduction, in turn, has lessened the economic interdependence of different households and longhouses that was formerly the only defense against this uncertainty.

This historic reduction in the economic interdependence of Kantu' society has been accompanied by a reduction in the intensity and scope of the ceremonial system. The greatest ceremony of the Kantu', the *gawa' bediri'*, has not been staged by the Kantu' of the Empanang valley for a generation. Although it was traditionally staged only on the occasion of taking a trophy head, its disappearance cannot be attributed entirely to contemporary constraints on head taking: Iban in remote parts of the valley still stage this ceremony on occasion, using (at least some of the time) old trophy heads taken from storage. The next greatest category of Kantu' ceremonies, those that mark childhood rites of passage (viz., first bathing, first walking, first hair cutting, ear piercing, and tooth filing) has also diminished. Only two ceremonies from this series (viz., those marking hair cutting and ear piercing) are still staged with any regularity (one was staged the year prior to my fieldwork).

The historical association between the diminished interdependence of the economic system and the diminished scope of the ceremonial system is reflected in the geographical association of rubber groves and ceremonies in the Empanang valley today. The ceremonial system remains most elaborate in the most remote parts of the valley (where, as noted above, the head-taking ceremony is still performed), which were also the last to be settled and the last to receive any plantings of rubber trees. In contrast, in the central parts of the valley, which were the first settled and the first to be planted with rubber trees, the ceremonial system is most attenuated. The latter area is typified by the longhouse Tikul Batu, which has some of the oldest and most extensive rubber plantings in the entire valley and which no longer stages the largest and most elaborate ceremonies.

This variation in the extent of rubber cultivation and its attendant economic independence is associated with variation in position within the Empanang valley's ceremonial system. Those longhouses with the most rubber and the greatest independence tend to be the most "popular" ceremonial partners, because they are more often able to exchange grain for labor and are less often in need of it themselves. This is the case with the longhouse Tikul Batu, whose members not only have a lot of rubber of their own, but also control the marketing of rubber from many other longhouses. As a result, in the words of the people of Tikul Batu, *Urang bukai ka' gawa' ngau kitai* (Others like to feast with us); and indeed they receive more invitations to ceremonies than they extend. With the longhouses whose invitations they accept, the people of Tikul Batu have largely balanced ceremonial and economic relations. With the longhouses whose ceremonial invitations they do not accept, the people of Tikul Batu have largely unbalanced relations, continually exchanging grain for latex or labor.

Conclusions

> Although the *gawai* is a religious occasion and the ultimate Iban rite, it is also a party, a time for eating and drinking, dancing, jollification, and drunkenness. (Jensen 1974:207)

> It is also important to realize that the major *gawai* of the Iban are serious religious occasions. To call them "feasts," as has become the popular practice, is to invite misunderstandings of their significance. True enough, all large-scale *gawai* are accompanied by much eating and drinking and a good deal of revelry, but this is always subservient to their primary purpose which is the invocation of gods so that certain definite advantages may be obtained. (Freeman 1970:263)

These passages present the two most common views of ceremony and drinking among Ibanic peoples, the first focusing on manifest form, the second on manifest purpose. Neither Jensen nor Freeman, nor indeed any other writer on this subject, suggests that there may be latent or structural forms and functions as well. My thesis here has been that this ceremonial drinking does have a latent structure and function, and that it involves the economic integration of these tribal societies.

I began my analysis by discussing the respective roles of host and guest in ceremonial drinking—the former associated with eagerness and the receipt of benefits, and the latter associated with reluctance and the experience of costs. This behavior, I suggested, is best explained with reference to the integrative role of drinking (as opposed to eating) within Kantu' society. Integration is a matter of concern in Kantu' society because their economy and ecology favor small, dispersed, and independent socioeconomic units, at the same time as they necessitate the regular exchange of grain and labor among these units. The relations that make these crucial exchanges possible are established, I argued, through the system of ceremonial drinking. Social units form, participate in, and dissolve ceremonial partnerships in accordance with their respective needs and abilities to exchange grain and labor with one another. This assignment of an integrative function to ceremonial drinking is supported by the fact that the people who drink the most are also the ones with the greatest responsibility for social integration, while the people who drink the least, or whose drinking deviates from the norm, are the ones with the least need for integration. Finally, I noted that with the introduction of cash crops to the economy, the overall need for socioeconomic integration has diminished, and this has resulted in a corresponding diminishment in the system of ceremonial drinking.

This analysis has several implications, both theoretical as well as policy oriented. The first concerns critiques of functional analysis, especially from Marxist scholars. One of their major critiques has been that functionalists demonstrate the association of some function with some social process, and then erroneously conclude that the purpose of the latter is therefore the former. This claim, they say, is unjustified without a further demonstration that the process in question was teleologically arranged to achieve the function in question (e.g., Friedman 1979). In the foregoing analysis of Kantu' drinking, I found evidence of this teleological arrangement in the symbolic structures surrounding the social process for which the function is claimed. That is, while the Kantu' themselves do not explicitly claim that the function of ceremonial drinking is to support regional socioeconomic integration, I demonstrated that a concern for this integration is implicit in the social and symbolic structure of these ceremonies, which suggests that this social process was in fact organized to perform this function. It is indeed at this level of social and symbolic structures, not explicit rules and aims, that evidence of teleological organization is best sought. The fact that functionalist scholars have not done so in the past is their failing and not that of functionalist theory per se.

The second major Marxist critique of functionalism concerns its supposed ignorance of systemic properties. As Friedman (1974:459) put it, "It is a deadly weakness of functionalism that it identifies the rationality of the element while ignoring the rationality of the system." This critique is indeed applicable to some of the early examples of functionalist analysis (see Diener, Nonini, and Robkin 1978 on Harris). Again, however, this failing is that of the practitioners and not that of the theory itself: there is nothing inherent in functionalist theory that limits it to the analysis of local social units, in ignorance of their relations with broader social, economic, and political systems. For example, in the foregoing analysis of Kantu' drinking, I did indeed focus on just a single element of the social system, namely ceremonial drinking. However, my analysis related this single element to the dynamics of the system (viz., the regional system) as a whole. To use Friedman's phrasing, I explained the rationality of the element in terms of the rationality of the system.

Another body of theory to which my analysis is relevant is that on the use and abuse of alcohol. As I stated at the beginning, this study—like most contemporary cross-cultural studies of drinking—has focused on the social causes and effects of alcohol use as opposed to physiological causes and effects. Recently, this approach has come in for some criticism. Room (1984) has suggested that ethnographic studies of alcohol use "deflate" the social and medical problems of this use in the societies under study. He believes that this deflation is inherent in the use of ethnographic methods in general, which, he says (ibid. 172) "are better attuned to measuring the pleasures than the problems of drinking." Regarding the use of functional theory in particular, he writes, "In my view, the deemphasis of the problematic side of drinking is not only a matter of oversight, but rather tends to be inherent in a functionalist perspective" (ibid.). Again, I suggest that this failing is falsely laid at the door of functionalism. In this study of the Kantu', far from ignoring the problems of drinking, I have focused on them—the ill-tasting liquor, the vomiting, the intoxication and delirium—and I have in fact explained the integrative function of drinking precisely in terms of these problems.

These theoretical implications aside, this analysis of Kantu' drinking also has clear implications for government policy in Indonesia. In Kalimantan, as elsewhere in Indonesia (and, indeed, in much of the developing world), the national government disapproves of the diversion of the time and resources of its peasants to the production and consumption of alcohol. During the time of this study, the provincial government of West Kalimantan imposed a ban on the holding of multilonghouse ceremonial feasts, arguing that they served no other purpose than to waste scarce resources and thereby frustrate government attempts to "develop" the rural economy. Quite to the contrary, my analysis suggests that ceremonial drinking and feasting is crucial to the integration and continued health of the rural economy in Kalimantan.[29] A successful prohibition of these feasts by the government will weaken or destroy the associated regional exchange system, thus greatly increasing the vulnerability of the Kantu' to the periodic failures of their swidden harvests.

The government's stance on ceremonial expenditure is, therefore, not in the best interests of the rural economy. It is, however, in the interests of the urban economy in which government officials more directly participate. If those Kantu' who chance to reap good harvests in a given year are prevented from investing the surpluses in the traditional exchange system—which would protect them should their harvests fail the following year—they are apt to spend them instead on nondurable consumer goods (cassette players, factory-made cigarettes, etc.). Such investments will not protect them against future harvest shortfalls and will do nothing for the local economy; but they will benefit the urban economy, by stimulating a net flow of capital out of the rural areas and into the manufacturing sector. This is one consequence of the government stance against ceremonial expenditure: the guarantee of local subsistence, by means of traditional systems of social security, is sacrificed in favor of stimulating the urban economy (Dove 1985a:28–31).

There is a second important consequence of the government's stance. According to this stance, ceremonial feasting is an economically irrational institution. This serves as the government's justification for attempting to do away with it; but it also—insofar as the institution nevertheless persists—serves as an apologia for problems experienced by the government in dealing with these communities. The national government tends to attribute all development failures and conflicts to the "irrationality" of the peasants, even when they are due—as is most often the case—to genuine differences between the interests of the governing circles and the interests of the peasants. The focus on supposedly irrational peasant institutions draws attention away from these real conflicts of interest, thereby sparing the government from any self-examination but also ensuring that its conflicts with the peasants continue.

I suggest that this association between government policy and the self-interest of the governing class is purposive, and that this association explains the existence of the policy. This is not to say that government officials purposively criticize and constrain the practice of tribal ceremony and drinking self-consciously in order to promote their own interests. Rather, I suggest that a concern for the officials' own interests, like the Kantu' concern for integration, is structurally expressed in their culture, and that it is this culture that leads them to criticize and constrain these tribal practices. Just as in the Kantu' case, there is evidence of teleological patterning between the social function and the social process by which it is attained. So we can conclude that, just as the purpose of Kantu' drinking—within their regional exchange system—is to pro-

mote their material welfare, so is the purpose of the government officials' view of this drinking—within their own economic system—to promote their own material welfare.

The fact that these two perspectives, these two systems, are not only
different, but in many respects mutually antagonistic, is known to the
tribesmen but not to the government officials. That is, the tribesmen
know that what they desire is in their own best interests, and that what
the government desires for them is not. The government officials, however, profess to believe—and in most cases do believe, in my opinion—
that what they want is also in the best interests of the tribesmen. This is
another example of the political axiom that those who possess power
and abuse it need to disguise this fact from themselves, whereas those
who are powerless and are abused have no such need for self-deception.
A first step in any program of genuine rural development is to end
this self-deception and oblige government officials to recognize that
the interests of the governed may in fact differ from those of the gover-
nors. Merely to recognize that the peasants have their own legitimate
interests is to go a long way toward safeguarding and promoting these
interests.

Notes

1. My study of the Kantu' was sponsored by the Indonesian Institute of Science (LIPI) and was supported with funds from the National Institute of General Medical Sciences, the Center for Research in International Studies (Stanford University), and the National Science Foundation (grant # GS-42605). I
benefited greatly from critiques of earlier versions of this paper by anonymous
reviewers and the late Michelle Z. Rosaldo.

2. I have carried out a similar study (Dove 1982), in which I explain the
Kantu' longhouse in terms of the ecological and economic imperatives of the
swidden system.

3. The swidden agricultural system of the Kantu' is described in detail in
Dove (1985b). A similar system in the adjoining Ketunggau River valley has
been described by Drake (1982). Swidden systems in Malaysian Borneo have
been described by Chin (1985) and Freeman (1970), and elsewhere in Southeast Asia notable descriptions have been provided by Condominas (1977), Conklin (1957), and Izikowitz (1951).

4. Compare Conklin's (1980:22) description of brewing rice wine among the
Ifugao of northern Luzon.

5. One of the most popular drinking chants is as follows:

Ia taca juam,	"She copulates with a bear,
Buluh sebam-sebam,	Its hair is wavy,
Bibir baka capan,	Its lips are like a winnowing tray,

Mua baka kangan,	Its face is like black calico,
Ntak lasak lalu tekan,	Its hairy erection presses in,
Ha' Hi' Ha'.	Ha' Hi' Ha'."

6. The figure of 370 kilograms of rice includes the cost of the pigs and chickens—expressed in rice equivalents, based on their respective values in the local markets—that are sacrificed during these ceremonies.

7. This one-third (viz., 123 kgs. of rice) is equal to the average household's consumption requirements for about two weeks. This can be compared with the 200 lbs. of maize—equal to more than one month's consumption requirements —that the average household devotes to brewing beer each year among the Tarahumara studied by Kennedy (1984).

8. Rice is the staple food of the Kantu' and the major ingredient of all meals except during periods of famine.

9. The hosting of ceremonies by households with grain insufficiencies is the exception rather than the rule, however. If the ceremonial activities and the grain supplies of the households of Tikul Batu are analyzed, for the years 1975 and 1976, a very strong association (P = .0003) between grain sufficiencies and hosting of large postharvest ceremonies is found.

10. Some Kantu' maintain, however, that in former times they ate the residue of the wine mash themselves.

11. The *beram* (rice mash) from which the wine is extracted—and from which all "coolness" has thus been extracted—is thought to be *angat* (ritually hot). Indeed, in Kantu' mythology this mash is said to be the source of fire.

12. The ability of rice wine to liberate some vital or essential part of the drinker is seen in the Kantu' myth of how the python *(Python reticulatus)* came to be a nonpoisonous snake. It is said to have gotten drunk and then vomited out its poison. This myth suggests that vomiting may be not just a side effect of the contemporary transfer of luck from guest to host—via drink—but an instrumental step in this transfer.

13. Personal injuries owing to drunken delirium, whether to the drinker or to bystanders, are extremely rare. This is probably due not only to the care that is extended to delirious drinkers, but also to Kantu' norms concerning behavior when "under the influence."

14. The divisiveness of food consumption can also be seen in the role that it plays in household partition. All foodstuffs (especially the rarer, more desired ones) are supposed to be shared equally among household members, regardless of age or gender. This rule is typically violated only when two married siblings, each with children, are living in the same household: in such cases, there is a tendency for the adults to favor their own children in the distribution of valued foodstuffs. Quarrels over such favoritism often provide the catalyst for the partition of households.

15. The central act of courtship is the nighttime visits by a young man to his beloved's mosquito net, which hangs in the apartment of her mother and father. In courtship as in drinking, therefore, the maiden plays the role of host.

16. During the postharvest feast of 1975 at Tikul Batu, one man caught his wife kissing another, at which point he started to berate and fight with her. Their adult son then interposed himself and started to fight with his father. The fracas was subsequently adjudicated by the longhouse headman, with the following result: the "other man" was publicly admonished, the husband was fined, and then he and his wife divorced one another and their *bilek* (household) was partitioned.

17. The Kantu' precisely fit Field's (1962) stereotype of an intemperate society, namely one that has great freedom of personal choice and expression, a nonhierarchical sociopolitical system, and bilateral descent.

18. This exchange of labor is also facilitated by variation among households in consumer/producer ratios (Dove 1984).

19. See Dove (1982, 1983, 1984) for further discussion of the constraints on the utilization of labor in the Kantu' swidden system and of the various means for overcoming them.

20. The two new households that were created at Tikul Batu in 1976 are not included in this comparison.

21. Of the remaining two households that experienced a shortfall in 1975, one made it up through trading ventures and the other had extensive stores of grain that it fell back upon.

22. Given an average population density of 11.5 persons or 1.5 households per square kilometer in the Kantu' territory at the time of this study, there will be *(cet. par.)* 115 households living within a radius of five kilometers of any given household and 460 households living within a radius of ten kilometers.

23. Kennedy (1984:70) has similarly explained the role of drinking in Tarahumara society, whose cultural ecology resembles that of the Kantu' in many respects: "Social obligations and the sure knowledge that assistance will be needed at some future time create pressures upon even the most isolated and self-sufficient families to occasionally brew corn beer for cooperative work gatherings."

24. Kirsch (1973:18) writes in a similar vein of the feasting pattern among the hill peoples of mainland Southeast Asia: "These feasts tend to even out any inequalities in diet, in agricultural skill, plot fertility, or 'luck'." However, Kirsch views the feasts themselves as the mechanism through which this "evening out" takes place, and I do not. As I noted earlier, the guests at Kantu' feasts never take home with them any food or drink, and whatever they consume during the feast is typically left there as vomitus. The Kantu' feasts themselves achieve not the actual distribution of the society's resources, but only a guarantee of this distribution.

25. This is not belied by the earlier described role of maidens in interlonghouse romance and marriage. Uxorilocal residence is the norm in interlonghouse marriages. The twenty-four couples present in Tikul Batu at the time of this study represented fourteen longhouse-exogamous unions and ten endogamous ones; postmarital residence was uxorilocal in nine of the former cases, but just three of the latter. Thus, while women are the objects of these interlonghouse relationships, it is the men that—by changing their residence—carry them out.

26. The *bilek* are also where the longhouse's maidens receive their lovers, the

sole instance in which visitors to the longhouse are not entertained in the longhouse gallery.

27. "Bingun" is a pseudonym.

28. In the event of a total failure of its swidden harvest, Bingun's household would, however, have needed the help of other households to replenish its stock of seed rice. Rice grain retains its powers of germination for less than a year; hence, grain stored from any harvest but the last one is of no use as seed.

29. In one of the few other studies of this matter, Dewalt (1979) similarly showed that drinking poses no threat to rural development. He found that heavy drinkers in highland Mexico were in fact slightly *more* likely to accept development innovations than were lighter drinkers.

References Cited

Burkill, L. H.
  1935   *Dictionary of the Economic Products of the Malay Peninsula.* 2 vols. London: Crown Agent for the Colonies.

Carneiro, Robert L.
  1960   "Slash-and-Burn Agriculture: A Closer Look at its Implications for Settlement Patterns." In *Men and Cultures: Selected Papers of the Fifth International Congress of Anthropological and Ethnological Sciences,* edited by Anthony F. C. Wallace, pp. 229–234. Philadelphia: University of Pennsylvania Press.

Chin, S. C.
  1985   *Agriculture and Resource Utilization in a Lowland Rainforest Kenyah Community.* Special Monograph no. 4. *Sarawak Museum Journal* 35, no. 56.

Condominas, Georges
  1977   *We Have Eaten the Forest: The Story of a Montagnard Village in the Central Highlands of Vietnam.* Translated by Adrienne Foulke. New York: Hill and Wang. (Original: *Nous Avons Mangé la Forêt de la Pierre-Génie Gôo.* Paris: Mercure de France, 1957.)

Conklin, Harold C.
  1957   *Hanuno'o Agriculture: A Report on an Integral System of Shifting Cultivation in the Philippines.* Forestry Development Paper no. 12. Rome: FAO.

  1980   *Ethnographic Atlas of Ifugao: A Study of Environment, Culture, and Society in Northern Luzon.* New Haven: Yale University Press.

Dewalt, Billie R.
  1979   "Drinking Behavior, Economic Status, and Adaptive Strategies of Modernization in a Highland Mexican Community." *American Ethnologist* 6:510–530.

Diener, Paul, Donald Nonini, and Eugene E. Robkin
  1978   "The Dialectics of the Sacred Cow: Ecological Adaptation versus Political Appropriation in the Origins of India's Cattle Complex." *Dialectical Anthropology* 30 (3): 221–241.

Doughty, Paul L.
[1971] "The Social Uses of Alcoholic Beverages in a Peruvian Commu-
1979   nity." In *Beliefs, Behaviors, and Alcoholic Beverages,* edited by Mac
        Marshall, pp. 64–81.

Dove, Michael R.
1982   "The Myth of the Communal Longhouse in Rural Development."
        In *Too Rapid Rural Development,* edited by Colin MacAndrews and
        L. S. Chin, pp. 14–78. Athens: Ohio University Press.

1983   "Forest Preference in Swidden Agriculture." *Tropical Ecology* 24 (1):
        122–142.

1984   "The Chayanov Slope in a Swidden Economy." In *Chayanov, Peas-
        ants, and Economic Anthropology,* edited by P. E. Durrenberger, pp. 97–
        132. New York: Academic Press.

1985a   "The Agroecological Mythology of the Javanese, and the Political
        Economy of Indonesia." *Indonesia* 39:1–36.

1985b   *Swidden Agriculture in Indonesia: The Subsistence Strategies of the Kaliman-
        tan Kantu'.* Berlin: Mouton.

Drake, Richard Allen
1982   "The Material Provisioning of Mualang Society in Hinterland Kali-
        mantan Barat." Ph.D. dissertation, Michigan State University. Ann
        Arbor: University Microfilms.

Ellen, Roy F.
1973   *Nualu Settlement and Ecology: An Approach to the Environmental Relations of
        an Eastern Indonesian Community.* Koninklijk Instituut voor Taal-,
        Land- en Volkenkunde, *Verhandelingen* no. 83. The Hague: Martinus
        Nijhoff.

Field, Peter B.
1962   "A New Cross-Cultural Study of Drunkenness." In *Society, Culture
        and Drinking Patterns,* edited by D. J. Pittman and C. R. Snyder, pp.
        48–74. New York: John Wiley & Sons.

Frake, Charles
1955   "Social Organization and Shifting Cultivation among the Sin-
        dangan Subanun." Ph.D. dissertation, Yale University. Ann Arbor:
        University Microfilms.

Freeman, Derek
1970   *Report on the Iban.* London School of Economics Monographs on
        Social Anthropology no. 41. London: University of London/Athlone
        Press.

1981   *Some Reflections on the Nature of Iban Society.* Occasional Paper. Austra-
        lian National University, Research School of Pacific Studies, Depart-
        ment of Anthropology.

Friedman, Jonathan
  1974   "Marxism, Structuralism and Vulgar Materialism." *Man* 9 (3): 444–469.

  1975   "Tribes, States, and Transformations." In *Marxist Analyses and Social Anthropology,* edited by Maurice Bloch, pp. 161–202. London: Tavistock.

  1979   "Hegelian Ecology: Between Rousseau and the World Spirit." In *Social and Ecological Systems,* edited by Philip Burnham and Roy F. Ellen, pp. 253–270. London: Academic Press.

Grijpstra, B. G.
  1976   *Common Efforts in the Development of Rural Sarawak, Malaysia.* Assen: Van Gorcum.

Hose, Charles, and William McDougall
  1912   *The Pagan Tribes of Borneo.* 2 vols. London: Macmillan & Co.

Hutchinson, Bertram
  [1961] "Alcohol as a Contributing Factor in Social Disorganization: The
  1979   South African Bantu in the Nineteenth Century." In *Beliefs, Behaviors, and Alcoholic Beverages,* edited by Mac Marshall, pp. 328–341.

Izikowitz, Karl G.
  1951   *Lamet: Hill Peasants in French Indochina.* Göteborg: Etnografiska Museet.

Jensen, Erik
  1974   *The Iban and Their Religion.* London: Oxford University Press.

Kennedy, John G.
  1984   *Tarahumara of the Sierra Madre: Beer, Ecology, and Social Organization.* Arlington Heights, Ill.: AHM.

King, Victor T.
  1979   *Ethnic Classification and Ethnic Relations: A Borneo Case Study.* Occasional Paper no. 2. The University of Hull, Centre for South-East Asian Studies. England.

Kirsch, Thomas A.
  1973   *Feasting and Social Oscillation: A Working Paper on Religion and Society in Upland Southeast Asia.* Data Paper no. 92. Ithaca, N.Y.: Cornell University Southeast Asia Program.

Leacock, Seth
  [1964] "Ceremonial Drinking in an Afro-Brazilian Cult." In *Beliefs, Behaviors, and Alcoholic Beverages,* edited by Mac Marshall, pp. 81–93.
  1979

Lemert, Edwin M.
  1954   "Alcohol and the Northwest Coast Indians." *University of California Publications in Culture and Society* no. 2:303–406.

Lumholtz, Carl
    1920   *Through Central Borneo: An Account of Two Years' Travel in the Land of the Head-Hunters Between the Years 1913 and 1917.* 2 vols. New York: Charles Scribner's Sons.

MacAndrews, C., and R. B. Edgerton
    1969   *Drunken Comportment: A Social Explanation.* Chicago: Aldine Publishing Co.

MacAndrews, C., and H. Garfinkel
    1962   "A Consideration of Changes Attributed to Intoxication as Common Sense Reasons for Getting Drunk." *Quarterly Journal of Studies on Alcohol* 23 (2): 252–266.

Madsen, William, and Claudia Madsen
    [1969]   "The Cultural Structure of Mexican Drinking Behavior." In *Beliefs,*
    1979   *Behaviors, and Alcoholic Beverages,* edited by Mac Marshall, pp. 38–54.

Mandelbaum, David
    [1965]   "Alcohol and Culture." In *Beliefs, Behaviors, and Alcoholic Beverages,*
    1979   edited by Mac Marshall, pp. 14–30.

Mangin, William
    1957   "Drinking Among American Indians." *Quarterly Journal of Studies on Alcohol* 18:55–66.

Marshall, Mac
    1979a   *Weekend Warriors: Alcohol in a Micronesian Culture.* Palo Alto, Calif.: Mayfield Publishing Co.

Marshall, Mac, ed.
    1979b   *Beliefs, Behaviors, and Alcoholic Beverages: A Cross-Cultural Survey.* Ann Arbor: University of Michigan Press.

Rappaport, Roy
    1968   *Pigs for the Ancestors: Ritual in the Ecology of a New Guinea People.* New Haven: Yale University Press.

    1979   *Ecology, Meaning, and Religion.* Richmond, Calif.: North Atlantic Books.

Room, Robin
    1984   "Alcohol and Ethnography: A Case of Problem Deflation." *Current Anthropology* 25 (2): 169–191.

Roth, H. Ling
    1896   *The Natives of Sarawak and British North Borneo.* 2 vols. London: Truslove & Hanson.

St. John, Spencer B.
    1862   *Life in the Forests of the Far East.* 2 vols. London: Smith, Elder.

Sandin, Benedict
    1967   *The Sea Dayaks of Borneo Before White Rajah Rule.* London: Macmillan & Co.

Singer, K.
  [1972] "Drinking Patterns and Alcoholism in the Chinese." In *Beliefs,*
  1979   *Behaviors, and Alcoholic Beverages,* edited by Mac Marshall, pp. 313–
          326.

Whittier, Herbert L.
  1973   "Social Organization and Symbols of Social Differentiation: An Eth-
          nographic Study of the Kenyah Dayak of East Kalimantan (Bor-
          neo)." Ph.D. dissertation, Michigan State University. Ann Arbor:
          University Microfilms.

6. Perception of Volcanic Hazards: Villagers Versus Government Officials in Central Java

P. M. Laksono

Abstract

This paper is based on an anthropological study of the hamlet of Gimbal on the southwestern slope of Merapi volcano in Central Java. Its purpose is to compare and assess responses to the volcanic threat to Gimbal by two different parties, the national government and the villagers themselves. The government's response has consisted primarily in attempts to resettle the villagers on one of Indonesia's outer islands. The villagers' response has consisted of trying to remain on the volcano and adapt to its hazards, using local systems of knowledge to both monitor (empirically) and explain (ontologically) the volcanic activity. Comparison of these two different responses to the volcanic hazard suggests that the government's is less objective, while the villagers' is less subjective, than is commonly thought to be the case.

Introduction

There are a multitude of ways to conceptualize the natural phenomena associated with natural disasters and a multitude of strategies for dealing with them. The manifest aim of all such strategies is to safeguard human life. However, natural disasters are not everywhere interpreted and assessed within the same conceptual framework. Hence, programs intended to prevent the loss of human life not infrequently lead to a conflict of goals, if not of means as well. This paper analyzes the way in which just such a conflict came about, in a small village in the shadow of an active volcano in Central Java.[1]

I propose to show how a dissimilarity in perceptions of environmental hazard, in this case the threat of volcanic eruption from Mount Merapi in Central Java, became a source of conflict between the central government and the local population. In 1961, the government declared certain areas on the upper slopes of Merapi to be too dangerous for human habitation. The villages lying within these areas—including Gimbal, the focus of my study—were stricken from official maps, their territories were reforested, and their inhabitants were relocated to Way Jepara in Sumatra under the government's transmigration program. Subsequently, however, some of the people of Gimbal returned on their own initiative from Sumatra to the site of their original village, thenceforth called Sumberejo. They rebuilt their homes and began to cultivate the land as they had done in the past. This rejection of the government's resettlement efforts was at first strenuously resisted by the government itself, but over time the villagers and the local government did manage to work out a *modus vivendi*.

I shall begin my analysis of these events with a description of village life in Gimbal-Sumberejo, followed by a description of the impact on this life of Mount Merapi's recent eruptions. I will then discuss the very different ways in which the national government and the villagers try to mitigate this impact. Finally, in comparing local and official views on the risks involved in living within a volcanically active zone, I will discuss traditional attitudes toward environmental hazards, in the hope that these attitudes may eventually be incorporated into Indonesian national policy on natural disasters.

Village Life on the Slopes of Mount Merapi

The village of Sumberejo is situated on the southwestern flank of Mount Merapi, at an elevation of approximately 700 meters (Fig. 6.1). It lies near the border between Central Java and the Special Region of Yogyakarta, and it is surrounded on three sides by other farming villages. At the time of this study (1979), the population stood at 238—117 males and 121 females. The village consists of *pekarangan* (mixed garden land), around which lie the *sawah* (wet-rice fields) and *tegal* (dry or unirrigated fields). Each house compound (averaging 25 meters by 25 meters in area) accommodates a house, a mixed garden, and livestock sheds, the latter usually being found in the front yard. All but two of the fifty houses in the village are occupied, and most are oriented to the south, with their backs to Merapi.[2] Built of wood or bamboo, the houses are easily dismantled and can be bought or sold separate from the land on which they stand. Sumberejo is unusual in that very little in the way of fruit trees or bamboo—common cultigens in Javanese villages—is grown. Even *salak* (palm fruit), found in all other villages near Merapi, is cultivated by only eight households. Instead, all of the dryfield land has been planted in cassava.

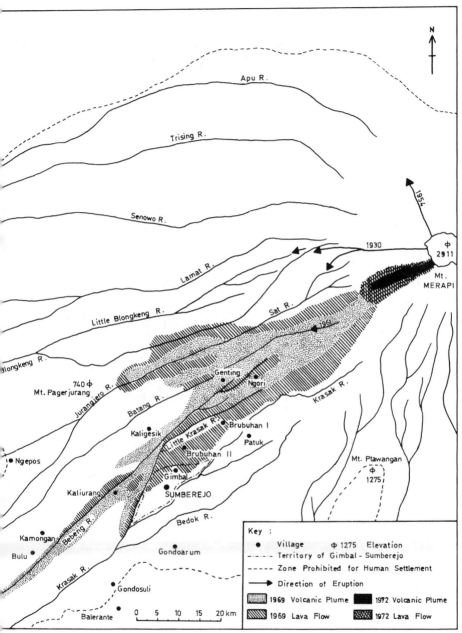

Figure 6.1 Mount Merapi

Residents of Sumberejo, which literally means "source of prosperity," believe that this new village name was aptly chosen. As they frequently and correctly observe, *Ngriki punika bumine taksih jembar* (In this place, the fields are still wide). Prior to the 1969 eruption, 130 households cultivated 40 hectares of irrigated land and more than 170 hectares of unirrigated land; after the eruption and the transmigration of the village's population, there remained 16.3 hectares of irrigated land and 153.7 hectares of dry land to be shared among the 48 households that returned from Sumatra or that never left. An additional 8 households from the nearby village of Kaliurang bought 2.8 hectares of land from one of the families that moved to Sumatra. Assuming that each of these 56 households owns and cultivates an equal proportion of the 173 hectares of combined *sawah* and *tegal* now available, each household has access to over 3 hectares of farmland, an extraordinary amount of land in comparison with the majority of villagers in Java.

Although more than half of Sumberejo's irrigated land was devastated by Merapi in 1969, wet-rice cultivation on the remaining irrigated terraces built along the Krasak River (see Fig. 6.1) continues much as before. This system of water control permits the farmers of Sumberejo to crop rice all year round. They claim that no matter what they plant in the irrigated fields, it always grows well. The unirrigated *tegal* fields, which constitute the greater part of their land, are not nearly so productive. They are situated further uphill near the boundary between Sumberejo and Brubuhan. Brubuhan itself is uninhabited, its residents having long since been evacuated to Sumatra. Beyond Brubuhan there is only forest, and beyond that, desolation, and then the mountain's crater. The belt of forest is thickly populated by wild pigs, which make regular forays down the mountain into the villagers' dryland fields. As a result, the villagers cultivate these fields only when, or if, they have any time left over from their more productive, and protected, irrigated fields.

The economy of Sumberejo is completely dependent on agriculture. Rice and maize are grown for household consumption, with occasional surpluses being taken to local markets in Balerante or Bulu (see Fig. 6.1) or sold to wholesalers from outside the village. Local strains of rice —*tumbaran, cempa, melati, hoing*—are double-cropped, while the introduced variety *taiwan* is triple-cropped. Production on irrigated land usually averages two tons (of unhusked rice) per hectare. A variety of other crops, including cassava, sweet potatoes, Irish potatoes, tobacco, and legumes, are also grown. As a result of overproduction, market prices for cassava are often very low, and so farmers sometimes leave it in the ground for up to two years.

With a few exceptions, everyone in Sumberejo does a little livestock raising on the side. Livestock holdings are distributed within the village as follows: sixty-one head of cattle are held by a total of thirty house-holds, eight head of water buffalo by eight households, and eighty-one goats by eight households. Cattle and water buffalo are kept as draft animals, and their dung is used to manure the fields. In addition, the farmers prefer to put savings in livestock as opposed to the bank, because every time the animals gain weight or give birth, they can liter-ally see their interest mounting up. Some villagers fatten stock for market, buying up thin animals and selling them at a profit when they get heavier. Others, who are involved on a lesser scale, raise young ani-mals until they are large enough to sell. Two men in the village have become "stock brokers," and so buying and selling livestock is never a problem.

Farming and animal husbandry together bring in a household aver-age of 550 rupiah a day, or 16,500 rupiah a month.[3] Rice consumption averages fifty-four kilograms per month for the average five-member household.[4] Contributions for births, circumcisions, and weddings average around 2,500 rupiah per month, and the average clothing expenses for an entire household are about 10,000 rupiah per year. Only twenty households have any school fees to pay, and only six of these spend more than 1,500 rupiah per month on this. Given these expenditures and the overall pattern of consumption, it can be said that, while no one in Sumberejo is rich, neither is anyone terribly poor. As one informant put it; "We get by. We don't go to bed on an empty stomach and we know where our next meal is coming from. That's what life's all about anyway—eating and sleeping. And if a man has a buf-falo, what more could he possibly want?"

As the foregoing comment suggests, the economic life of the villagers in Gimbal-Sumberejo is not too bad, certainly not when compared with many other regions of Java. The character of this life is directly related to the human and physical ecology of the area in which the village is sit-uated—with specific reference here to its proximity to Mount Merapi. This proximity explains both the fertility of Gimbal-Sumberejo's soils, due to the periodic infusions of ash, and the relative abundance of land for farming and grazing, due to the decline in population density that occurs (after a certain point) as distance from the volcano decreases and the level of risk increases.[5] It is necessary to look closely at this level of risk in order to assess the "cost" of the life depicted above.

Volcanic Hazards on the Slopes of Mount Merapi

According to historical records, between 1548 and 1968 the average interval between Merapi's eruptions was seven and a half years, with the shortest interval being one year and the longest seventy years

The December 1931 Eruption of Mount Merapi. (Reprinted from KITLV, ond. 613, bundel 3/157, p. 6.)

Lava from the 1931 Eruption Encroaching upon Wet-Rice Fields. (Reprinted from KITLV, ond. 613, bundel 3/157, p. 11.)

(Reksawiraga 1972:2). Phreatic explosions and/or pyroclastic flows have accompanied almost all of these eruptions. Lava, mud, and debris have periodically descended Merapi's slopes and turned adjacent forests, rivers, and fields into wastelands of sand and rock, taking numerous human lives in the process. According to surveys by the government's Vulcanology Department, Gimbal-Sumberejo, which lies only nine kilometers from the crater, is potentially vulnerable to this sort of destruction. The likelihood of destruction is a function of the direction of the eruption—which itself is determined by the profile of the summit, the location of the eruptive activity, and the direction of wind—and therefore it changes from one eruption to the next. The nature of the eruptions that occurred on Merapi in 1930, 1954, and 1961, and their impact on Gimbal-Sumberejo, serve to illustrate the difficulty of attempting to predict either the direction, magnitude, or effects of volcanic eruptions.

In 1930 both magma and volcanic plumes swept down the west and southwest sides of the mountain. One informant from Gimbal-Sumberejo claims to have witnessed the beginning of the lava flow at 8:00 A.M. on 8 December. He reports that at first there was not much of a flow, but as time went on, the volume increased. Then, between 17 and 19 December, there occurred explosive eruptions of sufficient magnitude to completely devastate thirteen villages and partially destroy twenty-four others, killing 1,367 people and 2,140 head of livestock (Kabupaten Magelang 1976:15). Hardest hit was the village of Pager Jurang, where no one escaped save for two girls who were visiting another village at the time. Informants who visited the village after the blast report having seen the charred remains of human shapes still kneeling with their foreheads to the ground, in the ritual position of Muslim prayer. Villages located in the Blongkeng-Sat watershed area, north of the Batang River, were totally destroyed, while those to the south and east of the Batang—an area that includes Gimbal-Sumberejo —were unharmed (Fig. 6.1).

A number of medium-scale eruptions followed the catastrophic 1930 blast, including ones in 1954 and 1961. In 1954 the direction of the blast shifted to the north, striking three villages in the Apu drainage area (Fig. 6.1), killing sixty-four people and injuring fifty-seven (Soebagio 1976:24; Reksawiraga 1972:25). In 1961 the direction of the blast shifted again, this time to the Batang River gorge, further south and much closer to Gimbal. Loss of life was much lower—five people and nineteen head of stock—because villages in the predicted target area were evacuated beforehand. Still, one village was totally destroyed and three others were partially destroyed. One of these, Kaligesik, was right next to Gimbal. Fortune smiled on Gimbal-Sumberejo, however, and once again the village escaped intact.

The Perception of Mount Merapi's Hazards
by the National Government

The Indonesian government responded to the 1961 eruption by forcibly removing 4,517 persons from Mount Merapi and resettling them in Sumatra. All of the 785 villagers in Gimbal were included in this resettlement, despite the fact that this particular village had not been touched by either the 1961, 1954, or 1930 eruptions. Nevertheless, Gimbal lost its administrative status, it was stricken from all official maps, and its inhabitants were sent to Way Jepara in Sumatra.

Many villagers were unhappy with this decision, the ostensible basis for it, and the way in which it was made. The *lurah* (village head) allegedly went to the regional government without prior consultation with the village council and handed over everyone's tax assessments, saying that the entire village had decided to transmigrate. Regardless of how it happened, once the decision had been taken, the people did not have the power to make the government reverse its position. Most of the villagers eventually gave in and, however reluctantly, went along with the resettlement plan. One informant has this to say regarding the incident.

> It was the *lurah,* you know. He had many children and not enough land, so when they offered him the chance to go to Sumatra, he didn't even ask us. He just said yes. Because of who he was, the government just moved a pen and "poof"—no more Gimbal. Now in Kaliurang, things were different. When they came to the *lurah* there, he said he'd have to see what everybody else thought. It turned out nobody wanted to go, so they didn't go. If our *lurah* had been like theirs, this village would still have plenty of people. Whoever wanted to go could have signed up and the rest of us could have stayed here to take care of the land.

In all, thirteen householders felt strongly enough about staying to risk opposing the government. They moved their residences lower down on Merapi's slopes, but they continued to tend their irrigated fields in Gimbal, avoiding roadblocks and police barricades to do so. When any of them happened to be caught inside the forbidden zone, they pretended to be taking a shortcut to land in the safe area.

Just as the villagers who refused to transmigrate experienced a variety of difficulties, so did those who agreed, both before and after the move. For six to nine months before leaving for Sumatra, the prospective transmigrants had to stay in government evacuee centers. One informant reported the general reaction toward these centers: "We never felt right staying in a place that wasn't our own." In addition, the villagers had difficulty getting enough food for themselves and their livestock. As a result, they would wait for opportune moments when no one was around to sneak back to Gimbal, dig up some tubers from their erstwhile gardens, and graze their stock on the slopes.

When the Gimbal villagers finally did arrive in Sumatra, there was little improvement in their situation. They were not all settled in the same village or even in the same resettlement block. Because conditions were not uniform, some adapted to their new surroundings quite easily, while others did not. The latter built a case for returning to Gimbal, on the grounds that there was too much sickness and death among them, the weather was too hot, and the natural environment was too harsh.[6] Eventually, thirty-four families returned from Way Jepara to take up residence again in Gimbal.[7]

This unofficial revival of Gimbal was not ignored by the local authorities. The government's edict to close Gimbal was still in effect, and the former transmigrants were visited on several occasions by officials who tried to persuade them to go back to Sumatra. There was also a question of land ownership, in that having forfeited their property rights (or rather the village headman having forfeited it for them), the returnees were now occupying land to which they had no legal claim. Nor did the returnees have anywhere to live: either they had sold their houses before they left for Sumatra or the police had demolished them to discourage resettlement in the area. So they had to rebuild from scratch. By night they slept in lean-tos made from *Imperata cylindrica,* while by day they worked on the construction of more substantial houses. As time went by, their numbers were swelled by the villagers who had originally refused to transmigrate, as well as by later returnees from Sumatra. They reopened their former agricultural lands and restarted the flow of irrigation water into their wet-rice fields. The yields from their irrigated and unirrigated fields together more than sufficed for their subsistence. In fact, there was a surplus of land for them to cultivate, since the total village population was now just a fraction of what it had formerly been.

In 1965, seeing that the village was doing so well and that Mount Merapi seemed to have quieted down, the local government relented and acknowledged the legality of the resettlement—on two conditions. The new settlement would have to be joined administratively to the nearby village of Kaliurang, and the villagers would have to pay a land registration fee amounting to 10 percent of the value of their individual holdings. The villagers eventually agreed to the first of these conditions, but the second has thus far remained unfulfilled.

With respect to future threats from the volcano, the government has undertaken a number of preventive measures—in addition to the transmigration program. To monitor volcanic activity, seven observation posts equipped with various types of sensory devices have been deployed around the volcano and linked up with the Merapi surveillance center in Yogyakarta. Communication is based on the use of telephones and *kentongan* (hollow log drums)—the former for interdepartmental contact between government agencies monitoring Mount Merapi, and the latter for direct contact with communities on the slopes.[8] In addition, escape routes have been laid out and marked with bold arrows, and emergency shelters have been constructed for villagers forced to flee their homes.

The Perception of Mount Merapi's Hazards by the Local Population

The reluctance of the inhabitants of Gimbal to transmigrate to Sumatra, coupled with their subsequent desire to return to Gimbal, suggests that the villagers' own evaluation of and response to the volcanic threat differ considerably from those of the government. The villagers have, in this respect, two basic needs. One is the need to predict and respond to the concrete hazards of the volcano. The second is the need to causally explain these hazards, and so reduce to a minimum the psychological stress attendant upon their vulnerability to them.

The potential amount of stress experienced by the villagers on Mount Merapi is a function of the relative unpredictability of the timing and force of eruptions and the location and extent of the damage caused by them (see also Hanson et al. 1982). This unpredictability gives rise to what appears to be a "chance" factor. For example, one house (or one village) may escape unscathed when all surrounding houses (or villages) are destroyed. Like other people who have had to deal with the apparent fickleness of a hazardous world, the villagers on Merapi have tried to see reason or cause where reason and cause (in their sense) do not exist (cf. Malinowski 1979:43). They do this by attributing volcanic activity to three classes of supernatural deities: the spirit of the volcano, the spirit of the south sea, and the spirits of departed ancestors.

This cognitive treatment of the volcanic hazard is made clear in the following invocation, which is recited by the *modin* (ritual expert) each time a *selamatan* (ceremony) is held in Sumberejo.

Sepindahan, ingkang kula perteni saklebetipun redi Merapi. Rambah kaping kalih ingkang wonten sak njawinipun redi Merapi. Pramila sedaya dipun perteni, kula sak ahli waris nyuwun wilujeng, lan sedaya para ahli kubur leluhur kula saking jaler saking estri, tebih celak ingkang mboten keruwatan lan keruwatan sedaya dipun perteni, kula nyuwun bakoh

langkep, kiyat slamet sak ahli waris kula sedaya. Rambah kaping tiga,
kangge merteni njeng Nyai Rara Kidul, mbok menawi utusan sak wanci-
wanci sageda kandheg kanankeringipun dhusun Sumberejo (Gimbal) mriki.

Praise be to you who dwell within the mountain. Praise be to all who dwell
without. Most humbly we implore you to accept this offering, that our days
may be spent in safety. To all who have gone before us, from among our men
and our women, near and far; to those still disturbed and to those already at
peace, we offer praise and thanksgiving. We beseech you to deliver us from
danger. Grant us strength and refuge. Glory to you, Nyai Rara Kidul. May
that which you see fit to summon forth, stop before our doors, and pass on
either side of us.[9]

This prayer contains an explanation for the destructive behavior of
Mount Merapi, by implying that it is related to the consummation of
marriage between the god of the mountain, *Kyai Sapujagad,* and the god-
dess of the south sea, *Nyai Rara Kidul.*[10] In Javanese cosmology, the
mountain and the sea are often seen as symbolic of the male and female
life force, respectively. Taken one step further, the ejection of lava from
the volcano during an eruption is associated with the ejaculation of
sperm from the male during intercourse. As the union of human beings
can be ritualized and controlled but not prevented, so too with the inevitable union of the male and female forces of nature. The mountain
communities do not attempt to deny *Nyai Rara Kidul* access to the volcano, therefore, but ask only that their village be spared when she sum-
mons forth its lava (viz., its male seed). Accordingly, they make ritual
offerings to keep favor with the gods and to divert their fiery path away
from the village. This belief that natural forces act in accordance with
certain principles of social order, such as the relationship between males
and females, is found elsewhere in Indonesia as well (see Van Wouden
1968).

The above invocation is part of a villagewide ritual called the *baretan*
(ceremony of village purification). This ceremony usually is staged during the Javanese month of *Sura,* on the evening before the Javanese day
of *Jum'at Kliwon.* A number of special ritual foods are prepared for this
ceremony: two servings of rice in the shape of a pyramid; two whole
cooked chickens, complete with head and feet; a dish of cooked potatos;
prawn crackers; red and white rice pudding; and saffron rice. These are
taken to the home of the village chief, where all the heads of households
gather. The *modin* burns incense and recites the invocation cited above,
as well as reciting an Islamic prayer in Arabic.[11]

In addition to responding through prayer and ceremony to the psychological stress of living on Mount Merapi, the villagers also respond
operationally to the physical threat of living there. They make continual

efforts to predict or divine the intentions of Merapi on the basis of various phenomena associated (in their experience) with the volcano's behavior. Informants claim they are able to tell that Merapi is becoming angry and dangerous from any of the following signs: three sharp cracks, as from a bullwhip, and a deep rumbling coming from the crater; lightning flashing on either side of the cone; a rise in air temperature; and the flight of wild animals from the upper slopes. When the volcano is just beginning to come to life, the villagers say, the following signs indicate that a cataclysmic eruption is imminent: lava flows down the slopes in fits and starts, clouds above the cone become pitch-black, and there is a deafening noise like thunder. The lava can also be seen from far away, even from as far away as the city of Yogyakarta: by night it appears as a glowing fire, and by day it appears as white smoke.

The villagers evacuate to safer areas as quickly as possible whenever they decide that Merapi is about to erupt. In my survey, 88 percent of the respondents said that in the event of another eruption, they would move to a safer village, either temporarily or permanently; 8 percent said they would trust to God to save them; and 4 percent said they would rely on the government for protection (Laksono 1977:26). The villagers' own accounts of incidents surrounding the 1969 eruption illustrate the way in which they perceive and adapt to this hazard. On 17 January of that year, Merapi burst into life (Kabupaten Magelang 1976:15). The eruption was only medium-sized, but heated gases, dust, and steam were ejected to a distance of thirteen kilometers from the crater, the furthest ever reached in the recorded history of the volcano. The gases poured down the Batang River gorge, crossed over to the Bebang River, and hit the western sector of Gimbal, killing three people (Fig. 6.1).

The summit area was clouded in thick smoke all morning before the eruption. The government issued a warning to leave the village, and all the villagers fled to the southerly village of Gondoarum among other places. By afternoon, however, the smoke had disappeared and the sky above the crater was clear. Deciding that it had been a false alarm, a number of the villagers returned to Gimbal, taking their livestock with them. One informant reports that he stayed up until midnight chatting with his neighbors. When the neighbors finally went home, he, his wife, and children went to sleep. Not long afterward, at around 1:00 A.M., Merapi began to pour forth both steam and lava. Fortunately, my informant's wife awakened and went outside to see what was happening. She found that lava was already flowing past the fields to the west of the house, and great billowing clouds of gas were gushing and roaring right over her roof top. She was momentarily stunned. When she came to her senses, she woke up her husband and children, and they all fled with no thought for their cattle or their other possessions, but only for their own lives. One of the children, who had gone to sleep with his radio, was still holding it in his hand when they fled down the mountain. This was the only possession the family had to sell during the lean times following the eruption. Two of their buffalo were burned to a crisp. The other two were so badly seared that they were slaughtered, and the meat was shared among their neighbors.

Another person, Sukardi, was not so fortunate with his radio. His neighbors could not wake him because they could not make themselves heard above the blare of a radio with which he too had gone to sleep. As a result, Sukardi was left behind. He, his home, and his radio were consumed in the fire from the mountain. The two others that perished in Merapi's onslaught were Atmo Giyo and his ailing mother Prawirorejo. The latter could not travel quickly, and when they attempted to cross the confluence of the Bedok and Krasak rivers they were caught in a torrent of *ladu* that poured down the bed of the Bebeng River and overflowed into the bed of the Krasak (Fig. 6.1).[12] Their bodies were later found thrown up on the sand at the point they had been attempting to cross. The eruption devastated the previously abandoned villages of Brubuhan, Kaligesik, and Ngori; but in Gimbal itself, it only destroyed a few houses in the westernmost quarter, one of which belonged to the ill-fated Sukardi. The overflow of lava from the Bebeng riverbed came to within one-half kilometer of the western edge of the village and turned approximately forty hectares of irrigated fields into barren sand and rock.[13]

After the eruption subsided, the villagers once again returned to Gimbal, but this time the government did not allow them to take up residence at the original site of settlement. They were instructed to move their houses approximately one kilometer to the southeast, to what was considered a safer part of the village territory, and they have remained there ever since. I was on hand for the beginning of this move in December 1969. At about this time the former village headman, who had also returned to Gimbal from Sumatra, had a change of heart and went back to the transmigration site; so the villagers felt free to join their settlement to the nearby village of Kaliurang as the local government had earlier requested. It was at this point that the village was granted administrative status as a hamlet and the name "Sumberejo."

Summary and Discussion

This discussion has made it clear that there is a difference in the perception of and adaptation to the hazards of Mount Merapi on the part of the government and the local villagers. Proof of this is contained in the fact that, first, after the 1961 eruption some of the villagers still did not want to transmigrate, and second, some of those who did transmigrate later returned to Merapi.[14] Further proof is contained in the fact that following the 1969 eruption, all of Gimbal's inhabitants remained at their village site and none of them transmigrated. This difference in perception and response between the government and the villagers is not a difference between truth and error. Neither side is necessarily right or wrong in its perception of the volcanic hazard. For example, from the government's point of view the return to Merapi of some of the Sumatran transmigrants led to the death of three of them during the 1969 eruption. On the other hand, from the point of view of the villagers, it is similarly true that their initial transmigration after the 1961 eruption—which did no damage whatsoever to their own village—led thereafter to the death of more villagers from disease and other environmental hazards than had been killed by the volcano in the previous three eruptions combined.

The magnitude of the volcanic threat to Gimbal-Sumberejo is a complex matter, therefore, and the government and the villagers differ less because of any miscalculation of this threat than because of the relative weight placed upon it. The villagers do not ignore or deny the importance of the volcanic threat; they merely do not consider it sufficiently important to justify moving away from the mountain.[15] Implicitly, they do not consider this threat to be greater than the threats that they would face in an alternative place of residence, such as Sumatra. The data do not yet exist to make a rigorous comparison of hazards to health and life on Mount Merapi and in the transmigration sites of Sumatra, but it is certainly clear that the latter place is not without its own hazards. It also seems clear that the villagers weight the hazards of Sumatra more heavily, because their lives there otherwise compare so unfavorably with their lives on Mount Merapi. On the other hand, the government is guilty of some bias in weighting as well. It is clear that the government, because of its massive economic and political commitment to transmigration, weights the hazards of life in Sumatra and on Mount Merapi respectively lighter and heavier than it otherwise might. Thus, the government appears to want to transmigrate villages in which there is any possibility of anyone dying from volcanic eruption. To the villagers, this makes no more sense than would a government policy that required city dwellers to move into the country in order to eliminate the possibility of deaths in urban traffic accidents.

This comparison of government and village views of the volcanic hazard on Mount Merapi shows not only that the two views differ, but also that each has its own validity. The fact that the villagers' assessment of hazard is colored by tradition and custom is no less inevitable and no more distorting than the fact that the government's assessment of hazard is colored by economics and politics. The real point of this comparison is that all such evaluations are ultimately subjective to some extent, the particular bias varying from case to case depending upon who makes the evaluation and for what purpose. To begin to deal with such subjectivity, we must first be aware that it exists.[16] Because of the differences in power between a national government and a tiny village, it more often happens that the latter is made aware of its subjectivity than the former. The purpose of this paper, then, is to suggest that there are some objective as well as subjective elements in the villagers' assessment of volcanic hazards on Mount Merapi and that there are some subjective as well as objective elements in the government's assessment as well.

Notes

1. I made two field studies in Sumberejo: the first, in September and October of 1977, as a research associate at the Population Studies Center, Gadjah Mada University; and the second, in June 1979, as part of the research for my bachelor's thesis in the Department of Anthropology, University of Indonesia. I am greatly indebted to the Population Studies Center of Gadjah Mada University for financing this research. I am also deeply grateful to my dear departed wife for the many hours she devoted to helping me in the field and organizing the data for my thesis. I would like to thank Gunarto and Ani Suyitno, my two field assistants, and the family of Diro Sumarto, in whose home I stayed during my fieldwork. And finally, to the people this study is all about, the people of Sumberejo: there are no words to express my appreciation for the way you welcomed me into your midst and gave of yourselves to help make this study possible.

2. The logic to this orientation is that in the event of an eruption, people need only run out of their front door and downhill to escape danger.

3. The exchange rate at the time of this study was 615 rupiah = US$1.00.

4. At the time of the study, rice was selling at approximately 150 rupiah per kilogram.

5. Taking Java as a whole, population density increases as proximity to volcanos increases, because of the soil-enriching properties of volcanos. In closest proximity to volcanos, however, passing from the regions that benefit from their activity to the regions that are actively menaced by them, population density begins to decrease with proximity—and it is this latter relationship to which the text refers.

6. One informant, the son of the village clerk, relates that less than two months after arriving in Sumatra, twenty-nine villagers had died. His own mother died in Brajamas, Way Jepara, just thirty-nine days after leaving Java.

7. Because four of these families eventually returned to Sumatra, and because of changes in the structure of some households as well as a difference between my definition of a household and the definition used by the local government (which regards each married male as the head of a household), my census of Sumberejo recorded only twenty-six households as having been transmigrated to Sumatra and then returned to Merapi.

8. Two drumbeats, continually repeated, signal an alert; four beats, continually repeated, signal that preparations to flee should be made; and continual beating signals that those in the danger zone should immediately flee.

9. In the invocation, the word *keruwatan* means roughly "those whose presence does not disturb us." However, in Sumberejo the pronunciation of *keruwatan* is often slightly altered to *kerumatan,* which means "those who are still cared for," meaning those whose graves are still visited and kept in good condition.

10. Another version holds that an eruption occurs when *Kyai Sapujagad* and *Nyai Rara Kidul* are in search of human beings to join the ranks of their phantom army (Susilowati 1981).

11. The dualistic nature of the villagers' response to supernatural powers is evinced by the Hindu-Javanese and Islamic elements in this ritual. For more on religious dualism among the Javanese, see Koentjaraningrat (1980).

12. *Ladu* is the local term for all ejecta thrown off by the volcano. This includes pyroclastic flows and material carried within volcanic plumes (ash, sand, gravel, pyroclasts, and gases).

13. In lower-lying areas it was possible to recover irrigated land buried under sand and rock by turning over the topsoil. In 1979 it cost approximately 125,000 rupiah per hectare to do so, the exact cost varying according to the depth of sand above the top soil. The deeper the sand, the greater the cost.

14. This also occurred in Sinila, in the Dieng plateau region, from which people were transmigrated following a poisonous gas emission. According to the junior minister for transmigration, Murtono, a total of forty-seven heads of households returned after learning that their land did not lie within the designated danger zone (*Kompas* 1982a).

15. Kiecolt and Nigg (1982) report a similar reaction in their study of mobility and perceptions of the threat of earthquakes in Los Angeles. Here, too, the proximity of seismic activity was not regarded as sufficient reason for moving. This also proved to be the case in the Tasik Malaya region of West Java. Following the eruption of Mount Galunggung in April 1982, the government set a target of 2,000 households to be evacuated and resettled on other islands. But by 17 May 1982, a grand total of only 197 households had actually been relocated. As a newspaper article at the time put it, "The crash program to relocate residents from high risk danger zones seems to be experiencing a setback" (*Kompas* 1982b).

16. For further discussion of this sort of self-consciousness on the part of researchers, see Mubyarto, Soetrisno, and Dove (1983).

References Cited

Hanson, R. O., D. Noulles, and S. J. Bellovich
    1982   "Knowledge, Warning, and Stress: A Study of Comparative Roles in an Urban Floodplain." *Environment and Behavior* 14 (2): 171–185.

Kabupaten Magelang
    1976   *Data on Mt. Merapi, Dati II Magelang.* Magelang: Community Protection Division, Dati II Magelang.

Kiecolt, K. J., and J. M. Nigg
    1982   "Mobility and Perceptions of a Hazardous Environment." *Environment and Behavior* 14 (2): 131–154.

Koentjaraningrat
    1980   "Javanese Terms for God and Supernatural Beings and the Idea of Power." In *Man, Meaning and History: Essays in Honor of Professor H. G. Shulte Nordholt,* edited by R. Schefold, J. W. Schoorl, and J. Tennekes, pp. 127–139. The Hague: Martinus Nijhoff.

Kompas
    1982a   "Enam Pola Pemukiman Akan Menjadi Dasar Program Transmigrasi" [Six settlement patterns will become the basis for the Transmigration Program]. *Kompas* (11 May): 1–5.

    1982b   "Di Pengungsian Korban Galunggung Berbagai Ekses Muncul Akibat Bantuan Terus Mengalir" [Various excesses occur in the evacuation of the Galunggung victims as the result of the assistance flowing away]. *Kompas* (17 May): 1.

Laksono, ed.
    1977   *Survey Sosial Ekonomi Budaya di Daerah Bencana Alam Gunung Merapi, Daerah Istimewa Yogyakarta dan Jawa Tengah* [Social, economic, and cultural survey in the hazardous area of Mount Merapi, Special Region of Yogyakarta and Central Java]. Yogyakarta: Population Studies Center, Gadjah Mada University.

Malinowski, Bronislaw
    1979   "The Function of Religion in Human Society." In *Reader in Comparative Religion,* edited by William A. Lessa and Evon Z. Vogt, pp. 36–46. New York: Harper & Row.

Mubyarto, Loekman Soetrisno, and Michael R. Dove
    1983   "Problems of Rural Development in Central Java: Ethnomethodological Perspectives." *Contemporary Southeast Asian Studies* 5 (1): 41–52.

Reksawiraga, L. J.
    1972   "Melengkapi dan Sebagian Merevisi Peta Daerah Bahaya Gunung Merapi Jawa Tengah" [Completion and partial revision of the map of the dangerous zone of Mount Merapi in Central Java]. Unpublished. Bandung: Directorate of Geology, Subdirectorate of Vulcanology.

Siswowijoyo, Suparto, and L. Pardyanto
  1976   *Gunung Merapi* [Mount Merapi]. Bandung: Directorate of Geology,
          Subdirectorate of Vulcanology.

Soebagio
  1976   "Bahaya Peletusan Gunung Merapi" [Danger of Mount Merapi's
          eruptions]. Paper read in the Department of Geological Engi-
          neering, Faculty of Engineering, Gadjah Mada University.

Suryo, Ismangun, and K. Kusumadinata
  1973   "Gunung Merapi dan Bahaya-bahaya Letusannya" [Mount Mera-
          pi and the dangers of its eruptions]. Unpublished. Bandung: Direc-
          torate of Geology, Subdirectorate of Vulcanology.

Susilowati, Trisno
  1981   Unpublished field notes.

Van Wouden, F. A. E.
  1968   *Types of Social Structure in Eastern Indonesia*. Translated by R. Need-
          ham. The Hague: Martinus Nijhoff.

7. The Mentawai Equilibrium and the Modern World

REIMAR SCHEFOLD

Abstract

The inhabitants of Siberut in the Mentawai Archipelago lived until the present century according to a late stone age cultural tradition. Their way of life is characterized by a striving to maintain balanced relations among themselves as well as toward the natural environment. Modern outside influences threaten this equilibrium. This paper gives a short outline of the traditional culture and describes a project aimed at helping the Mentawaians to develop in a manner that will not destroy their cultural identity.

Introduction

The concepts of "cultural identity" and "national identity" often relate to quite different things. Various cultural traditions can coexist within one nation, and one cultural tradition can also subsume parts of several nations. The American anthropologist Clifford Geertz pointed out as early as 1963 that this potential discontinuity between culture and nation is often experienced as a threat by the emergent states of the Third World. They are afraid that "primordial attachments," the links with local traditions, may prove stronger than the feeling of belonging to a new state, perhaps calling in question the unity of the nation. This fear is pronounced in Indonesia, with its unmatched profusion of historical and regional traditions.

Indonesia's ethnic minorities have their own fears, namely, that the values of the nation will be equated with those of the most numerous group, the Javanese. The larger minorities, such as the Batak, Minangkabau, and Balinese, are strongly aware of their own existence and are in a position to assert it. This is less true of the smaller ethnic minorities. Their traditions are often archaic and are thus under double pressure. They are faced not only with the problem of how they can make their voices heard in the concert of Indonesian cultural traditions, but also with the fundamental question whether there is any place at all today for such archaic traditions. Can they develop so as to participate in a meaningful way in modern society? Can they accurately assess the various possibilities open to them and then choose the course of development of most benefit to them in the long run?

This paper examines these questions and proposes a possible answer within the context of traditional Mentawaian culture on the Indonesian island of Siberut.[1]

Siberut

Siberut is the northernmost and the largest island in the Mentawai Archipelago, some 100 kilometers to the west of Sumatra, Indonesia (Fig. 1). It has a surface area of 4,480 square kilometers, nearly the same size as Bali, and has the shape of a protracted rectangle. The eastern side, facing Sumatra, falls gently away into the sea and is easily accessible. Here, in general, the sea is calm. Bays and tongues of land with white coral beaches alternate with mangrove swamps. Everywhere, there are little coral-ringed islands to be seen. Those who travel in a small boat along the coast can see, every few kilometers, dark openings—the estuaries of rivers winding their muddy way into the sea. The western side offers a very different picture. This is the outermost edge of the Asian continent, a straight and frequently sheer coastline, on which a powerful surf breaks as it arrives across the ocean from the direction of Africa. Only in the estuaries of the Sagulubbe River in the south and the Simalegi River in the north are there bays with any degree of protection, and even these are only fair weather anchorages.

The interior is hilly, with a maximum elevation of 384 meters. Since the ground is soft and relatively free of rock, the surface reveals extraordinary erosion patterns with steep slopes and sharp ridges, between which little streams twist and turn their way to join the rivers. The larger rivers, with their fertile, alluvial plains, break the interior up into wide valleys. There is no rainy period as such. On average, it rains every second day, but the rainfall is at its heaviest in the months of April and October, when a river can rise by more than five meters in a matter of hours, turning an entire valley into one huge lake. The only protection against erosion is the dense tropical rain forest, which covers more than 90 percent of the island. As a result of the prolonged geographic isolation, some estimates say as much as half a million years, this forest is rich in an animal and plant life found exclusively in this region. The four different kinds of Mentawaian primates have, in particular, recently attracted the attention of zoologists.

The Mentawaians

There are about 20,000 people on Siberut—about five persons per square kilometer. The population is concentrated along the island's rivers. The cultural roots of this population reach directly back into the Neolithic (viz., the late stone age). At that time, more than three thousand years ago, various mainland peoples migrated into Indonesia and gradually settled the various islands. This Neolithic culture was later transformed on most islands, though not Mentawai, by the early metal age cultures of Southeast Asia, namely, the Dongson cultures, which include the Batak, Dayak, and Toraja. Other changes followed the introduction of Hindu culture, currently still found in Bali, and finally Islam, the prevailing religion in Indonesia today. As a result, the traditions of the Neolithic are more intact on Siberut, today, than anywhere else in Indonesia except New Guinea. The inhabitants of Siberut no longer fashion their tools from stone, however. For many generations, they have traded coconut and rattan for bush-knives and axe-heads from Sumatran fishermen and traders. It is only in legend that evil ogres called the *silakokaina* use tools made from stone. The archaic cultural tradition of the Mentawaians is more apparent in their organization of daily life.

The traditional economy of Siberut takes its character from the fertility of the soil, the abundance of land, and the profusion of foodstuffs. The main staple is sago. The pith of sago palm, when pounded and washed, yields flour on which a family can subsist for weeks; and there are entire forests of palms in the marshy lowlands that are waiting to be eaten. Planting and processing sago is men's work. Other crops are cultivated by women. They plant taro in fields near the rivers, where the soil is enriched by floodwaters. Further from the rivers, where the valley floor marches up into hilly forests, men and women make clearings in which other tubers, as well as bananas, are planted. They do not use fire when clearing the forest, for fear of offending the forest spirits. After a number of years of cultivation, when the fertility of the soil has diminished, they plant fruit trees in these clearings. As a result, the natural forest in these areas is gradually replaced with a forest than can be harvested. In addition to these several horticultural activities, the Mentawaians (both sexes) rear chickens and pigs, which also are fed mainly sago.

A Mentawai Siberut *Uma* (House)

Two Women Adorned for a *Puliaijat* (Ritual)

There are other subsistence activities as well. Women fish in the streams with nets for shrimp and small fish. In the hilly forested areas between river valleys, the men hunt with bow and poisoned arrows. The most prized targets are monkeys, deer, and wild boar. The forests serve also as a source of rattan, firewood, and trees for dugout canoes and house timbers. The Mentawaians use their slender, mobile dugouts to carry home the crops from upstream or downstream gardens, and also to visit neighboring settlements. They also paddle down to the estuaries to fish in the shallow waters, or into the open sea to hunt for turtles. When they plan to do the latter, they first lash outriggers to the canoes for greater stability. There were originally no settlements on the coast itself, because the slight inclination of the major valleys causes the brackish water to extend far upstream at high tide.

Within this subsistence system, labor is divided according to gender. The Mentawaians base this division on differences in physical strength. They see use of the axe, for example, as particularly strenuous, so they reserve it for men. When building a house, the men use axes to fell trees for the timbers, while the women use bush-knives to cut palm leaves for the roof. The division of labor has a spatial component as well. A man's sago and coconut trees are apt to be spread out over an entire valley and may keep him away from the settlement for days at a time. In contrast, a woman's taro and banana fields are typically close to home. Similarly, hunting takes men deep into the forests, whereas women usually do their fishing in the vicinity of the settlement.

The unit of production in this subsistence system is the family, but it is not the focal point of Mentawaian life because it is not in itself a viable unit. The demands of daily existence constantly surpass the capabilities of a single family. Family resources alone are inadequate to supply the needs of illness, old age, and defense. Thus, the focal unit of Mentawai life is the *uma*. This term refers both to the residential group and to the traditional residence of the Mentawaians, namely, five to ten families living in a group house constructed atop large wooden pilings (see Kis-Jovak 1979).

Equilibrium and Disequilibrium in the Mentawai World

The world of the Mentawaians is characterized by built-in tensions or conflicts and by marked human efforts to reduce them and maintain (or restore) equilibrium. These tensions arise in three areas: intragroup relations, intergroup relations, and relations between humans and the environment.

Within the *uma,* unqualified solidarity prevails. The fruit of an individual family's labors belongs to it, but it must be ready to assist any other *uma* family that needs help. The principle of solidarity is particularly marked in eating practices. For example, it is taboo to eat meat alone. When a man is successful in the hunt, he must divide his prize in such a way that every other family in the settlement receives the same amount of meat. Before big festivals, the entire group gets together and discusses how many pigs each family should contribute. The number depends upon individual assets. If one family has more pigs than others with less luck in breeding, it must give more. The animals are brought to the settlement and slaughtered. Then the individual contributions are pooled and redistributed so that everyone presents receives an equal portion.

This practice poses a potential dilemma for the individual pig owner. There is always a shortage of pigs. They are regularly decimated by illness, traded to neighboring groups for other goods, or used as gifts in social interaction with such groups. The dilemma lies in the conflict between the need to comply with the requirements of the *uma* and the desire to use pigs for personal ends. It sometimes happens that an individual refuses to contribute to a festival the number of pigs that the others feel can be expected of him. Such incidents are among the most frequent causes of conflict within a group. They are dealt with by open discussion. The group, including the women and the children, comes together and talks the matter over. Since the *uma* traditionally has no leader who can make a final judgment, it is not uncommon for such discussions to drag on for days or even weeks. A solution is acceptable only if all parties are convinced of its fairness. Sometimes, despite all such efforts, the group is unsuccessful in reaching agreement. In order to prevent open hostilities, there is only one recourse. One faction moves away and establishes its own settlement. This represents a weakening of the community and is seen as a last resort. All ceremonies contain symbolic reminders of the necessity for togetherness and solidarity.

The nature of relations between groups resembles that within the *uma*. The ideal life for people on Siberut is peaceful coexistence, in which no one gets in another's way. There is a countervailing ideal, however, involving pride and the desire of each group to surpass all others. Every *uma* jealously guards its rights and position and is instantly ready to suspect its neighbors of covetous intentions. There is a pattern of rivalry, mistrust, and tension that can at any time produce open hostilities. The tendency to such rivalry is balanced, however, by a need for some amount of intergroup cooperation. Neighboring groups must be called upon for major undertakings, such as the construction of an *uma* joint house, which are beyond the resources of any one community. In addition, each community must look to other groups for its wives. All of the families in any given Siberut *uma* are descendants of the same male line. Wives are taken from other *uma* communities. Upon marrying, a woman becomes a member of her husband's community. (If a woman is widowed, she returns to her natal community, where she will receive land and participate in the household of a brother or nephew.)

The need to transfer wives helps to make intergroup cooperation possible. There is no political integration among the indigenous peoples of Siberut. There are no traditional chiefs who can impose peace by fiat. Rather, peace is maintained, or restored, through intergroup alliances. Each group tries to make alliances with as many other groups as possible, based largely on the transfer of wives. In every marriage, all members of both the wife-giving and wife-taking groups ideally contribute to the brideprice and the return gift. This creation of ties between all of the members of both communities forms the basis for a bond between the two *uma*.

The ideal of equilibrium and harmony in the relationships within and between groups also applies in the supernatural sphere. Here again, there are no dominant forces. There are spirits everywhere—in the forests, in the sky, in the sea, and under the earth. Every entity, whether human, animal, plant, or object, has its own personal soul. All of these spirits and souls interact and work upon each other. Without the intervention of man, the Mentawaians believe, these forces are in a state of equilibrium. In the course of his subsistence activities, however, man interferes with this equilibrium. He must kill in order to survive, to keep alive not only his body but also his soul. If life becomes too miserable, if there is not enough to eat, if plentiful feasts cannot be had from time to time, his soul will lose its will to live and pass on to join the ancestors. When this happens to a man's soul, his body dies. The Mentawaians nevertheless regard any intervention in the environment as sinister. It disturbs the equilibrium that exists in the environment and, just as with disturbances on a social level, this is potentially dangerous. The objects of such intervention (e.g., a felled tree) may rebel against the use to which they are put and turn on man. Their anger can make him ill.

Conflict between one human group and another can be moderated by forming alliances and by mutual consideration and reciprocation. The same principle is applied to relations between humans and their environment. Entities in the environment cannot just be utilized by man; they are not just objects at his disposal. They are actors that may allow themselves to be used or not. Any prospective human user must first establish a relationship with them. Before the Mentawaians kill a pig that they have reared, for example, they explain and excuse what they are about to do. They tell the pig why they are killing him. They remind him that he is only so big and fat because he has always been well looked after and sheltered from the rain and bad weather. They ask him not to take his death too hard, reminding him that his ancestors all experienced the same fate. These conciliatory efforts also include sacrifices to the entities in question. The same attitude is the origin of a great many taboos. All important undertakings are accompanied by a number of ritual proscriptions. For example, when men are engaged in hunting, they are forbidden to eat certain kinds of food, to bathe in the river, or to engage in sex. By refraining from these activities, they try to compensate for their interference in the environment. If this does not succeed and someone falls ill, ceremonies are staged to appease the entities that have been violated and to restore the original balance.

Thoughts of illness and premature death are central to the life of the Mentawaians. This preoccupation is associated with very high rates of mortality: for example, an average of only two children from each marriage survive to adulthood. This grim reality is interpreted in terms of the concept of man's soul and the conditions of everyday life. Thus, Mentawaians believe that man must be good to his soul just as he is good to his body, and he must respect the souls of the things in his environment just as he must respect the needs of his friends and neighbors. Everywhere, good relations must be established and maintained, for everything is subject to the law of balance and harmony.

These ideas find their most complete expression in the major religious feasts of the *uma*, the *puliaijat*, held several times each year. A complete *puliaijat* can last several weeks and is carried out in complete isolation from other groups. Once it has started, strangers are not allowed into the *uma*. Only at the beginning are shamans from neighboring groups invited to assist with the ceremonies. In return for their help, they are presented with a pig or two when they leave. These gifts reveal a central social theme of the feasts. They stress the unity of the group, within which alone human existence is possible, and they reject the outside world, which always represents a potential threat. At the same time, and reflecting the tensions discussed earlier, they show the dependence upon friendly relations with other groups in the valley. A second theme of the ceremonies involves the relations of the Mentawaians with their natural surroundings. All subsistence activities that might disturb the harmony in the environment are proscribed during the feast. In addition, prophylactic ceremonies to appease particular local flora and fauna are carried out.

Toward the end of the feast, the entire group removes itself to a camp in the forest and hunts for monkeys for several days. The kill consists typically of just a few animals, which are quickly consumed. The effort seems greatly out of proportion to the results of the hunt, but the animals are important less for their numbers than for what they represent, namely, the property of the spirits. During the ceremony, the community slaughters and sacrifices its domestic animals. If the spirits are satisfied and approve of the *puliaijat,* they show this by presenting the community in return with some of their own animals, as prey for the hunters. The climax of the ceremony is the enticement of the individual souls. In daily existence, a person often has to neglect that which his soul expects of him. Now people try to please their souls and bind them to life again. Everybody adorns himself, the *uma* house is decorated with carvings and blossoms, great banquets are held, and there is dancing throughout the night.

Modern Impacts on Mentawaian Life

Modern influences arrived relatively late in Siberut. Because Siberut held no economic interest, the Dutch colonial government intervened very little in the old ways of life. There was just a single administrator and a tiny police force stationed on the coast, who collected a small tax per head and did their best, with varying degrees of success, to prevent feuds between the groups and to subject disputes to colonial legislation. Major changes did not occur until after Indonesia's independence. By this time, both Protestant and Catholic missionaries had settled on the island. Then, in 1954, the government issued a decree banning the island's traditional religion and stating that all islanders had to decide within three months whether to follow Christianity or Islam. Anyone choosing neither was threatened by the police or the missionary teachers with punishment, and his religious implements were burned. Concurrently, the government took steps to centralize and resettle the scattered *uma* communities into a smaller number of easily supervised villages, each one with a church and a school. At the same time, the government forbade all signs of unseemly primitiveness, including the long hair, glass beads, and loin cloths worn by men, as well as their custom of filing their teeth to points and tatooing their bodies. Finally, and most recently, commercial loggers started large-scale operations on the island, with the intention of harvesting all of its forests in the course of a twenty-year contract.

The Mentawaians were ill prepared for such a massive onslaught on their traditional ways of life. They had lost the habit of warring some fifty years earlier, so there was no violent resistance. Only in the interior of Siberut do large groups of people still pursue their old traditions to any extent. At the time of my initial fieldwork (1967–1969), one of these groups, the Sakuddei, still lived in remarkable isolation and had not yet been affected by the modern developments elsewhere on the island. They had heard about them and thought of them as a vague threat, but they did not believe that one day such developments would reach them. As an elder of the Sakuddei said to me upon my departure in the spring of 1969, "Now you know just what I know and what I have learned from my ancestors. This is what I shall tell my children and what they in turn will tell their children. This is how it will always be."

During my initial stay on Siberut, I made some attempts to mediate with the authorities on behalf of the Mentawaians, and upon my return from Siberut I tried to extend these efforts. I thought it should be possible to demonstrate to government officials that the life that the Mentawaians had led for thousands of years, and which had given them a meaningful existence, should not be wiped out at a stroke. It was clear to me that certain changes were inevitable, if only because Siberut was no longer an isolated community, but was now part of a larger nation-state. The question was, how could the Mentawaians be given an opportunity to develop in their own fashion, in a manner that they could understand and that would not destroy their cultural identity?

In her essay on development in New Guinea, Margaret Mead (1970) wrote that speculation on the possibilities of maintaining tribal cultural traditions is purely sentimental. She said that the backwardness of today's tribal societies is a result of their prolonged isolation, tantamount to an "unfair' treatment by history. According to her view, all means, including the most modern, should be used to induce such societies to adapt their ways of life as quickly as possible to industrial, Western civilization. This extreme stance is difficult to comprehend. Certainly a culture such as that on Siberut, with its conflict-laden social fragmentation, is far removed from Rousseau's concept of the "noble savage"; and there is a clear moral imperative to, for example, combat the frightful tropical diseases of Siberut with modern means (accompanied, however, by steps to prevent overpopulation). On the other hand, it is also clear that Mentawaian culture has a positive side. The Mentawaians are able to give their lives an institutional order that enables each individual to develop his personality in many directions, perhaps in ways more diverse and more meaningful than those typically attained in modern, Western society. But even if the value of such ways is questioned, the value or at least attainability of Mead's proffered alternative seems at least as dubious. The Western standard of life, with which the tribal societies are to be blessed, owes at least part of its force to the lower standards in developing countries. Inevitably, the real alternative for tribes like those on Siberut is to support but not enjoy these standards, in the role of unskilled laborers in the Third World.

Viewed objectively, the Mentawaians can live much better from their own largely self-sufficient economy than they could by selling their labor within the broader national and international economy. Moreover, within this self-sufficient economy there are possibilities for gradual development (although not necessarily along Western lines) that would not destroy the present order of their lives. However, the basic question is: What do the Mentawaians themselves want? Will they choose a development of their original tribal life that will enable them to take up a distinct place within the nation of Indonesia, or will they choose a life that is a poor copy of Western consumerism, a life dependent on paid labor and involving the surrender of their identity? In most other times and places, the latter choice has prevailed. Innumerable tribal cultures have disappeared within the past several centuries, living on only in travelers' tales or in the vague recollections of subsequent generations. Yet few if any of these peoples had the opportunity to make a genuine choice. They were overrun like the people of Siberut today. Even where no force was involved, there was rarely if ever a sufficient understanding on the part of the victims to foresee the consequences of their choices. Drawn by the temptation of hitherto unknown novelties, they did not realize, or realized too late, that the acquisition and maintenance of these meant increasing dependence with no turning back.

Any attempt to assist the people of Siberut, therefore, must involve creation of the preconditions for this type of understanding. The Mentawaians must be able to reflect on their own traditions and confront these with the real alternative, of the nature of which Mead shows so little understanding. They must also learn to understand their proper role in modern Indonesian society, which includes obligations but also rights and ways to make themselves heard. It is clear that assisting them to such an objective self-appraisal constitutes a major interference in ethnocentric tribal thinking; but it is equally clear that the time of isolation for individual tribes is over. To try to fossilize a situation of this kind, to enclose the people in a kind of a human zoo, can only be described as a misguided and patronizing form of romanticism.

Concern for social change on Siberut cannot be divorced from concern for environmental change. Almost all the trees on Siberut are part of a primary rain forest never before affected by man. This fact alone is extraordinary in today's world. The forests of Siberut have developed a unique composition as a result of the island's hundreds of thousands of years of geographical isolation. They contain a large variety of plants that have evolved here over the ages and occur only here. The same applies to the fauna that live in the forest. The four kinds of primates found only in Mentawai have already been mentioned. A number of other endemic species have arisen by adaptation to the local situation

and live nowhere else (McNeely 1978). Any disruption of this environment would threaten these life forms with extinction. The fissured
nature of Siberut's topography means that disruption resulting from
commercial deforestation is exceptionally severe. Every felled tree takes
the surrounding vegetation with it. Moving the trees by bulldozer
leaves deep swaths between which only thin strips of woodland are left
standing. The inevitable result is erosion, the exposed earth being
washed away in no time by the constant rainfall.

It is appropriate, therefore, to combine the two concerns, namely
assistance for the people and protection of their environment. The traditional ecological balance on the island did not, in any case, exist in
spite of the people. It existed with them. The Mentawaians long ago
evolved ritual prescriptions and proscriptions that, expressing their ideology of harmony, prevented any ruthless exploitation of the environment. For instance, strict taboos traditionally prevented Mentawaian
hunting from overexploiting the animal life. Wildlife will be threatened,
however, if forested areas are diminished by logging and if abrupt social
change leads the Mentawaians to abandon their hunting regulations. A
governmental prohibition of monkey hunting, for example, would not
address the first of these problems, and it would only increase the likelihood of the second, since the symbolic significance of hunting is a central pillar of traditional ritual prescriptions. It would be more appropriate, for example, to restrict hunting to particular occasions and to limit
the kinds of weapons used to the traditional ones.

The Siberut Project and the Future

In early 1973, a project designed to address some of these problems was
formulated under the auspices of Survival International (London). It
was later further developed in collaboration with the International
Union for the Conservation of Nature, the World Wildlife Fund, and
the Dutch and Indonesian governments.[2] The project, which finally
commenced in 1978, contained two basic components. First, it was
designed to strengthen the future economy of the people of Siberut; and
second, it was designed to stimulate the people to choose—consciously
—their own way of development.

There are several possibilities for achieving the first economic objective through the use of traditional techniques of production. One possibility involves improvement of the supply of meat. Along the rivers are
extensive grassland areas that have never been exploited, which would
make excellent grazing lands for water buffalo. Experiments have
shown that water buffalo can also be given sago as an additional food.

To introduce water buffalo, the Siberut project will make breeding animals available on loan to different island communities in turn. Inland, each community will be encouraged to build ponds that can be stocked with fast-growing species of fish. Fry and equipment will be made available at the start. Fishing nets will be provided, and appropriate techniques will be taught to encourage exploitation of the rich coastal fishing grounds. Finally, an investigation will be made into pig and fowl epidemics, in the hope of developing vaccines to control them. Once meat and fish are more readily available, a limitation of hunting to a certain quota per *uma,* corresponding to the traditional amount hunted, can be more readily introduced.

Government plans to resettle people in coastal villages also merit reexamination. Such plans complicate the breeding of pigs, for example, which traditionally are kept upstream close to the fieldhouses. Coastal resettlement would also render traditional agricultural practices more difficult by increasing the distances between house and plantation. Resettlement programs were originally developed in Indonesia to cope with the phenomenon of shifting cultivation. This is not an issue in the case of the Mentawaians, however, since their agriculture is based on permanent sago and taro plantations. In fact, their agricultural methods are highly efficient and could probably support a much larger population (McNeely 1978:18). Since Indonesia does not produce enough foodstuffs for domestic consumption, long-term possibilities for exporting sago from Siberut to Sumatra can even be envisaged. At the same time, possibilities for rice cultivation should also be investigated. Another aim of the resettlement program, namely that of better communication, might be more easily and cheaply attained by constructing country roads than by relocating the entire population.

Even within a subsistence economy, modern developments (education, the acquisition of new tools, etc.) necessitate some flow of cash. Hitherto, the main cash crops on Siberut have been coconuts and rattan. In addition to these and perhaps sago as well, the possibility of raising nutmegs and cloves for export should be investigated. They can be grown with existing crops without any great difficulty. Tourism, which will inevitably not leave Siberut untouched, also merits attention. In conjunction with the World Wildlife Fund, plans have been prepared for two- and three-day guided tours to certain areas of scenic beauty, which will as far as possible bypass populated areas while still producing some income for the island. At all times, the guiding principle will be to exploit the possibilities of the island while relying as little as possible on external resources. In this way, adverse ecological consequences, which often attend the introduction of new elements into a closed environment, can be avoided.

To these economic objectives must be added another one: to stimulate the people's consciousness of their own cultural traditions, so that they can decide for themselves how to integrate these new elements into their future way of life. The project must assist the people to establish a way of life that will fulfill their material needs without damage to the environment and that will create and maintain a critical awareness of the value of their cultural identity within the context of the wider Indonesian community. The ultimate goal of the project must be to make external aid superfluous. In the end it must be the people themselves who, with their newly acquired awareness of belonging to a nation, determine how much they want to contribute to the rich cultural variety referred to in the motto of Indonesia's national emblem, "Unity in Diversity."

Notes

1. An earlier version of this paper was published in Schefold (1980), and a portion of it was included in Schefold (1979/1980). The author lived on Siberut from 1967 to 1969, carrying out anthropological fieldwork among the Sakuddei, a group living in the center of the island. A second visit was made in the autumn of 1974, during which the film *The Sakuddei* was made, in conjunction with a film team from Granada TV, London. (This film is available on request from the Survival International Office in London.) It is intended to show the changes to which the inhabitants of Siberut are increasingly exposed. The author made a third visit to Siberut in 1978 to prepare (among other things) for the Survival International project.

2. See Schefold (1980) for further details on the history of the project.

References Cited

Geertz, Clifford
  1963   "The Integrative Revolution: Primordial Sentiments and Civil Politics in the New States." In *Old Societies and New States: The Quest for Modernity in Asia and Africa,* edited by Clifford Geertz, Glencoe, Ill.: The Free Press.

Kis-Jovak, J. I.
  1979   *De traditionale architectuur van Siberut.* Delft: Volkenkundig Museum Nusantara.

McNeely, J. A. ·
  1978   Siberut: Conservation of Indonesia's Island Paradise. *Survival International* 3 (1): 18–20.

Mead, Margaret
    1970   "The Rights of Primitive Peoples." In *Cultures of the Pacific,* edited by
             T. G. Harding and B. J. Wallace. New York: The Free Press.

Schefold, Reimar
    1979–   *Speelgoed voor de Zielen/Spielzeug für die Seelen.* Delft: Volkenkundig
    1980   Museum Nusantara/Zurich: Museum Rietberg.

    1980   "The Siberut Project." *Survival International* 5 (1): 4–12.

PART IV: SOCIAL RELATIONS/ SOCIAL CHANGE

8. Social Rank and Social Change among the Maloh of West Kalimantan

Victor T. King

Abstract

The system of social inequality of the Maloh people of interior Kalimantan is examined in terms of the concepts of class, status, and power. A synchronic and functionalist interpretation of the traditional system of stratification reveals three politico-economic classes of aristocrats, commoners, and slaves; four named status levels of *samagat, pabiring, banua,* and *pangkam;* and two classificatory categories of "superior" and "inferior" people. A diachronic analysis of changes in this system indicates that the traditional system of ranks has been undermined and the former economic, symbolic, and political position of the aristocrats is now in question. Ascriptive inequality has been replaced by competition among Maloh for key resources that determine relative degrees of superiority and inferiority. These processes of change were initiated by Dutch political, administrative, and religious innovations in village society during the colonial period, and they were continued by the efforts of the postindependence Indonesian authorities to "democratize" village life.

Introduction

The Maloh are a distinctive Dayak population inhabiting the upper Kapuas region of the Indonesian province of West Kalimantan. In 1972–1973 they numbered about 11,000 people, and their villages were scattered along various tributaries of the upper Kapuas River, including the Leboyan, Embaloh, Lauh, Palin (Nyabau), Sibau, Mendalam, Mandai, Peniung, and Kalis, and along the Kapusa River itself above the regional adminitive center of Putus Sibau (Figs. 8.1 and 8.2). Their close neighbors are the culturally different Kantu', Iban, Kayan, Suruk, Mentebah, Punan, and Bukat. Maloh also have close contacts,

219

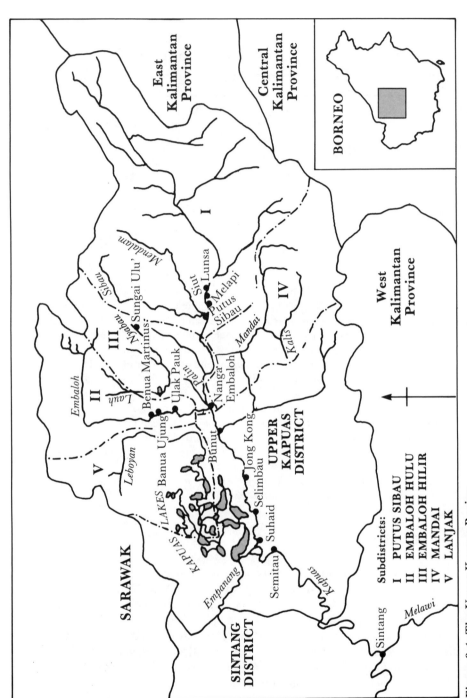

Figure 8.1 The Upper Kapuas Region

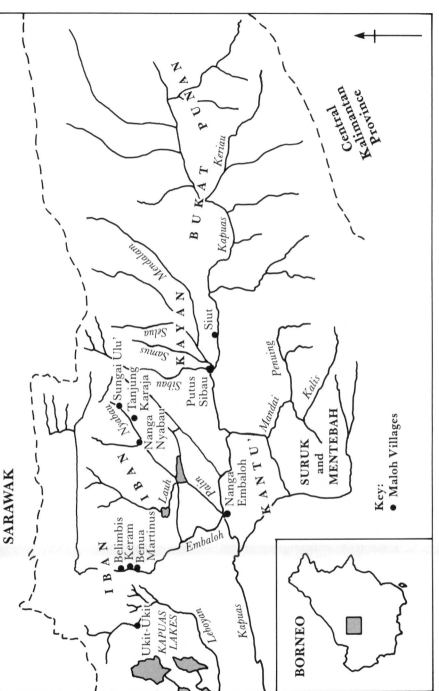

Figure 8.2 Important Maloh Villages and Surrounding Ethnic Groups

particularly of an economic kind, with the Chinese and Malays who dominate the trade of the area.

The Maloh economy is based on the shifting cultivation of dry rice, supplemented by a significant amount of swamp rice grown in water-logged areas. Most farms are located on rolling and gently undulating quaternary and tertiary formations that are covered in places by fertile alluvial soils. The Maloh are diligent and conscientious rice farmers. They also grow a variety of fruit and vegetable crops, either in or around their rice fields or in separate garden plots near their dwellings. Cultivated food crops are supplemented by jungle fruits and tubers. A vital source of protein is fish. Maloh keep domestic animals such as cows, pigs, goats, and fowl, most of which are sold, exchanged, or slaughtered for ritual purposes. Very rarely are domestic animals killed for daily food. Instead, animal meat is largely obtained from hunting wild animals such as feral pig, monkey, bear, and civet cat. The main sources of cash are tapping rubber, gathering tallow nuts, logging, and working for wages either locally or across the border in Sarawak.

The Maloh are probably the only indigenous Bornean people who have specialized in the manufacture of ornamental silverware; and this craft, probably more than any other cultural trait, distinguishes them from other ethnic groups. In the past, the main market for their wares were the Iban of Sarawak. Itinerant smiths traveled long distances to sell or exchange their goods. Recently this Maloh craft has been declining in importance because of falling demand for traditional adornments and associated competition from imported or Chinese-made bazaar jewelry. In the Sarawak literature Maloh are usually referred to in the context of their metal-working activities (Baring-Gould and Bampfylde 1909:18–19; Harrisson 1965:244; Hose and McDougall 1912:118–120, 253; Morrison 1948:249–255; St. John 1862:44), and in the Iban mind "Maloh" is virtually synonymous with "silversmith."

Maloh can also be distinguished from other Dayak by language, certain aspects of life crisis rites, particular oral traditions, and some items of material culture. But apart from silversmithing, stratification was the main distinguishing feature of Maloh society noted by early observers (Bouman 1924:179–180; Enthoven 1903:60, 64–65; Helbig 1939:72; Huijbers 1931:204–209, 237–243; 1932:151–162; 1934:93–104; Scheuer 1932:3; Werkman n.d.:11). The Maloh system of social stratification, which formerly comprised aristocrats, commoners, and slaves, was a major focus of my own fieldwork among them.[1] In this paper I will first describe the traditional ranking system and then analyze the changes that occurred in it, first during the Dutch colonial period and then following Indonesian independence.

I base my reconstruction and analysis of the traditional Maloh system of ranks on published literature, unpublished archival material, and verbal information collected during fieldwork. By "traditional" I mean the social system that existed prior to and during the early stages of Dutch colonial intervention in the Maloh area (viz., before about 1920). There are many problems inherent in any historical reconstruction of a preliterate society. I have relied to some extent on information supplied by present-day Maloh. The consciousness of the past may combine ideal with actuality, alter past events to fit with present ideas, and emphasize certain aspects of the society at the expense of others. Any informant presents a fragmented vision of the past colored by his or her interests, age, gender, and rank. Frequently, Maloh do not distinguish between "what was" and "what is," and some informants, especially aristocrats, stress the continuity of certain social and cultural institutions that to the outside observer have clearly disappeared or been radically altered. The data I have extracted from Dutch secondary sources are similarly fragments of a vast series of events, ideas, and personalities channeled through the senses of particular colonial observers with particular commitments and created as historical objects. While I recognize the contingency of social and cultural forms, I have brought together (rather like Lévi-Strauss' *bricoleur*)[2] bits and pieces of material from different time periods and orders of phenomena in an attempt to grasp synchronically the main features of the Maloh ranking system before European intervention began seriously to undermine it. The accuracy of this reconstruction is attested to by the considerable congruence among the data from both Dutch and Maloh sources. The justification for the reconstruction lies in the value of the past in illuminating the present. Without an appreciation of traditional Maloh society we cannot fully comprehend the form, content, and direction of changes in Maloh rank in the modern era (viz., 1920 to the early 1970s).

Following this reconstruction, my second task is to examine the effects of Dutch colonialism on Maloh society. In the early stages of Dutch colonial rule, Maloh aristocrats largely retained their privileged position in society, but gradually European policies undermined the system of ranks. I suggest that this was due more to politico-juridical and religious factors than to economic ones. However, I do not assume a simplistic cause-effect relationship between "external" dynamic forces and "internal" passive reaction. The Dutch, as well as eroding the traditional system of stratification, opened new channels of mobility by means of which individual Maloh responded dynamically to remodel elements of their social organization.

Finally, I examine Maloh stratification during the postcolonial era, first during the immediate postindependence period, and then, at greater length, during the early 1970s. I suggest that it is difficult to arrive at a clear picture of Maloh hierarchical groupings during this period because it is a changing situation in which some features of the traditional ranking system can still be found, while others have disappeared or been considerably modified.

My analysis of changes in the Maloh ranking system is based throughout on Weberian conceptual distinctions among class, status, and power (Weber 1947:424–429; 1971:250–264; and cf. Runciman 1969:45–63).[3] This tripartite division is employed to analyze different dimensions of rank and changes in analytically separable kinds of inequality. The three dimensions of rank are interrelated, but they do not necessarily coincide. Nor do the Maloh necessarily explicitly identify these dimensions and classify ranked social categories in these terms. The concepts "social stratification," "rank," and "ranking system" in this paper refer to the static placement of groups of individuals in vertically ranked strata based on such criteria as wealth, prestige, and political power; and the concept of "social inequality" refers to the process of unequal distribution of, and/or unequal command over, key resources such as material goods, labor, ritual objects, and knowledge and skills (cf. Béteille 1969:13).

The use of the Weberian scheme in investigating traditional Maloh stratification reveals three politico-economic classes—aristocrats, commoners, and slaves—and four named status levels—*samagat* (aristocrats), *pabiring* (middle rank or high commoners), *banua* (ordinary villagers or low commoners, together comprising a politico-economic class of commoners or freeman), and *pangkam* (slaves).

The Traditional Ranking System

Economic Aspects of Rank

In traditional Maloh society, aristocrats comprised the dominant economic class. They had significant control over labor resources since only they could own slaves. The slaves captured in war lived in their masters' households and performed domestic chores such as cleaning, washing, cooking, and collecting firewood. They also cleared and farmed the forest for the aristocrats, thus enabling the latter to establish rights to large areas of land, because the first felling of virgin forest gave rights to that land in perpetuity. Slaves could be exchanged for goods or used in bridewealth and in the payment of fines and ransoms. They could be summarily executed if they committed an offense, and aristocrats arranged their slaves' marriages and disposed of their children (A.S. 6 Jan. 1933).[4] Slaves also provided entertainment such as dancing and wrestling at festivals (Huijbers 1931:205).

The ability of aristocrats to impose fines on their villagers, coupled with the fact that fines due to aristocrats were higher than those for offenses against commoners (A.S. 26 July 1920; and cf. Whittier 1973:70–71), meant that the latter sometimes got into debt. Indeed, in interrank disputes the maxim was "Aristocrats always win." Those in debt to aristocrats might then become debt or field slaves. These lived in their own households and were allowed to farm and work for themselves, but they were subject to the whims of their masters. They could be called at any time to perform duties on his behalf, and they had to give tribute to their masters, in particular to help finance ceremonies. Theoretically, aristocrats also held the rights to the land that their debt slaves worked, and they could regulate their marriages also (cf. Morris 1980:305). The categories of debt slaves and captive slaves together constituted a separate class called *pangkam* (anything that is owned).[5] They were coerced into labor on behalf of aristocrats and treated as instruments of production.

The commoner class (both *pabiring* and *banua*) also had obligations to the aristocracy. Commoners had to offer to their headmen a portion of any game taken in the hunt and any fish caught within the village territory. They also had to contribute food and drink to village festivals. Of most importance, they had to perform corvées for the aristocrats (Enthoven 1903:64–65; Huijbers 1931:206). At the start of certain phases of the farming cycle (viz., clearing the forest, sowing, and harvesting) aristocrats were entitled to one day of corvée from every adult member of every household in the community (Huijbers 1931:204). No commoner household was allowed to commence that phase on its own farm until these labor services had been performed. Unlike slaves, commoners were not at the aristocrats' beck and call, however, and to a large extent they controlled their own productive activities and the product of their labor. Their corvées were seen as *mangoroki samagat* (assisting the aristocrats), done not at the command but at the invitation of the aristocrats.

Their control of labor and their rights to various prestations released the Maloh aristocracy from manual labor. They were a leisured class, though they did hunt and fish. They had the time to organize trading expeditions. They had rights in large areas of land. They possessed numerous valuable heirlooms such as gongs and jars (Huijbers 1931: 205). The surpluses that they commanded were used in trade, in financing impressive ceremonies (aristocrats provided the main ritual sacrifices of slaves and animals), and in high bridewealth payments.

Political Aspects of Rank

The Maloh aristocracy also comprised a ruling class. They controlled village politics. A Maloh village *(banua)* formerly consisted of one or more longhouses *(sau)*. These were massive wooden structures, well-fortified, raised on stilts, and containing a number of individual households occupying separate apartments. Village and longhouse headmen were always aristocrats. Indeed, the term for headman was *samagat*—the same term as that for the aristocratic rank as a whole. Conceptually the two were inseparable, because the headmanship was under the collective control of the aristocrats. All aristocrats participated in decision making. They selected the headman from among their number and they benefited from the advantages attached to his office. They could also remove an unsatisfactory headman. In villages consisting of one longhouse, the house headman was by definition also village headman. In a multilonghouse village, only one of the house headmen served as village headman. He was referred to as *indu' banua* (mother of the village). Again, the *indu' banua* was selected by all the aristocrats. Sometimes the office rotated among the aristocrats of the village's constituent longhouses.

The village was defined primarily in territorial and residential terms. Each village had its own broadly recognized boundaries, usually demarcated by natural features such as streams and watersheds. As custodian of the village estate, the headman settled all disputes over its use (Huijbers 1931:205–206). He also had the power to confiscate his own villagers' property should they displease him, retaining it for his own use or redistributing it to others as he wished. If outsiders wanted to exploit a portion of the unclaimed village estate, they had to obtain the headman's permission and give him an agreed upon percentage of the agricultural or natural products extracted (A.S. 10 May 1921; Enthoven 1903:69). In a very real sense the territorial integrity of the village was maintained by, and expressed in, the position of this aristocrat cum headman. The village territory was seen as aristocratic "property." However, territory was virtually useless without people to exploit it, so an important aristocratic prerogative was control over the movement of villagers. Village members could not move out of the community without the headman's permission and without paying him a *sarakan paulun* (fine) (A.S. 4 July 1919). The crucial role of the laboring classes is also seen in the term for a village—*banua*—which is also one of the words used to refer to low commoners, who constituted the majority of the population. An alternative term for low commoners—*suang sau* (contents of the longhouse)—has a similar connotation.

The aristocrats, represented by the headman, were custodians of customary law. They played a conspicuous and crucial role in village discussions. Any adult from the lower strata, with the exception of slaves, could also voice an opinion, but the views of the aristocrats and a few prominent commoners carried the most weight. These influential commoners, called *tau rá* (big men), assisted aristocrats and sat on a council of elders (cf. Rousseau 1974:417–427). These nonaristocratic elders consisted of the most capable *pabiring* and *banua*, who had established reputations for economic success, wisdom, oratory, knowledge of customary law, fair-mindedness, generosity, and bravery in war. These big men rubbed shoulders with aristocrats, but unlike them their position was achieved and not ascribed. More important, their main political role was in mediating minor legal disputes between commoners, sometimes with the intervention of aristocrats, and in guarding the commoners against aristocratic abuse of power. The council of elders, in particular the aristocrats, handled extravillage relations involving such matters as intercommunity crimes (e.g., theft, injury, murder). The headman and other aristocrats were also the most important war leaders, and it was they who mobilized forces to raid for slaves and heads. The aristocracy were not only responsible for protecting their village but also for negotiating peace settlements between villages. One of the main mechanisms for ending hostilities was intervillage marriage between aristocrats.

While the aristocracy was drawn together by common bonds of kinship, alliance, and mutual interest, it was occasionally driven apart by the conflicting personal ambitions of its members. One of the main causes for community fission was conflict between aristocrats in the same village or house (cf. Rousseau 1979:299–300). Sometimes, disagreement between the headman and another aristocrat might lead to a decision to split the longhouse (A.S. 14 May 1936). This could only be done by members of the aristocracy. The usurper had to secure a following before he could form a viable house, and this was done by capitalizing on any ill will that the commoners felt toward their current headman (A.S. 4 June 1931). Although such conflicts within the aristocracy were by no means uncommon, they were not responsible for the historic decline in the aristocrats' capacity to operate as a ruling class.

Symbolic Aspects of Rank

The aristocracy as a political-economic class was differentiated from the other strata by a host of status symbols, which were largely religious or cosmological in nature. The aristocracy was considered sacred by reason of their descent from founding ancestors and legendary heroes and by their possession of heirlooms invested with supernatural powers. They kept long and detailed genealogies *(tutulan),* and the deeds of aristocratic heroes and heroines were glorified in long sagas. As descendants of ancestral spirits who were still invoked in important ceremonies, aristocrats—represented by the headman—were essential par-

Maloh Boat in Route to a Ceremony at Another Village

Maloh Girls Wearing Their Finest Beadwork and Silverware

ticipants in ritual. The headman addressed and made offerings to supernatural beings in rituals associated with, for example, the building of a new longhouse (A.S. 11 Aug. 1920), the construction of a new village charnel house or deathhouse *(kulambu)* (A.S. 25 July 1920), and the agricultural cycle. During such ceremonies the aristocrats sat either on gongs or on specially elevated seats (Huijbers 1931:205). Distinctions were also made between ranks in rites of passage: symbols appropriate to one's status level were displayed at birth, marriage, and death. During marriage ceremonies, the items of bridewealth passed from the groom's family to the bride's were differentiated according to rank (A.S. July 1930). When aristocrats died, slaves were sometimes sacrificed to accompany them to the land of the dead (Harrisson 1965:147, 339–340). Their coffins were decorated with aristocratic motifs and were placed either on high shelves in the village deathhouse or in a separate deathhouse draped with silk cloth. They were also entitled to long and onerous mourning prohibitions, which were observed by the whole village.

These ritual distinctions were reflected in a variety of cosmological symbols. Certain designs painted on coffins, offering trays, deathhouses, canoes, longhouse posts, and apartment walls were specific to the aristocrats. The main elements in Maloh art were human bodies and faces, dragons, and hornbills. The human motif was the sole preserve of aristocrats. It represented a slave, and only aristocrats possessed slaves. The face design was employed by both aristocrats and high commoners but never by low commoners. Only an aristocrat could use a full dragon design, while high commoners could use the dragon's head on their coffins, offering trays, apartment walls, and support posts; low commoners who had proven themselves in war could display it on their coffins and offering trays. Finally, the hornbill motif was permitted to aristocrats on their coffins, offering trays, apartment walls, and support posts; a less elaborate hornbill design was allowed on the coffins, trays, walls, and posts of high commoners and on the coffins and offering trays of very worthy low commoners.

Various items of clothing and bodily adornment were also symbols of rank. Tiger teeth, worn in the upper shell of the ear, were reserved exclusively for male aristocrats, as were war cloaks made of the skin of the orangutan, sun bear, and clouded leopard. All male commoners who had been on headhunting expeditions could wear leopard teeth (in their ear lobes) and cloaks or tunics made from the skin of lower animals such as the civet cat, monkey, and gibbon. Aristocrats wore the long feathers of the helmeted hornbill in their headdresses, while high commoners, as well as low commoners who had distinguished themselves as warriors or shamans, could use the feathers of the rhinoceros hornbill.

The households of aristocrats and high commoners were situated toward the upstream end of the house. The Maloh view upstream regions as sources of goodness, health, and life. They are also the homes of benevolent spirits and, in Maloh cosmology, associated with the upper world. Aristocrats and high commoners, who are classified as *tau mam* (good people),[6] were associated with this upper world, as they were also associated with warfare, bravery, and strength (Huijbers 1931:206; 1934:94). Strength was in turn associated with the male gender, the right hand, and the sun. Weakness, the female gender, the left hand, and the moon were, by contrast, associated with low commoners, who were categorized as *tau ajau* (bad people). Their longhouse apartments were situated downstream of those of the high commoners, just as the village's deathhouse was downstream of the village itself. In Maloh cosmology downstream regions lead to the sea, the land of the dead, and the underworld. The ranking system was thus linked to, and hence supported by, a perpetual and universal cosmological and sacred order. The association between this order and the ranking system was not always unequivocal, however. The rank of high commoner, which was so critical to the maintenance of the overall system of rank, stood in an ambiguous position with respect to the cosmological order. In certain symbolic usages the high commoners were assimilated to aristocratic rank, while in other usages they were like low commoners.

Dynamic Aspects of Rank

In practice, the stratification of Maloh society was not rigid. Low-ranking but able and enterprising individuals could attain prestige in their communities through becoming big men, warriors, or shamans, or by sponsoring, organizing, or playing a key role in major ceremonies.[7] While prestige could be earned, however, high rank could not. Ultimately, rank could be altered only through marriage. Most marriages followed a rule of rank endogamy, which sustained the ideological and practical exclusiveness of ranks (A.S. 3, 11 June 1920; Huijbers 1931: 206).[8] Despite this rule, there were always some interrank marriages. For example, a high-ranking man might take a low-ranking wife if he was unable to muster sufficient resources for bridewealth, a situation that might be caused by, for example, disownment by his parents (Huijbers 1931:207) or a sharp decline in his family fortunes (A.S. 1 Aug. 1924). In such marriages it was the children of the marriage who benefited or suffered in terms of changing rank position and not the parties to the marriage (or their own parents), for the ranks of the latter did not change. A Maloh man of low rank could, for example, gain prestige by marrying into a higher rank or by contracting a marriage for his daughter to someone of high rank, but this gain would not encompass a change in rank for him or his daughter. One inherited rank, one did not achieve it, even through marriage. The child of an interrank marriage, however, took the rank of the parent in whose household he or she was born.

Interrank marriage complicated the ranking system and led, in practice, to gradations within ranks and to a blurring of rank boundaries, which were theoretically rigid. However, it was a necessary mechanism to bring rank levels into line with the changing economic and political fortunes of the members of Maloh society. It maintained the given structure of the society by allowing enterprising individuals to channel their energies into acquiring higher rank for their descendants rather than challenging the existing system. Interrank marriages also provided a means of demoting "failed" aristocrats (cf. Rousseau 1979:230). Decline in an aristocratic household's economic and political position was often followed by marriages with people of lower rank. After a few generations the household concerned would be reclassified as "high commoner" (Huijbers 1934:94).

The dynamic aspect of rank is best seen in the context of the high-commoner rank *(pabiring)*. Terminologically, symbolically, and legally distinct, this status level was, in a very real sense, transitional between aristocrat and low commoner. *Pabiring* means "those at the edge, those on the sides" and, indeed, *pabiring* was a middle rank comprised of both fallen aristocrats and aspiring commoners.[9] As noted earlier, the *pabiring* were grouped with the aristocrats with respect to some rank symbols, although in terms of class they were clearly more like the low commoners. They worked their own fields and cooperated with the low commoners in ad hoc work groups when sowing, weeding, and harvesting. They also intermarried with upwardly mobile low commoners. Like these latter, the high commoners had to make prestations of both goods and labor to the aristocrats, and they similarly had no say in the selection of the headman.

The high-commoner rank can be interpreted as a means to accommodate social movement between ranks and so to maintain them all as an ongoing system. Such movement (whether upward or downward) may also have served to regulate any increase or decrease in the population of any one rank relative to the others. Despite the possible functions fulfilled by the high-commoner rank, however, its members were in an ambiguous position. Huijbers indicated that all high commoners he knew could trace at least some descent lines to aristocrats (1934:94). Some high commoners had aristocratic names; some played a role in legal disputes and in organizing major ceremonies; and some even maintained that they were still aristocrats. Huijbers cited the case of one

Sanggum, for example, a high commoner who "claims he is fully royal and who tries to get his subjects back" (1934:94–95).

Rousseau's remarks on the Kayan *hipuy* are relevant to the Maloh *pabiring*. He argues that this middle rank is important at the "structural level," that it is "essential to the *reproduction* of the system because it protects the ideology which justifies the structure of inequality" (1979: 232). In other words, this intermediate rank maintains the distance between the dominant group and the bulk of the population, while also regulating the number of aristocrats and permitting the removal of non-functional aristocrats. In the absence of this rank, changing socioeconomic circumstances would have caused some aristocrats to become low commoners (and vice versa) in a relatively short time. This direct transformation would have made it more difficult to sustain an ideology that posited an intrinsic difference between aristocrats and commoners.

Regional Aspects of Rank

The system of rank was also partly maintained by external means. The Maloh lived downstream from forest nomads such as Punan, Bukat, and Bukitan. The Maloh acted as middlemen between these nomads and the Malay and the Chinese traders from further downriver. The Maloh exchanged such items as tobacco, salt, iron, and cloth from the latter for forest produce and handicrafts from the former.[10] On the Maloh side, this trade was run by those of aristocratic rank, which helped them to maintain their economic position. In addition, the aristocrats replenished their supply of slaves by raids against these same nomads. Relations with surrounding settled Dayak cultivators such as Kayan and Iban also supported the ranking system. Maloh aristocrats contracted marriages with the leading families of other Dayak communities in order to cement alliances, maintain political relations, and secure external sources of power. One function of the Maloh aristocracy, therefore, was to regulate relations with potentially hostile neighbors.

Among the Maloh's external ties, those with Muslim Malays were perhaps the most important. The Malays were concentrated in trading and fishing settlements at the mouths of the main tributaries of the Kapuas, such as at Bunut (Fig. 8.2). The majority of the upper Kapuas Malay population derived not from Malay migration into the area but from local Dayaks (including Maloh) who converted to Islam and became Malay. The pace of such conversions accelerated in the nineteenth century. One of the reasons for Maloh conversions to Islam was mutually advantageous alliances between Malay rulers and Maloh aristocrats. Such alliances were normally cemented by marriage and a gift of slaves from Maloh to Malay. The Malay rajah might marry a woman from a leading Maloh family or receive a male aristocrat to wed his daughter.[11] In this way the rajah gained allies and ensured trading relations, while the Maloh leaders enhanced their political and economic position with the promise of external support, protection, and favorable terms of trade. If a Maloh aristocrat moved on marriage to a Malay settlement under these circumstances, then he (or she) became Muslim. On occasion, ambitious aristocrats deprived of the headmanship, or aristocrats who were in danger of falling in rank, moved away, married Malays, and converted to Islam as an expression of their discontent with the prevailing Maloh social order. There were also some dissatisfied commoners who fled their villages and turned to Islam for salvation. Finally, there was some actual proselytizing by the Malays, particularly those living in the upper Kapuas state of Bunut.

As with their external relations with other Dayak, Maloh relations with Malays in general supported rather than undermined their ranking system. Islam and Malay culture provided a different set of values for some of the prestige-seeking and power conscious aristocrats, as well as for those aristocrats and commoners who were dissatisfied with, and/ or who had failed in, their own society and culture. These opportunities in the Malay communities did not threaten Maloh society, rather they drew disaffected elements out of it. In addition, trade and alliance with the Malays enabled the Maloh aristocrats to strengthen their position in situ.

The Colonial Era

The Dutch Government

The advent of the Dutch was primarily responsible for transforming Maloh society, in particular the ranking system. Despite Dutch mercantile contacts with the West Borneo coastal sultanates of Sukadana and Sambas dating from the seventeenth century, it was only after the Anglo-Dutch Convention of 1814 and the brief British interregnum in the Indies that the Dutch began to take any real interest in interior Borneo (Veth 1854:xxxvii). The first journeys of exploration along the Kapuas were carried out in the 1820s by such people as L. C. Hartmann and George Müller (Enthoven 1903:127, 160, 179, 190; Posewitz 1892:19–20). Then the Java War (1825–1830) and the financial burden it placed on the Netherlands Indies government forced a cutback in activities in Borneo. Subsequent Dutch involvement in the "culture system" in Java prolonged this period of neglect in Borneo until the 1840s (Veth 1856:443). The establishment of James Brooke's

Sarawak in 1841 and the fear of the southward extension of British power and influence in Borneo revived Dutch interest in their Borneo possessions. Accordingly, the Dutch government began in 1843 to sponsor further journeys of exploration and also began in 1846 to establish an administrative framework for the interior (Irwin 1967:156). As part of this exercise, treaties were concluded with the various Malay states along the Kapuas (Enthoven 1903:96). The Maloh villages did not fall within the sphere of influences of any of these states, so they were placed (theoretically) under the direct rule of the Dutch (Enthoven 1903:55).

The main objective of the Dutch was to extend their political control in the interior.[12] To this end one of their priorities was to establish law and order and stamp out headhunting (Ozinga 1940:79). Their attempts to combat intertribal hostilities were chiefly directed against the Iban. They considered peoples such as the Maloh and Kayan relatively peaceable. In addition, the Maloh villages had early acknowledged Dutch authority, partly to ensure protection from raids by Sarawak Iban. To help finance their administration, the Dutch established some control over trade and introduced taxes. In 1857, for example, they appointed the Maloh headman of the village of Ulak Pauk as the collector of government taxes on forest products for the Embaloh region. He received no salary but was entitled to a small percentage of the taxes he received (Salam 1936:16).

Initially, these administrative and legal innovations (instituted from the 1850s onward) were only indifferently and sporadically put into practice among the Maloh. European personnel were few in number, and until the end of the nineteenth century the Dutch were preoccupied with troubles elsewhere. They had to put down two Malay rebellions in the middle Kapuas in 1859 and 1864 (Niclou 1887:44–47), and throughout the 1870s and 1880s they had to deal with Iban headhunting and migration in the northern areas bordering on Sarawak. By the 1890s, therefore, despite Dutch policy statements to the contrary, government involvement in the local affairs of the Maloh in the Leboyan, Embaloh, and Palin rivers had been relatively slight. The aristocracy carried out some government orders but, for example, in the Palin River area, the Dutch officials visited villages so infrequently that headmen had little inclination to cooperate with Europeans (Enthoven 1903:60, 69–70).[13] Thus, up to the 1890s the Maloh to the north of the Kapuas River watershed retained a considerable degree of autonomy. The appointment of some aristocrats as tax collectors and administrators during this period served only to consolidate the traditional power structure.

It was not until 1895 that the Dutch established a district officer at Putus Sibau, in charge of a newly created Upper Kapuas administrative subdivision, which included all of the Maloh areas of settlement (Enthoven 1903:56). The first household tax on Dayak was introduced there on 1 January 1896. It comprised 2 percent of a household's income with a minimum assessment of one guilder per year (Enthoven 1903:57, 92). To ensure tax collection in the Embaloh region, the Dutch established a small fort at Benua Ujung with a corporal in charge. In addition, "village service" was introduced, whereby every adult had to contribute to the upkeep of footpaths and bridges in the village territory (Werkman n.d.:3). Larger projects such as road construction were accomplished by paying local workers a small wage. This taxation and paid work resulted in the gradual introduction of money into the region.

This extension of Dutch control eventually had a marked impact on the role of aristocrats in Maloh society. This was in part because the aristocracy was co-opted into the colonial administration to collect taxes and administer local justice, at the same time as their traditional roles as war leaders and slave owners were weakened by the Dutch interdiction of intertribal warfare. The Dutch also legislated out of existence the aristocrats' jurisdiction over the crime of homicide as well as their powers of life and death over slaves. The Dutch officially abolished slavery in 1896, although the institution hung on until the 1920s and 1930s. Eventually, the Dutch even eliminated the prerogative of aristocrats to fine commoners who wished to leave their village (Bouman 1924:178–180).

The Catholic Church

Apart from the political, administrative, and legal innovations set in motion by the colonial government, a number of important changes were brought about by Christian missionary activity. To ensure continued peace in the area, especially in Iban territory, the Dutch controllor of Semitau suggested that the "civilizing" influence of Christianity might accomplish more than the use of military force. In 1908 he succeeded in getting the Roman Catholic Capuchin order to establish a mission at Lanjak in Iban territory (Maxandrea 1924:176–177). But the enterprise failed, with the priests deciding that the Maloh in the nearby Leboyan and Embaloh offered the best opportunities for conversion. In 1913 the Capuchins established a mission at Benua Martinus, between the villages of Benua Ujung and Keram along the Embaloh River (A.S. April 1913). Situated in the center of the Embaloh area and on a main route to the Leboyan River system, the missionaries had an accessible base among a relatively large, stable, established population (in marked contrast to the priests' experience with scattered, mobile Iban living in remote hill country).[14] By December 1913, eighty-eight baptisms had been performed in the Embaloh area. The first church burial took place in 1916 (A.S. 22 Sept. 1916) and the first church wedding in 1917 (A.S. 16 March 1917). In 1918 the church took the first steps leading to the eventual abandonment of the Maloh charnel houses (A.S. 27 May 1918; 18 Aug. 1924).

Some Maloh aristocrats were anxious to accept Christianity and education. They saw it in their interests to cooperate with the Dutch and thereby secure continued protection from the Iban. In addition, they felt that since the Dutch were obviously more powerful than the Malays, their religion was thus more prestigious than Islam (A.S. 21 July 1920). Indeed, conversion to Islam decreased among the Maloh after the introduction of Dutch missions. While the aristocrats saw conversion to Christianity as one means of maintaining and even strengthening their position, some Maloh commoners saw it as an opportunity to end their obligations to the aristocracy.

Christianity undermined the whole range of practices and beliefs related to the traditional Maloh ranking system. Although the Dutch officially abolished slavery in the 1890s, for example, it was mainly the preaching and actions of the missionaries that led to its later, de facto disappearance from Maloh society (A.S. 30 Jan. 1920). Over time the ritual legitimation and expression of aristocratic superiority and sacredness was also challenged as a result of the broader challenge to Maloh religion by the missionaries. The traditional ranking system was challenged directly as well. The Dutch missionaries clearly disliked the Maloh ranking system, in particular the practice of arranged marriages within ranks (A.S. 8 Nov. 1935), differential fines according to rank (Huijbers 1932:162; 1934:94), and slavery. They saw these institutions as "brutal," "primitive," "pagan," and "foolish"; and the priests communicated and enforced government edicts relating to them. In addition, the missionaries made their protection and assistance available to those who thought they had been mistreated or fined unfairly by aristocrats and to young people who did not wish to be a party to an arranged marriage (e.g., A.S. 8 June, 2 July, 8 Dec. 1919; 26 July 1920; 19 Jan., 4 July, 26 July, 15 Aug. 1921).

In time, some commoners realized that acquiring European education and religion was an alternative means to acquire wealth, status, and power not only outside of but also within Maloh society. The Catholic missionaries had considerable success in education. A government subsidized mission school for boys was opened in November 1914 in Martinus (A.S. Jan. 1920), and in 1917 the mission began to take girls for instruction in domestic subjects (A.S. July 1921). The children who received mission education began to question traditional authority. Particular issues of conflict were arranged marriages, respect for elders and for *adat* customary law, and the various services due to aristocrats. The conversion of some Maloh, especially commoners, also led to a certain amount of village schism. Tensions between pagans and others often revolved around the problem of which *adat* rulings to apply to Christians if they avoided customary obligations (e.g., A.S. 30 Nov. 1920). However, while conflict between pagans and Christians accelerated the breakup of some longhouses (Burgemeestre 1934:6), village cohesion was already in decline as a result of the cessation of intertribal hostility and the removal of longhouse fortifications.

Rubber Cultivation

The role of economic forces in transforming the traditional Maloh ranking system during the colonial era has not been stressed here, but some economic changes must be mentioned. The most important of these was the development of rubber cultivation. The rubber tree was introduced into West Borneo in 1909 (Uljee 1925:74), and Dutch priests began to cultivate it in Martinus in 1915 (A.S. 18 Jan. 1915). It was quickly adopted by the Maloh and grown on a smallholder basis. Rubber provided a source of cash with which the Maloh could pay their taxes, buy their children's school supplies, and purchase trade goods. This cash cropping facilitated the social leveling of the Maloh. Many commoners initially used the proceeds from their rubber groves to raise their positions in the ranking system, but as consumer goods became increasingly available and as the ranking system began to decline in importance, cash was used instead to buy goods or to set up in trade. Traditional heirlooms, some of which had been used as symbols of rank in bridewealth, in *adat* fines, and in ritual, slowly lost their significance as people began to sell or exchange them for consumer goods.

The Postindependence Era

The above changes continued and in some cases accelerated after the departure of the Dutch, the brief Japanese interregnum, and the winning of Indonesian independence in 1949. During the subsequent years, as the government bureaucracy grew apace, many Dayak became government workers. By 1972–1973 the district offices at Putus Sibau and Sintang were employing a number of Maloh men, and in Martinus the subdistrict officer and his staff were all local Maloh. Maloh even occupied some provincial posts in Pontianak. The greater opportunities in government have led to a change in values among young Maloh, to greater physical mobility to pursue education and paid work, and to a further diminution in the prerogatives of traditional rank. But offices and schools have not spawned a new, separate class of Maloh. Salaries are nominal, payment is often delayed, and office hours are short and irregular. Male office employees and teachers typically live in their home territories and work their own rice fields and rubber gardens. In general, government salaries are no more than a useful supplement to other sources of income for low-level, white-collar workers.

Two positions that existed under the Dutch administration, village headman and *adat* chief, were continued in the postindependence era. During colonial times these positions were reserved for aristocrats, but independence saw the introduction of democratic elections and literacy requirements for candidates.[15] Even so, aristocrats continued to dominate the position of *adat* chief, and some of them became elected headmen as well (although the government insisted that they now be called by the Malay term *kepala kampung* (village head), and not by the traditional Maloh term, *samagat,* with its connotations of rank. Many commoners were also elected headmen, but the impact of such election was diluted by the fact that modern headmen have little real power, command only a nominal salary, and are vulnerable to being voted out of office. Indeed, there has often been a dearth of willing candidates for election to this office.

These several political and administrative changes led to an *adat* conference in the Embaloh valley in 1970, the intent of which was to democratize Maloh society by reformulating customary law, equalizing fines and bridewealth, and eliminating rank differentials in rites of passage. The resulting regulations formally acknowledged some changes that had already taken place and introduced new ones as well. By 1972 these changes had not yet been completely accepted by some Maloh (viz., along the Leboyan and Palin rivers), but negotiations were still in progress.

The Maloh Today

By 1972–1973 it was no longer possible to discern traditional politico-economic classes of aristocrats, commoners, and slaves in Maloh society, nor was it yet possible to discern any newly formed classes. Maloh society was in transition, certain trends of which can be highlighted. Differences in control over labor and other resources no longer differentiate economic classes of aristocrats, commoners, and slaves. With the elimination of corvées and the abolition of slavery, aristocrats have increasingly had to work in their fields like everyone else, with the result that by 1972–1973 they no longer constituted a leisured class. Although a stigma still attaches to some people of slave descent, it is forbidden in Maloh law to call someone publicly a slave or a descendant of a slave. Former slaves have increasingly acquired rights to land, intermarried with ordinary villagers, and now identify themselves as commoners.

Economic Aspects of Rank

In 1972–1973 I attempted to determine whether there remained significant wealth differences between aristocrats and others.[16] It was difficult to arrive at a clear picture as regards household rights in land, because most rights were shared by groups of individuals *(kapulungan)* tracing descent from a common ancestor who had originally cleared the forest. However, I collected approximate data on income and sources of income from thirty households in one Embaloh village (here called village X) and supplemented them with more superficial data from three other villages—one other village in the Embaloh valley, one in the Leboyan valley, and one in the Palin valley. These data pertain to household production and consumption of rice in 1972–1973 and the income from the sale or exchange of fruit, vegetables, rubber, tallow nuts, and animals; from paid labor in teaching, office work, logging, and agricultural work; and from trade and shopkeeping. In addition, data were gathered on the size and quality of dwellings and the material goods contained in them.[17] The overall findings suggest that while wealth is obviously an indicator of class position, any differentiation of people in terms of their wealth alone is necessarily based on arbitrary divisions that cannot be equated with "classes" (Table 8.1). There are three reasons for this.

Table 8.1. Association between Rank and Wealth

Household Wealth (in rupiahs)	Household Rank		
	Aristocrat	High Commoner	Low Commoner
> 600,000 rp	1	0	4
450,000–600,000 rp	1	1	1
300,000–450,000 rp	0	1	9
150,000–300,000 rp	0	1	6
< 150,000 rp	0	0	5

Note: Household wealth is based both on annual income and the value of household property.
N = 30 Maloh households
$X_c^2 = .733$
$P < .99$

First, the households within each category (or within any two adjacent categories) do not see themselves as forming a distinct group in relation to the households in any other category, either in terms of ideology or in terms of preferential marriage patterns. The two aristocratic households, in the two highest wealth categories in the sample, still try to set themselves apart from the rest of the village; but these attempts are based more on their status as aristocrats and less on their status as wealthy people, and they are unsuccessful in any case. Some commoners maintain that there is no longer any basis for, or logic to, the doctrine of aristocratic superiority—not in terms of wealth, type and pattern of work, birth, education, or political power. This reality is reflected in the absence of a stated desire, among any of the wealthy commoners in village X, to marry into aristocratic households.

The second reason for not equating these wealth categories with classes is that they are quite fluid. For example, the eight households in the upper two categories in the sample were placed there on the basis of data gathered in 1972. Some of these households would not have been placed there if the data had been gathered instead in 1971 or 1973. This largely subsistence-based economy is characterized by considerable short- and long-term fluctuations in the fortunes of individual households. Unforeseen illness or death, periodic social commitments such as marriage, and varying environmental conditions such as drought and crop pests all can dramatically affect household income. The new economic opportunities, though still secondary to rice cultivation, have magnified this fluid situation. So no group of households in village X has yet been able to consolidate a position of economic superiority.

Third, none of these wealth categories can be defined as a class in terms of productive relations and the division of labor. Formerly the aristocracy were a leisured class with control over labor and the slaves were workers with no control over labor. But by the 1970s all households in village X were equally involved in farming. There is no distinct rentier or landowning class. Every household has farming rights in at least some area of land. Furthermore, no segment of the village population is released from manual labor. The wealthiest households (viz., in categories 1 and 2) do not all employ farm labor; and those that did so in 1972–1973 did not all do so in either the following or preceding season. In any case, only households short of rice in a given year will consider working for others, and since most Maloh households only find themselves in this position on an irregular basis, they only seek out employment on an irregular basis. Moreover, villagers who need to secure extra income often travel to other areas to find better paid work than is available within their community. It is neighboring Iban, rather than Maloh, who are usually drawn into the Maloh economic system as hired farm laborers.

Thus, the contemporary, wealth-based divisions of Maloh society cannot be equated with classes; nor do they equate with the traditional class divisions of this society. The correlation between wealth differences and traditional rank in the sample is far from being significant at the .05 level (Table 8.1). Similarly, in one village close to village X, the two most wealthy households are both of low commoner rank. The head of one is a teacher at the Catholic school who, using his contacts with the church, secured a loan on favorable terms to buy a small motorboat and set himself up as a trader. The other household has three males who work periodically in the logging industry, and the head of the household is a Sunday school teacher who also has two large rubber gardens. Neither of these households has any desire to marry with aristocrats since, being strong Catholics, they do not value that traditional status. In another village in the Leboyan valley, the aristocratic households have declined to the point that the village is dominated by four Catholic households, all of whom are wealthy high commoners. The head of one of them is headman of the village, and a young man in another has been trained as a bible teacher. Two of these households are also involved in trade. Thus, small-scale traders and a number of teachers and government employees (some of whom have close contacts with the Catholic church) have all been able to acquire a degree of wealth outside the traditional class system. These new groups, rather than intermarry with aristocrats, have mainly tried to deny and undermine the traditional criteria of status. The ability to make an effective claim to high status has increasingly come to depend on economic success, political position, education, Catholicism, and "white-collar" employment, and not so much on hereditary rank. The partial exception seems to be in the more isolated Palin River valley, where traditional status still carries some weight, and where some economically successful people of lower rank still marry into aristocratic circles.

Political Aspects of Rank

The decline in aristocratic dominance, and the challenge from new groups, is also evident in the political arena. Democratic elections for village headmanship have resulted in a number of commoners becoming headmen, as noted earlier. Among the twelve current villages in the Embaloh valley, only three headmen come from aristocratic households; three come from the households of high commoners, and the remaining six come from low commoner households. Even in the remote Palin valley, one of four villages has a low commoner headman and another, which was headed by an aristocrat in 1973, had been previously headed by a man of low commoner rank. In contrast to village headmanship, however, the aristocracy has continued to retain control of the position of *adat* law chief.

In addition to changes in the rank of the people who occupy these various offices, there have been changes in the scope and responsibilities of the offices themselves. One dramatic change in village headmanship has been the reduction in the range of the headman's powers. The village today is the lowest administrative unit in the wider local, regional, and national political systems, and consequently the headman is subordinate to all those above him in the government bureaucracy. His immediate superior, apart from the *adat* law chief (whose powers have also been curtailed), is the subdistrict officer, who is usually appointed from outside the region. Neither the headman nor any other traditional leader has control any longer over the movements of the villagers. Travel passes are now vetted and issued by the local subdistrict officer and by military patrol posts. Nor do the local leaders any longer have a monopoly on the use of physical force in intervillage affairs. Even within the village they cannot exact physical punishment on guilty parties. Extravillage government officials have jurisdiction over crimes such as homicide; and even disputes involving such crimes as theft, adultery, and assault, which are still largely the preserve of village headmen and *adat* law chiefs, may lead to the intervention of the subdistrict officer or the police. Further, the former association of headmanship with the spiritual integrity and physical well-being of the village has been gradually severed, and with it the supernatural sanctions that headmen could traditionally apply. Once the aristocracy—which was formerly seen as responsible for the maintenance of a balance between the human and supernatural worlds—no longer monopolized village headmanship, the religious aspects of village leadership were undermined.

These changes have resulted in the common complaint among headmen and *adat* law chiefs that theirs is a thankless task. The general feeling is that the meager rewards of office are hardly adequate compensation for the stresses and strains incurred. The headman, in particular, is in an ambivalent position in contemporary Maloh society. He is a government officer who must at times enforce unpopular government edicts. In addition, he must reconcile customary law with new government regulations, with Catholic mores, and with the values emerging from secular education. In the absence of traditional sanctions, the headman must secure a much wider measure of agreement for his decisions than formerly, which vastly complicates the governing process.

The ambiguities and dubious rewards of headmanship mean that men are often reluctant to run for the post and that elected headmen are frequently turned out by dissatisfied voters. For these reasons the headmanship has not been greatly sought out by aristocrats desiring to recoup their lost political power, although it is still one possible avenue for the social advancement of commoners.

The question remains: Does the aristocracy play an indirect but nevertheless influential role in village politics? In village meetings and internal legal disputes, some aristocrats who are not headmen do play an active role in the discussion of precedent and the fine points of customary law. Other aristocrats, however, appear to have ceded any political voice they might have had. In terms of political power as in terms of wealth, therefore, there is no longer a clearly defined ruling class. New sources of knowledge and legitimacy have entered into village decision-making processes. The aristocracy still has some influence because of their knowledge of customary law and their retention of the position of *adat* law chief, but increasingly they must justify this influence in terms of such criteria as education, literacy, former employment in government offices, knowledge of new government procedures, and achievements in the economic sphere. They do this perforce, in the face of challenges from enterprising commoners who have become shopkeepers, teachers, headmen, and government employees.

Symbolic Aspects of Rank

The parallel between the decline of the aristocracy's political power and the decline of their ritual status has already been noted. This is explained by the increasing number of headmen from commoner ranks and by the consequent weakening of the association between the ritual well-being of the village and the well-being of its headman cum aristocrat. Furthermore, to the extent that aristocrats no longer monopolize the position of headman, they can no longer play a crucial organizational and supervisory role in large-scale rituals. In any case, the traditional villagewide ceremonies, performed at various stages of the agricultural cycle and supervised by aristocrats, are being replaced by small-scale rites conducted by individual households.

This decline in the ritual preeminence of the aristocracy has gone hand in hand with the waning of the oral traditions that formerly expressed and validated it. In the Embaloh and Leboyan valleys, old people remember much of their oral tradition; but young people below about twenty years of age, many of whom have been brought up as Catholics and educated in the mission school, no longer express any interest in it nor fully understand the archaic language in which it is delivered. An even greater blow to the retention of this literature has been the progressive disappearance of the ceremonial events (e.g., funerary rites) in which myths and sagas were recounted. Formerly these were led by the aristocracy and were occasions for the symbolization of rank. However, the 1970 *adat* law conference in the Embaloh valley officially abolished all such symbols, which in many instances was no more than a ratification of what had already come to pass. Today everyone is given the same type of burial, supervised by a Catholic priest. No charnel houses can be built; and the only way to honor a dead relative is through construction of a cement headstone. The district government has contributed to these developments by decreeing that, for health reasons, all coffins must be buried as opposed to being left above the ground in charnel houses; nor can bodies lie in state in the house for long periods. In the Palin valley, on the other hand, the oral tradition is still vigorous. Only a few people are nominal Catholics, and the majority of those who converted to Islam have moved away. Most of the main ceremonies, in which elements of the oral tradition are recounted, are still performed. The people still live in longhouses, they still use charnel houses, and they have retained much of the traditional funerary ritual, in which some symbols of rank are still present. In this valley the special ritual status of the traditional aristocracy is still expressed by word and deed.

The ritual status of the aristocracy has also been affected by the disappearance of the Maloh longhouse in many areas. Formerly, in accordance with the Maloh classification system, the aristocracy had their apartments at the upstream end of the longhouse, as discussed earlier. As villages of dispersed single-family houses grew up in the Embaloh, this pattern changed. In most such villages the houses of the aristocracy are intermixed with those of other ranks. Even in the Leboyan valley, where longhouses are still in use, some aristocrats' apartments are no longer found at the upstream end of the house. In the Palin valley, on the other hand, the traditional pattern still largely prevails.

In addition to architectural symbolism, other symbols of rank have also declined, as the result not only of the proscription of such things as the deathhouses but also the general decline of Maloh art. Even where longhouses are still present, in the Leboyan and Palin valleys, there are no decorations on the apartment walls and support posts. In the Palin valley some decorative art forms indicating rank differences are still employed on coffins and offering trays, but even there the practice is in decline. Other symbols of rank that were common in the past, such as tiger teeth and animal skin cloaks, have fallen into almost complete disuse. Such symbols as the feathers of the rhinoceros and helmeted hornbills and designs in beadwork clothing have lost their former connotations and are worn irrespective of rank.

Overall, the ritual basis of aristocratic superiority has largely disappeared in the Embaloh and Leboyan valleys, although some elements have remained in the Palin valley. The clearest changes are in the disappearance of a number of villagewide ceremonies (some being replaced by Christian rites) and, with them, the role of the aristocracy in religion. While some Maloh in the Embaloh and Leboyan valleys still hold curing rituals and give offerings to the spirits, they no longer work through the aristocracy. The religious status of the aristocrats in the Palin valley has not declined as markedly, but it has been undermined by the gradual weakening of their economic and political dominance.

Marriage Patterns and Rank

The ranking system is not supported by marriage patterns to the same extent it once was. By 1972–1973 the majority of marriages were still rank endogamous, and many aristocrats were still attempting to maintain their status by marrying close relatives of the same or adjacent rank. Nevertheless, the incidence of interrank marriages—which jeopardize the maintenance of status levels—has been increasing. Added to this are the changes in Embaloh *adat* law eliminating rank differences in bridewealth and, therefore, one of the former obstacles to cross-strata marriage. In the Leboyan and Palin valleys bridewealth is still differentiated according to rank, but even there the system is being undermined by the increasing use of money for marriage payments.

Summary and Conclusions

In this analysis of traditional Maloh rank I posited the existence of three economic classes—aristocrats, commoners, and slaves—based on the control of key resources—labor, rights to land, and material wealth. There was a close correspondence between these economic classes and political status: the aristocrats were rulers, the commoners were freemen with rights under law, and the slaves were totally subordinate. A third system of classification was based on four hereditary status levels —*samagat, pabiring, banua,* and *pangkam*—and a basic classificatory division between "good" and "bad" people. All three of these bases of inequality demarcated a dominant stratum of aristocrats. This stratum was not impermeable. Enterprising commoners could translate economic and political success into status gains through marriage into higher status levels, followed by the adoption of symbols of rank and the assimilation of their descendants into the aristocracy. Similarly, unenterprising aristocrats might be forced to marry down, eventually leading to their descent to commoner status.

This movement between ranks addressed structural tension deriving from the incongruence of talent and ascribed status, and thereby reinforced the ranking system and the position of the aristocracy within it. The system was similarly reinforced by the partial diffusion of decision-making abilities to a council of elders, which included commoners. The council brought some commoners on a par politically with aristocrats and also acted as a sanction against the latter's excesses. It channeled energetic commoners into structurally supportive roles and gave them aspirations to higher status, all of which tended to protect the position of the aristocracy. Finally, the aristocracy's position was also supported by the regional relations of the Maloh. The Maloh aristocracy took slaves from among neighboring forest nomads and husbands and wives from the leading families of neighboring Malays and other Dayak. The Malay communities also functioned as a place of refuge for disaffected aristocrats and commoners.

Dutch colonization of Kalimantan led to dramatic changes among the Maloh. Many changes in the Maloh ranking system came about as the result of Dutch measures to secure law and order by the establishment and financing of an administration in the upper Kapuas region. These measures included stamping out inter-Dayak warfare, using Maloh aristocrats as administrative intermediaries and tax collectors, and depriving traditional leaders of various political prerogatives. The Dutch also introduced a money economy via taxation, wage labor, and the cultivation of cash crops such as rubber. These developments undermined traditional Maloh rank, although such was not their principal intent; nor did they stem from any negative evaluation of the indigenous system of stratification per se by the Dutch. On the other hand, some ancillary aspects of the ranking system did suffer from European disapprobation. The official Dutch decision to abolish slavery and corvée labor was based on moral grounds, and was supported by the missionaries. Some of the Dutch missionaries also disliked and set themselves against what they saw as "primitive" customs, meaning arranged marriages, differentiation of fines according to rank, and pagan ceremonies such as funerary rites. The abolition of these aspects of Maloh culture was gradually brought about through Catholic conversion, mission education, and priestly intervention in village life.

Externally imposed change was inextricably intertwined with dynamic, internal response. Some aristocrats saw that they could maintain their superior position only by using it to grasp the opportunities, such as education and government office, that the Dutch presented to them. In contrast, commoners saw such opportunities as a chance to advance their own positions at the expense of the aristocrats. The availability of alternative institutions and values also helped the commoners to question the traditional system that had asserted that they were intrinsically inferior.

The increasing democratization of village life has been one of the most significant features of the postindependence era. This was symbolized by the government's introduction of village elections for headmen who, in turn, select the *adat* law chiefs. These leaders were required to be literate and to consult with other educated Maloh, including government employees, teachers, and merchants. Pursuit of this ideal of equality and democracy has been compromised, however, by the relative impotence of village officials within the broader provincial and national context. Village leaders, for very small rewards, are often caught between the conflicting demands of the villagers they represent and the supravillage political and administrative bodies of which they are agents. The maintenance of law and order is difficult for the village leaders because they cannot impose sanctions to enforce their decisions and those who can are remote from the village.

In examining contemporary Maloh rank I argued that it is no longer possible to differentiate strata of aristocrats, commoners, and slaves; nor is it yet possible to distinguish new classes or status levels, because some elements of traditional rank can still be found while others have been eliminated or altered.[18] The situation is further complicated because external influences and internal responses have varied in different parts of Maloh country. The Embaloh area, for example, has been the object of much government and mission attention, while the more remote Palin region has not and has thereby avoided some of the more radical transformations.

None of the three aspects of traditional stratification—economic strength, political power, and ritual preeminence—exclusively differentiates the aristocracy from other Maloh today. Regarding economics, strata can no longer be easily differentiated on the basis of the ownership and/or control of labor or land, nor in terms of the distinction between manual and nonmanual occupations, nor in terms of annual income or relative wealth. Whereas formerly aristocrats were a leisured class, wealthy and important in trade, now they have to work their fields like other villagers. Some are comparatively poor, and even well-endowed aristocrats are not necessarily the richest individuals in the village. Aristocrats do not monopolize trade or other nonagricultural occuaptions; most of the traders are from other ranks, and teaching, clerical posts, and wage labor are open to all. In general, today's wealthiest households are not united but divided by different status evaluations and marriage alignments.[19]

In terms of political power, with the recent incorporation of villages into a wider administrative framework, the bureaucratization of village leaders, the holding of elections for village office, and the creation of a local militia and police force, the village (and by extension the aristocrat cum headman) has lost much of its former political autonomy. What political power remains is diffuse, since no one rank can monopolize the headmanship today. Some aristocrats are still headmen, they still dominate the position of *adat* law chief, and they frequently have influence in decisionmaking. But with the removal of many traditional aristocratic powers, with the ability of successful commoners to achieve political office should they desire it, and with the questioning of village customary law by young, educated Maloh, it is problematic to talk about either an aristocratic class or a new ruling class of any type in Maloh society today.

In terms of ritual status, most aristocrats, rich or poor, influential or not, have attempted to retain their superiority by continuing to emphasize traditional status criteria. Indeed, as the economic and political foundations of aristocratic superiority are increasingly threatened, the aristocracy is tending to fall back on traditional status distinctions, some of which are relatively easy to preserve. However, this strategy will ultimately fail, because the bases of status are themselves changing.

In contemporary Maloh society the various dimensions of social inequality no longer coincide (with the partial exception of the Palin valley people). Current economic and political positions are not in line with traditional status levels, and there is little effort or desire to bring them into line. All of this is producing an increasing number of conflicts over status evaluation. Any analysis of present-day stratification among the Maloh must take this flux into account, and it must also recognize the new role of the broader, extra-Maloh world in creating and sustaining this flux.

Notes

1. Fieldwork was undertaken in the upper Kapuas for twelve months between September 1972 and September 1973. The research was generously supported by grants from the Social Science Research Council, the Evans Fund, and the British Universities Student Travel Association. I studied the Maloh of the Leboyan, Embaloh, and Palin (Nyabau) areas. While much of what I say has relevance for all Maloh, it must be constantly borne in mind that there were and are differences, particularly of a cultural kind, between Maloh communities in different river systems; and their experiences under the Dutch also varied in form, content, and intensity.

2. Lévi-Strauss (1966:1–33).

3. This analytical orientation is used in an interesting way in Rousseau's work on the stratified Kayan of Sarawak (1974, 1979). My debt to him will

become obvious in this paper. This kind of analysis can also be detected, although not so explicitly, in Morris' writings on the Melanau (1953, 1976, 1978, 1980) and in Whittier's study of the Kenyah (1973, 1978). The existence of hereditary, formalized, named ranks distinguishes certain Borneo societies such as the Maloh, Kayan, Kenyah, and Kajang-Melanau from surrounding, more egalitarian peoples such as the Iban, Bidayuh, Rungus Dusun, and Selako.

4. A.S. plus date of entry refers to the "Archief Statie" (see References Cited).

5. Watson (1980:1–15) stated that one of the main defining features of slavery is that it is a form of bondage in which humans are a form of property or chattels and treated as "things."

6. For similar symbolic divisions among the stratified Kayan and Kenyah see Rousseau (1979:218–219) and Whittier (1973:69; 1978:110–111), respectively. Maloh slaves were not included in the system of symbolic classification, nor were they ascribed any origin in Maloh myth.

7. These symbolic distinctions of the Maloh, and the graded scale of feasts upon which they depended, are modest when compared to the Kenyah *suhan* grades and impressive *mamat* rituals (Whittier 1973:74–76, 162–163, 167, 175–176).

8. See also the Kayan (Rousseau 1978:86), Kenyah (Whittier 1978:113), and Melanau (Morris 1978:48–49).

9. Rousseau pointed out that Kayan *hipuy* (structurally equivalent to *pabiring*) appears to be a residual category without a distinct role (1974:389).

10. See Rousseau for similar relations between Punan and settled Kayan and Kenyah in Sarawak (1975:41–42).

11. The Dutch writer Enthoven recorded a number of genealogies of Malay rulers, and many of these contained Maloh aristocrats. For example, Abang Barita, the first Malay ruler of Bunut, had kinship links with the Maloh: Barita's father, one of his sons-in-law, and the grandfather of another of his sons-in-law were all Maloh aristocrats (Enthoven 1903: genealogy pp. 96–97).

12. See Whittier for similar comments on Dutch policy in East Kalimantan (1973:32 seq.).

13. Even in 1972–1973 it was apparent that the Maloh in the Palin area had been less influenced by outside forces than those in the Embaloh and Leboyan rivers.

14. There was very little missionary activity, on the other hand, among the Maloh in the remote Palin River system.

15. See also Whittier on Kenyah headmanship in East Kalimantan (1973:51).

16. Even traditionally, relative wealth was never a clear defining criterion of classes although it was broadly correlated with it. Formerly rises and falls in fortune were, however, translated into movements up and down the status scale.

17. It was impossible to ascertain the amount of capital tied up in rubber gardens and wet-rice fields because there was no sale and purchase of land.

18. The themes of "transition" and "classes in formation" are familiar ones in the macrosociological literature on Third World social stratification. See

Evers (1973:108–131), Roberts (1978:92 seq.), Roxborough (1979:70–106), and Worsley (1967).

19. Divisions based on "vertical ties" of status, ideology, religion, and ethnicity, which cross-cut horizontal relations among people of broadly the same economic position, can also be seen in Geertz's (1963, 1965) and Wertheim's (1969) work on *aliran* in Java, and in Adas' (1974) analysis of "plural society" in Burma.

References Cited

Adas, Michael
    1974   *The Burma Delta: Economic Development and Social Change on an Asian Rice Frontier, 1852–1941.* Wisconsin: University of Wisconsin Press.
Archief Statie (A.S.)
    1912–   Unpublished journal of the Dutch Catholic Mission at Benua Mar-
    1946   tinus on the Embaloh River. 4 vols.
Baring-Gould, S., and C. A. Bampfylde
    1909   *A History of Sarawak under its Two White Rajahs, 1839–1908.* London: Sotheran.
Béteille, André
    1969   Introduction in André Béteille, ed., *Social Inequality,* pp. 9–14. Harmondsworth: Penguin Books.
Bouman, M. A.
    1924   "Ethnografische Aanteekeningen omtrent de Gouvernementslanden in de boven-Kapoeas, Westerafdeeling van Borneo." *Tijdschrift voor Indische Taal-, Land- en Volkenkunde* 64:173–195.
Burgemeestre, J. E. L.
    1934   "Memorie van Overgave van den Gezaghebber van Semitau, 1930–34." *Memorie van Overgave.* Amsterdam: Royal Tropical Institute.
Enthoven, J. J. K.
    1903   *Bijdragen tot de Geographie van Borneo's Wester-afdeeling.* 2 vols. Leiden: Brill.
Evers, Hans-Dieter
    1973   "Group Conflict and Class Formation in South-East Asia." In *Modernization in South-East Asia,* edited by Hans-Deiter Evers, pp. 108–131. Singapore/Kuala Lumpur: Oxford University Press.
Geertz, Clifford
    1963   *Peddlers and Princes: Social Development and Economic Change in Two Indonesian Towns.* Chicago: University of Chicago Press.
    1965   *The Social History of an Indonesian Town.* Cambridge, Mass.: M.I.T. Press.
Harrisson, Tom
    1965   "The Malohs of Kalimantan: Ethnological Notes." *Sarawak Museum Journal* 13:236–350.

Helbig, Karl
1939   "Op Landwegen in Acht Maanden door Borneo." *Tropisch Nederland* 12:67–72.

Hose, Charles, and William McDougall
1912   *The Pagan Tribes of Borneo.* 2 vols. London: Macmillan.

Huijbers, H. J.
1931   "De Embaloeh-Dajak." *Koloniaal Missie Tijdschrift van de Indische Missie-Vereeniging* 14:171–181, 204–209, 237–243.

1932   "De Embaloeh-Dajak." *Borneo-Almanak* 22:151–162.

1934   "De Embaloeh-Dajak. Pabirin." *Borneo-Almanak* 24:94–104.

Irwin, Graham
1967   *Nineteenth-Century Borneo. A Study in Diplomatic Rivalry.* Singapore: Donald Moore Books.

Lévi-Strauss, Claude
1966   *The Savage Mind.* London: Weidenfeld & Nicolson.

Maxandrea
1924   *De Dajaks in de Binnenlanden van Ned. Borneo.* Grave: Missie der PP Capucijnen.

Morris, H. S.
1953   *Report on a Melanau Sago Producing Community in Sarawak.* London: Her Majesty's Stationery Office.

1976   "A Problem in Land Tenure." In *The Societies of Borneo: Explorations in the Theory of Cognatic Social Structure,* edited by George N. Appell, pp. 110–120. Special Publication no. 6. Washington: American Anthropological Association.

1978   "The Coastal Melanau." In *Essays on Borneo Societies,* edited by Victor T. King, pp. 37–58. Hull Monographs on South-East Asia no. 7. Oxford: Oxford University Press.

1980   "Slaves, Aristocrats and Export of Sago in Sarawak." In *Asian and African Systems of Slavery,* edited by James L. Watson, pp. 293–308. Oxford: Blackwell.

Morrison, Hedda
1948   "Maloh Silver-smiths in Sarawak." *Geographical Magazine* 21:249–255.

Niclou, H. A. A.
1887   "Batang-Loepars-verdelgings-oorlog. Europeesch-Dajaksche Sneltocht." *Tijdschrift voor Nederlandsch-Indië* 16:29–67.

Ozinga, J.
1940   *De Economische Ontwikkeling der Westerafdeeling van Borneo en de Bevolkingsrubbercultuur.* Wageningen: Zomer & Keuning.

Posewitz, Th.
   1892   *Borneo: Its Geology and Mineral Resources.* London: Edward Stanford.

Roberts, Bryan
   1978   *Cities of Peasants: The Political Economy of Urbanization in the Third World.* London: Edward Arnold.

Rousseau, Jérôme
   1974   "The Social Organization of the Baluy Kayan." Ph.D. thesis, Cambridge University.

   1975   "Ethnic Identity and Social Relations in Central Borneo." In *Pluralism in Malaysia: Myth and Reality,* edited by Judith A. Nagata, pp. 32–49. Contributions to Asian Studies no. 7. Leiden: Brill.

   1978   "The Kayan." In *Essays on Borneo Societies,* edited by Victor T. King, pp. 78–91. Hull Monographs on South-East Asia no. 7. Oxford: Oxford University Press.

   1979   "Kayan Stratification." *Man* 14:215–236.

Roxborough, Ian
   1979   *Theories of Underdevelopment.* London: Macmillan.

Runciman, W. G.
   1969   "The Three Dimensions of Social Inequality." In *Social Inequality,* edited by André Béteille, pp. 45–63. Harmondsworth: Penguin Books.

St. John, Spenser
   1862   *Life in the Forests of the Far East.* 2 vols. London: Smith, Elder & Co.

Salam, Abdul
   1936   "Notes on Embaloh Adat." Unpublished ms. Dutch Catholic Mission at Benua Martinus.

Scheuer, W. H. E.
   1932   "Memorie der Afd. Sintang." *Memorie van Overgave.* Amsterdam: Royal Tropical Institute.

Uljee, G. L.
   1925   *Handboek voor de Residentie Westerafdeling van Borneo.* Weltevreden: Visser.

Veth, P. J.
   1854–   *Borneo's Wester-afdeeling. Geographisch, Statistisch, Historisch, voorafgegaan*
   1856   *door eene Algemeene Schets das Ganschen Eilands.* 2 vols. Zaltbommel: Noman.

Watson, James L.
   1980   "Introduction. Slavery as an Institution: Open and Closed Systems." In *Asian and African Systems of Slavery,* edited by James L. Watson, pp. 1–15. Oxford: Blackwell.

Weber, Max
　1947　*The Theory of Social and Economic Organization*. New York: Free Press.
　1971　"Class, Status and Party." In *Sociological Perspectives,* edited by K. Thompson and J. Tunstall, pp. 250–264. Harmondsworth: Penguin Books.

Werkman, E.
　n.d.　"Memorie van den Gezaghebber van Smitau." *Memorie van Overgave.* Sintang: KalBar.

Wertheim, W. F.
　1969　"From Aliran to Class Struggle in the Countryside of Java." *Pacific Viewpoint* 10:1–17.

Whittier, Herbert L.
　1973　"Social Organization and Symbols of Social Differentiation: An Ethnographic Study of the Kenyah Dayak of East Kalimantan (Borneo)." Ph.D. dissertation, Michigan State University.
　1978　"The Kenyah." In *Essays on Borneo Societies,* edited by Victor T. King, pp. 92–122. Hull Monographs on South-East Asia no. 7. Oxford: Oxford University Press.

Worsley, Peter
　1967　*The Third World.* London: Weidenfeld and Nicolson.

9. Ritual Feasting and Resource Competition in Flores

Hans J. Daeng

Abstract

This paper analyzes the former system of competitive feasting in Ngadha, central Flores. The manifest fuction of this feasting, which was marked by the slaughter of large numbers of livestock, was to measure the differences between clans in wealth and status and on this basis to settle disputes over land. The feasting also performed a latent function, which was to reduce population/land pressure by optimizing the distribution of the human population on the land and by reducing the size of the livestock population. Many of these same functions are performed today, following the disappearance of the competitive feast, by a newly evolved system of adjudication. Other of the functions of the historic feast have been replaced by the contemporary system of competitive marital payments, following a replacement of the central role of land and livestock in Flores society by people and bureaucratic power.

Introduction

The phenomenon of social and ceremonial feasting has long been an object of anthropological research. In recent times, such feasting has become the focus of some concern in developing countries, including Indonesia, with many government officers arguing that it is a waste of scarce resources and a hindrance to economic development. In this paper I suggest that anxiety over competitive feasting, and attendant attempts to proscribe it, are misplaced. As has been shown in other studies, such feasting performs a definite, often critically important function within the society that carries it out.

I will first describe the traditional system of competitive feasting, with an emphasis on one type of feast in particular, the *boka goe,* as it existed in one district in particular, Ngadha. This will be followed by an analysis of both the manifest and the latent functions of this feast, which in turn will be followed by a discussion of recent changes on Flores, involving the disappearance of the *boka goe,* the development of a judicial system for settling land disputes, and the efflorescence of the system of brideprice and dowry. The data that will be presented are derived, in part, from a review of the relevant literature and, in larger part, from my own observations in Flores, where I was born, raised, and educated.

The *Boka Goe*

The people of Flores traditionally believed that their ancestors owned all of the land. The *mori tanah* (clan chief) merely held the land in trust for the ancestors. He shared it out among the clan's *sipopali* (extended families), each of which shared it out among its own constituent *sa'o/dhoro* (nuclear families). There was no intraclan competition for land, or if there was it was settled by the clan chief. All competition over land was interclan, and it was traditionally settled by means of the *boka goe* (to slip and fall backwards) competitive feast, of which examples have also been described from Sumba (Onvlee 1973) and Timor (Ormeling 1957: 88–89).

Ceremonial feasting was formerly a salient part of clan life on Flores, being staged not only to settle land disputes, but also on the occasion of moving the village to a new location, erecting megaliths to the ancestors, building a new meeting house, or preparing for a wedding. These feasts entailed great expense. Arndt (1963) reports that when the village of Wogo of Golewa subdistrict in Ngadha was moved to a new location, three hundred head of buffalo and an untold number of pigs were slaughtered. The cost of the move, in terms of the amount of livestock and rice needed for the celebrations, was borne by the members of all the clans living in Wogo. No costs were spared in making the feast as grand as possible. The village's paramount objective on this occasion was to bring no shame upon itself through being unable to entertain its guests on a befitting scale or being unable to provide each of them with enough meat and rice to take home.

The logic of the *boka goe* was based on the assumption that the ancestral spirits knew who was the rightful owner of each plot of land, even if the living did not. For the spirits of the ancestors to make their decisions known, both parties to the dispute had only to compete in a livestock slaughter. Whichever side held out longest by virtue of having the most stock was adjudged to be true owner of the land. This validation by the spirits was backed up by the manifest support of the living, who would

Guests Assembled at a Feast. (Reprinted with permission from P. Arndt, "Die Wirtschaflichen Verhältnisse Der Ngadha," *Annali Laternensi* 22.)

Buffalos Slaughtered for a Feast. (Reprinted with permission from P. Arndt, "Die Wirtschaflichen Verhältnisse Der Ngadha," *Annali Laternensi* 22.)

gather in large numbers to strengthen the respective claims of each side. These supporters received food and drink at the feast and also had to be given generous portions of meat and rice beer to take home with them. Enormous quantities of livestock and rice were sometimes expended for this purpose, in particular when feasts went on for a month or more, with large groups of supporters coming in daily from other villages. As in the case of the feast described by Arndt, cost was no object. Land, the sacred trust of the ancestors, was at stake. As long as one did not disgrace the ancestors by losing the slaughtering competition, they would ensure that there would be enough livestock for another day.

Only clan leaders could sponsor *boka goe* (or other large feasts or ceremonies). However, all clan members could attend, indeed had to attend, the principle being that anyone who used the land of the clan leader had to attend his feast. In addition to clan members, some members of allied clans would also attend a *boka goe*. On the other hand, hostile clans would not attend. This distinguishes (in terms of attendance) the *boka goe* from a feast like the North American potlatch, which brought together not allies but rivals. Just as the clan leader commanded the attendance of clan members at his *boka goe,* so too did he command their material support. The main resource expended during the *boka goe* was livestock, and most were provided by the clan members, not the clan leader.[1] The clan members also helped to provide rice, *tuak* (rice beer), and accommodations for the guests. Some of the livestock was also provided by the members of allied clans who attended the *boka goe.* Any such contribution set up a reciprocal obligation for the recipient clan leader to contribute an equal number of livestock to future *boka goe* held by the contributors. (The reciprocal obligation was calculated on the basis of the horn length, not body weight, of the animals contributed, as Onvlee [1973] noted on Sumba.) No such obligation was established by contributions made from within the clan sponsoring the *boka goe.* On the other hand, the contributions that the common clan members made to the *boka goe* were not totally lost to them. Indeed, most of each animal contributed to the feast by a clan member was returned to that same member during the course of the feast in the form of prestations of butchered meat, and the amount returned to each member was proportionate to the number of livestock he contributed. Thus, the *boka goe* did not function simply to redistribute the wealth of the clan from those members who were well-off to those who were not so well-off.

The ancestors were thought always to select the side that slaughtered the most livestock with the longest horns (in the case of cattle) or tusks (in the case of pigs), which provided the most drink, whose feast lasted the longest and was attended by the most people, and who received the most material support from other clans; that is, the ability to slaughter more animals and so forth was seen as proof of greater righteousness in the land dispute question. (This connection among livestock, supernatural favor, and personal prestige was reflected in the custom of adorning one's house with the horns and tusks of animals slaughtered during a *boka goe*.) The decision of the ancestors was made known through the local rajah. Either he or one of his representatives attended each *boka goe* and declared the outcome based on his observation of the number of animals slaughtered by each party to the dispute. Some evidence also indicates that the rajah based his decision not solely on the number of animals slaughtered during the *boka goe*, but also on the number of animals slaughtered (or not) and then presented to him.

This description of the *boka goe*, as it formerly existed in Ngadha, central Flores, can be compared to similar mechanisms for settling disputes elsewhere in Flores. In East Flores, for example, up until twenty years ago the ultimate recourse in intervillage or interclan land disputes was the *perang tanding* (competitive war), an open battle between the contending sides that was conducted under the observation and mediation of the rajah of Larantuka (just as the local rajah supervised the *boka goe* in Ngadha). It seems likely that this *perang tanding* was the evolutionary precursor to the *boka goe*, the former developing into the latter (at a differential rate across the island) in response to increasing criticism of warlike activities from the traditional rulers of Flores, as well as from the Dutch colonial administration.

The Function of the *Boka Goe*

The manifest function of the *boka goe* was to settle disputes over land, while the latent function appears to have been to settle disputes over relative status or prestige. The importance of this latent function is suggested by cases in which the amount of land disputed was so minuscule as to be of no economic importance. Competition for prestige has been cited as the function or purpose of many other traditional feasting systems as well, both in Indonesia and other countries. However, in too many of these analyses the prestige associated with feast making is interpreted (sometimes implicitly, sometimes explicitly) as the "explanation" of the feasting. This is an incomplete explanation. The fact that people acquire prestige by staging feasts does not explain the function of feasting. To discover this function it is necessary to ask what lies behind the prestige, what critical cultural values are being encoded in social prestige. In the present case we must ask: Why is prestige important to the people of Flores? Relative prestige is important, in the context of the *boka goe,* because it strengthens and validates a claim to scarce and disputed land. It is the thesis of this paper that the association between relative prestige and the disposition of disputed land is a functional one.

Functional analyses of ritual or ceremonial behavior have been common for some time (e.g., Moore 1965, Harris 1966). One notable and relevant example involved reexamination of the aboriginal potlatch on the northwest coast of America. Piddocke (1965) concluded that the potlatch historically functioned to optimally distribute the produce from an environment characterized by overall abundance punctuated by local shortages. This sort of analysis attained perhaps its greatest development in the work of Rappaport (1968). He demonstrated that the cyclic pattern of warfare and pig festivals in highland New Guinea functioned to regulate the balance among land, people, and pigs. Part of this regulation was achieved through the display of relative strength (in numbers of warriors) during the pig festivals. The purpose of such epideitic display is to compare the strength of two competing organisms or groups without resorting to open conflict and then, based on this comparison, to achieve an optimal distribution of resources throughout the population involved in the system. It seems clear that comparison and redistribution were also main functions of the *boka goe* in Ngadha, Flores. It seems clear, that is, that the actual latent function of the ceremony was not so different from its manifest one: the latter was the redistribution of land based on juridical principles, while the former was the redistribution of land based on principles of human ecology.

My theory that the former function of the *boka goe* was to regulate the balance between population and resources, in this case land, is derived from the initial premise that this balance needed periodic adjustment and readjustment because of periodic changes in the demographic structure of one clan relative to another due to varying rates of population growth and to clan fission and fusion. To the extent that such changes caused variation in the population/land balance of one clan relative to another nearby clan, it would have tended to exacerbate competition and disputes over land. The *boka goe* resolved such disputes through the public display of the size of the human and animal population of the rival clans. The number of people who attended the feast was a measure of the clan's size (as well as that of allied clans), and the number of livestock slaughtered was a measure of the size of its herds (as well as an indirect measure of its human population, given a fairly constant ratio of livestock to people). Accordingly, when disputed land was awarded to the winner of the *boka goe,* it was thereby awarded to the clan with the most people and animals—or the most users of land—meaning the clan with the greatest relative need of the land.

This means of settling land disputes would not always have resulted in an optimal distribution of landed resources as seen from the perspective of the individual clan. A clan that lost some of its land as the result of a *boka goe* would definitely be worse off. However, from a population-wide, multiclan perspective, this system of dispute settlement would have achieved an optimal distribution of land in relation to people, since it would have continually awarded land to the largest clans with the greatest need of it.

The land conflicts that led to the *boka goe* and the redistribution of disputed land were a function of population/land pressure. The *boka goe* functioned to reduce this pressure by distributing the finite and scarce resource of land more optimally among the human population. As noted, however, in some cases the amount of land involved in the dispute was so small as to make it questionable whether its redistribution could have had any possible effect on population/land pressure. In these cases, the *boka goe* still had a beneficial effect on land pressure. The effect was accomplished, however, not by the redistribution of land as a result of competititve feasting, but as a result of the feasting itself, specifically as a result of the slaughter of livestock for the feast. This slaughter achieved a large, absolute reduction in the herds of both parties to the dispute. It typically took a clan years to replenish its herds after staging a *boka goe*. There may even have existed a causal relationship between the length of this interval and the length of the interval between the *boka goe* staged by that clan. It is possible, that is, that pressure from growing livestock/land ratios ultimately triggered the staging of the *boka goe,* the *boak goe* thus being staged at times when the herds were at their maximum sizes and not at other times. Rappaport (1968) described a similar situation in the New Guinea highlands, where the major ceremonial feasts—in which large numbers of pigs were slaughtered—were staged whenever the domestic pig population outgrew the tribesmen's capacity to feed and care for it.

The reduction in the livestock population achieved by the *boka goe* would have benefited the human population both indirectly and directly. The indirect benefit was that the environment would improve in the wake of the reduction in herd size, because the land cover would have a greater opportunity to grow back, erosion would diminish, and so on. The direct benefits of this reduction are several. In the case of cattle, the fewer the animals, the smaller the amount of labor that has to be devoted to cutting grass for them and/or supervising them while they graze and also the smaller the amount of land that has to be diverted from the production of food crops to the production of fodder. This is true in the case of pigs, too: the fewer the animals, the smaller the amount of foodstuffs (e.g., cassava tubers) that have to be diverted from human consumption to animal consumption. And in both cases, the fewer the animals, the smaller the amount of damage done by them to food crops and hence the smaller the amount of labor that has to be devoted to fencing fields against the threat of such damage.

To understand this analysis of the ecological function of the *boka goe,* it is also necessary to understand the broader role of contest and competition in Flores society. I suggest that while this ecological function was critical to the operation of this society, the *boka goe* itself was not. That is, the function was critical but the means by which it was fulfilled—the *boka goe*—was arbitrary. I suggest that the ecological function was in fact filled by the *boka goe* because, of the various socio-cultural mechanisms that conceivably could fill it, socially or ritually regulated competition was the most well developed in traditional Flores society. (I take this development as a given: I am not trying to explain the origin of the competitive element in Flores society.) Tests and displays of strength historically formed one of the most important mediums of interaction between individuals or groups in Flores as well as one of the most important ways of resolving the problems attendant upon such interaction. Examples of such competitive interaction included the *parang-memarang* (sword-fight) waged over the carcasses of animals killed in group hunts, the postharvest *pesta etu* (fisticuffs), and the postharvest *pesta para.* The data on the *pesta para* are especially intriguing in the context of my current analysis because it involved men fighting against water buffalos, whereas in the *boka goe* men fought against one another through water buffalos (among other animals), by slaughtering them in a competitive context. These and other instances of competitive interaction are associated with a very old and pervasive aspect of the cosmology of Flores: the blood of animals (and men) must be sacrificed to the earth (*membasahi bumi,* "water [the] earth") to keep it fertile.

This evidence of the pervasiveness of contest and competition in Flores life suggests that, given the need to regulate the population/land balance, the mechanism that evolved to meet this need would likely involve social competition. My suggestion that this competition— namely the *boka goe*—did indeed help to regulate the population/land balance is supported by data on the immediate causes of individual feasts. Most *boka goe* were precipitated by interclan conflicts over land. Some were precipitated by conflicts over use of the land by livestock (e.g., grazing on land or destroying crops belonging to another clan). In both cases, the immediate stimulus of the *boka goe* was thus related to population/land pressure, which supports my theory that the staging of the *boka goe* helped to reduce that pressure.

Contemporary Changes

The Rise of Competitive Adjudication

Since independence, the Indonesian national government has made increasing efforts to regulate the traditional pattern of ceremonial feasting in Flores, prompted by a concern that such feasting is an unwise use of scarce resources and hence an obstacle to development. The government has demanded that certain types of feasts not be staged without governmental permission and supervision—especially as regards the number of livestock that can be slaughtered—and it has levied a tax on each animal slaughtered. Other types of feasts, including the *boka goe,* have been altogether proscribed by the government. This official pressure has been supplemented by similar pressure from such institutions as the Farmers' Union and the Catholic Church, the latter of which has attempted to minimize the number and scale of feasts by incorporating them into the church's celebration of first communion. These pressures have largely achieved their stated aim, at least in the case of the *boka goe.* The last *boka goe* in Ngadha was staged in 1943/1944.

Since the disappearance of the *boka goe,* land disputes have been settled by traditional moots or, in the event that these do not produce a mutually acceptable decision, by the state court system. In the latter case, decisions are based on the oral testimony of the disputants and witnesses, and on the inspection of boundary markers. In addition, each party to the dispute uses the social, political, and especially economic influence at its disposal to sway the government to its point of view. In this endeavor, moreover, the parties to the dispute—for example, two households—are not limited to the use of their own resources. Typically, each party draws on the material resources of its entire clan. Such influence is crucial to the outcome of judicial proceedings over land disputes and is even, it is said, more important than the existence of ties of friendship or kinship between the disputing parties, on the one hand, and the adjudicating officials, on the other.

The evidence suggests that the contemporary system of settling land disputes by adjudication functions in much the same way as did the historic system of *boka goe.* That is, the evidence suggests that the contemporary system also functions to redistribute land to the most populous of the disputants, thus contributing to an optimal distribution of the land-using population over the land. This is suggested by the fact that influence is brought to bear upon the judicial proceedings by the entire clan whenever one of its constituent households is party to a land dispute. Hence, the outcome of a case is typically determined by the resources not of the landowning household alone but by those of his entire clan, the traditional land-holding and land-using unit. It follows that the larger the clan, the more financial resources it can muster during litigation and the greater its chances of winning the dispute. Just as in the *boka goe,* therefore, the larger group—the group that probably needs it more—is more likely to win the disputed land.

This suggestion that the contemporary system of adjudication achieves optimal land distribution by, in effect, evening out population/land ratios, is supported by the remarkable fact that the system overrides ties of friendship and kinship. One would expect such ties to influence the settlement of these land disputes. However, one would not expect this influence to optimize the population/land distribution, because there is no reason why the strength of these ties should increase as group size increases. Thus, the fact that ties of friendship and kinship are overriden supports the thesis that group size (as reflected in the amount of resources and influence brought to bear on the judicial proceedings) has been the determinant factor in the evolution of this system of dispute settlement and land distribution.

In addition to suggesting that the current system of adjudication distributes the population optimally over the land, I also suggest that it reduces the pressure from livestock on the land in the same manner as did the *boka goe.* In order to amass financial resources for use in a court case, the extended family or clan members typically have to sell large numbers of their livestock, thus automatically reducing the pressure on land (viz., grazing from the herds) among the parties to the dispute. This interpretation seems particularly applicable in cases in which very small amounts of land are involved or cases in which livestock-related issues initially gave rise to the dispute.

The Rise of Competitive Marriage Payments

I have suggested that the disappearance of the competitive feast, the *boka goe,* is partially explained by the transfer of its role in optimizing the distribution of land and people to the contemporary system of competitive adjudication. A second factor has also contributed to the waning of the *boka goe,* namely the transfer of the locus of power in Flores society from land to people. In the traditional agrarian societies of Flores, power was based on the amount of land that one controlled and the amount of livestock and agricultural products that one could derive from it. In contemporary Flores, this locus of power has increasingly shifted to the extent of one's influence on the government bureaucracy and to the number of benefits that one can thereby procure. Influence on or participation within the government bureaucracy is based, in large part, on education. Hence many of the resources that clans formerly expended on competitive feasting over disputed land are now expended—collectively—for the higher education of clan members. This expenditure is competitive in the sense in which a clan with more educated members, working for or with the government, is likely to be stronger and wealthier than a clan with fewer such members. More openly competitive are the expenditures on marriage payments, also carried out collectively by the clan, which determine which clan will benefit from the skills of the best educated young people, following their marriage.

The institution of marriage payments is one element of traditional custom that is still strongly upheld throughout Flores. It has undergone some changes, however. In addition to the social status of the couple and their respective parents, the degree of education acquired by the bride and groom is now often applied as a standard in setting the size of marriage payment. Other considerations include the young people's skills and talents and, particularly in the case of the girl, physical attractiveness. In setting the amount of bridewealth, the girl's clan will in effect set the standing of both families in the community as well as the clan. It is a common practice for the boy's kin to ask for a slight reduction in bridewealth, although the amount they eventually pay is usually still high. No matter how much bridewealth is requested, however, the boy's kin will almost never retract a marriage proposal once it is made. They would rather lose everything they own than suffer the ignominy of being unable to come up to the bride's clan's estimate of their financial-cum-social status. The clan will try with all the means at their collective disposal to make all the requested bridewealth payments. These usually take the form of livestock, jewelry, elephant tusks—of a circumference and length (from one half to one meter) in keeping with the family's social position—and cash payments of up to millions of rupiah. The preferred payments in Manggarai and Ngadha are horses and water buffalo; in Ende-Lio, gold jewelry, cash, and horses; in Sikka, cash and tusks as well as ivory bracelets; and in East Flores, ivory and cash.

While the element of "bargaining" in the families' discussion over the bridewealth gives the impression that the bride is being "bought," to take this impression at face value is to miss the whole point of marriage payments. For every article given in payment of bridewealth, the girl's family must reciprocate with a return gift of equal value, for not to do so would constitute a serious loss of self-respect. To guard against this, the girl's dowry will frequently exceed her bridewealth. In addition to uncooked foodstuffs (e.g., milled rice and pigs) and cooked foods (e.g., steamed rice, pork, and traditional cakes), the dowry will also include presents of hand-woven cloth, customarily given to all who help carry the bridewealth to the girl's house. All bridewealth and dowry gifts will be displayed to clan members visiting the homes of the bride's and groom's parents, and they in turn will tell everyone else what sorts of gifts, and in what amounts, were given as bridewealth and dowry.

There is one principal reason why so great an effort is made to complete marriage payments. It is the completion, or noncompletion, of these payments that decides where future children will live and whose lineage they will join. This accordingly determines which clan will receive additional manpower in the form of an adult female and all the children she will subsequently bear. Every extended family or clan desires increments in membership, since the greater their number, the more leverage they can exert on government bodies. Thus, the competition evinced during negotiation and settlement of marriage payments (including the dowry as well as the brideprice) reflects competition over people as a critical resource, a competition that has partially supplanted the historical competition over land evinced in the *boka goe.*

Summary, Conclusions, and Recommendations

I began this paper with a general description of the *boka goe,* the competitive feast by which the clans traditionally settled their land disputes. I proposed that these feasts did not merely settle land disputes; they also redressed the land pressure that gave rise to them, in two ways. First, they caused the disputed land to be awarded to the clan that slaughtered the greatest number of animals, which was likely to be the larger of the clans involved and hence the one more in need of that land. Second, regardless of which disputant received the land, both slaughtered many livestock, and this reduction in the size of the herds reduced the pressure on the land. I suggested that this functional interpretation of feasting is supported by the particular importance of competition and contest in Flores society and by the fact that the immediate stimulus for staging a *boka goe* was usually related to land pressure. Looking at recent changes in Flores attendant upon the disappearance of the *boka goe,* I suggested that the *boka goe* has been replaced by the contemporary system of adjudication, which achieves the same end in the same ways: it reduces population/land pressure by redistributing land optimally and by reducing herd size absolutely. I suggested that the function of the *boka goe* has also been supplanted by the contemporary system of marriage payments, as competition over people has partially displaced competition over land. Influence with the government bureaucracies is more important today than the control of land. It is most easily attained by those with education, and educated young people are in effect fought over, through dowry and brideprice, by their respective clans.

Based on this analysis, I can conclude, first, that there has been an ongoing, dynamic relationship between land pressure and the structure of the indigenous societies of Flores. As this pressure has changed historically, so has the society's method for dealing with it. Thus, it appears that when land pressure was lowest (although not nonexistent), land disputes were resolved by open warfare. When land pressure and population density increased beyond a certain point, such disputes came to be resolved by competitive feasting. In the most recent development, as land pressure and population density have reached even higher levels and as competitive feasting has been restricted, a system of competitive adjudication has evolved through which land disputes are now resolved. The second conclusion that I can make is that human behavior of a social, ceremonial, or religious nature is not necessarily unrelated or irrelevant to behavior that is economic and ecological in nature. More specifically, as the classic studies by Harris (1966), Rappaport (1968), and Moore (1965) long ago demonstrated, critical material relations are often regulated, especially in tribal societies, by ceremonial mechanisms—as I have indeed found to be the case in Flores.

Both of these conclusions, but especially the latter, are relevant to government policy making. There is a strong prejudice within most development policy and planning against ritual or ceremonial activities and expenditures of resources. At a time when so much funding is needed to develop Indonesia and attain higher standards of living, many officials regard the passing of practices such as the *boka goe* with no great regret. To them, ceremonies of this nature are wasteful and, if not actively suppressed, they should at least be altered to a more "productive" form. My analysis clearly suggests that the *boka goe* did not jeopardize the historic productivity of the clan economy on Flores. Quite the contrary, the *boka goe,* by regulating the balance among people, livestock, and land, and by thus safeguarding the health of the environment, safeguarded the productivity of the agricultural system that depended on this environment. This suggests that development planners need a less naïve, more sophisticated view of the functions and values of traditional customs and beliefs (cf. Ormeling 1957:89).

Enough has been said in this paper to express my views on customs and traditions as a way of keeping trust with our ancestors. That these customs and traditions seem no longer in keeping with the spirit of the times is no justification for doing away with them. Yet, as they stand now, they are not completely viable, since they do have elements not necessarily conducive to development. Accordingly, it is necessary to conduct further in-depth studies in communities where such traditions and customs still prevail in order to know which of them should be maintained and utilized in development.

Note

I. Livestock fulfill a number of functions on Flores (Onvlee 1973): (1) they have important economic significance; (2) they are used in ceremonies involving ancestor worship, which is still important among many of the island's ethnic groups, even those that have adopted one of the "world religions"; (3) they are a means of enhancing social status, enabling their owner to stage elaborate celebrations and entertain numerous guests; (4) they are needed to pay brideprices; and finally (5) they are used for competitive feasting by clan leaders (Arndt 1963).

References Cited

Arndt, P.
    1963   *Die Wirtschaftliche Verhältnisse der Ngadha,* vol. 27. Rome: Annali Lateranensi (The Vatican).

Harris, Marvin
    1966   "The Cultural Ecology of India's Sacred Cattle." *Current Anthropology* 7:51–59.

Moore, Omar Khayam
    1965   "Divination—A New Perspective." *American Anthropologist* 59:69–74.

Onvlee, L.
    1973   *Cultuur als Antwoord.* The Hague: Martinus Nijhoff.

Ormeling, F. J.
    1957   *The Timor Problem: A Geographical Interpretation of an Underdeveloped Island.* Groningen/Jakarta: J. B. Wolters.

Piddocke, Stuart
    1965   "The Potlatch System of the Southern Kwakiutl: A New Perspective." *Southwestern Journal of Anthropology* 21:244–264.

Rappaport, Roy A.
    1968   *Pigs for the Ancestors: Ritual in the Ecology of a New Guinea People.* New Haven: Yale University Press.

PART V: EVALUATION

10. Costing Social Change

G. N. APPELL

Abstract

One of the most pressing problems of developing nations such as Indonesia is the management of social change. Anthropological research has shown that social change often entails costs that are neither expected nor planned for. In order to examine these costs, this paper will present and discuss seven principles of social change. Attention to these principles, it is argued, will make it possible to plan for social change with a minimum of unintended and deleterious consequences. A key element of such planning is a focus on the community level, which enables planners to utilize the strengths of the local community, including its knowledge of the local ecosystem and its potential for adaptation.

Introduction

A major focus of anthropological inquiry for a number of years has been the processes of social change. The social anthropologist as a clinician of social systems is uniquely qualified to contribute to the planning of social change, to the evaluation of the costs of social change, and to the management of the dysfunctional reactions to social change. But seldom are anthropologists so employed in the developed countries, much less in the lesser developed countries such as Indonesia. The reasons for this are complex, but they include a lack of knowledge of the uses of anthropological inquiry. In this paper I will consider this lack, in the hope of delineating both the uses to which anthropology can be put and the further directions in which anthropology should develop to become yet more useful in the management of social change. This will involve an analysis of the seldom considered consequences of social change.

271

Seven Principles of Social Change

Development, modernization, and social change have all become hallowed, unchallenged goals, as a result of which their full impact on society is seldom considered. This impact can be discussed as a series of principles.

1. Every act of development or modernization necessarily involves an act of destruction.
2. The introduction of a new activity always displaces an indigenous activity.
3. The adaptive potential of a population is limited, and every act of change temporarily reduces this potential until such time as that change has been completely dealt with.
4. Given such reduction, each act of change has the potential to cause physiological, psychological, and/or behavioral impairment in the subject population.
5. Modernization erodes support and maintenance mechanisms for managing social stress.
6. Change always produces psychological loss, as well as compensation for such loss.
7. Change threatens the nutritional status of a population.

Development and Destruction

One purpose of development is to increase the productivity of a society. To achieve this, ecosystems are modified, agricultural systems and work regimes are changed, new knowledge is introduced, and old ways are discouraged. Development often entails, therefore, destruction of the indigenous system of knowledge, the indigenous structure of articulation to an ecosystem, and the indigenous biological mechanisms used to adapt to an environment. I do not oppose development per se any more than I oppose radiation treatment for a cancerous tumor. In radiation treatment, however, we know in advance what the cost benefits of the tissue destruction are. Development, on the other hand, often destroys without first assessing the potential costs. Development planning tends to make use of partial social models that do not incorporate these costs, often because of the explicit devaluation of the culture and members of the target society (Appell 1975a, 1975b). I will devote the remainder of this paper to assessing the value of what is destroyed in developing societies and the ability of anthropological inquiry to establish this value, estimate the social costs of its loss, and, if necessary, minimize the dysfunctions of this loss.

I have elsewhere illustrated the role of indigenous knowledge in the growth of Western civilization, ranging from pharmaceuticals to medication, from new species of crops to new uses of wild plants (Appell 1975a, 1975b, 1975c). This critical indigenous knowledge was easily incorporated into expanding Western society, because change was not too fast nor was the difference in levels of socioeconomic integration between developer and developed too great. The situation today in the developing countries is very different. When social change is consciously engineered in the small communities of these countries, their more fragile cultures can disappear almost overnight, with tragic losses of indigenous knowledge. As yet, there are insufficient mechanisms in development planning to either assess this loss or preserve what is of value. An example of what is needed is given in the work of some anthropologists on indigenous systems of agricultural knowledge, in which they have attempted to assess the empirical worth of this knowledge and its potential use in externally stimulated agricultural development (cf. Freeman 1970; Dove 1985).

It has been estimated that for the whole world there are ten million distinct organisms or species, including plants, animals, bacteria, viruses, and so forth, only 10 to 15 percent of which have been identified and described by biologists (Raven, Berlin, and Breedlove 1971: 1210). An estimated 90 percent of this immense variety of life forms is to be found in the tropics alone (Myers 1977:4). The tropical forest contains up to two hundred different species of trees alone per hectare, which compares with an average of just ten species per hectare in the temperate woodlands of the Northern latitudes (IUCN 1977:1). Unfortunately, it is precisely this environment that is most threatened by change today. The International Union for the Conservation of Nature estimates that at the present rate of conversion (by logging, by the spread of farmlands, by dam building, etc.), the rain forests of Southeast Asia will almost have disappeared by the end of the 1980s (IUCN 1977:1). As a result of the modification of this ecosystem by development, many of its life forms are being lost and will be lost before they have been identified and evaluated by science for the contributions they might make to man's future adaptation to this limited biosphere. Raven, Berlin, and Breedlove (1971:1210) estimate that at the current rate of species extinction due to development, and in view of the limited manpower available for studying them, it is doubtful that even 5 percent more of the world's organisms will be added to our inventory before the remaining 80 percent become extinct.

Thus, the evaluation of these biological resources for potential uses as medicines, foods, petroleum substitutes, and so on cannot be left to the botanist alone. One solution is to tap the accumulated storehouse of knowledge found in the indigenous societies around the world. Each society, through interacting with its environment, develops a variety of cultigens and domestic animals unique in their genetic composition. In Borneo, for example, ecotypes of dry rice, each with different character-istics, are found extensively throughout the interior. These important sources for cross-breeding and hybridization are rapidly being lost, however, as refined cultigens from the agricultural centers of the world displace them and as people leave the countryside for the cities, discard-ing as they go their agricultural heritages. These processes are leading to the permanent loss of many of the traditional cultigens, because no consistent effort has been mounted to survey and preserve them (Appell 1970). The potential magnitude of this loss is illustrated by the recent "discovery" by the American National Academy of Sciences of a remarkable but relatively obscure bean plant that may go a long way toward alleviating the protein shortage in the humid tropics. It is the winged bean *(Psophocarpus tetragonolobus),* formerly grown only as a back-yard crop in Papua Guinea (National Academy of Sciences 1975:56). Man has depended on such biological mechanisms, evolved over bil-lions of years, to adapt to his world. Today this inheritance of critical germ plasm is being wasted precisely when it is most needed.

Displacement of Indigenous Activities

A too common characteristic of development projects is a tendency to view the target society as an empty vessel to be filled, not realizing that every introduced activity displaces an extant, indigenous one, possibly more critical to the survival of the target population. Three examples will illustrate.

In many schools in Indonesia as elsewhere in the developing world, Western-style calisthenics and games are being introduced, even though the societies involved already possess their own forms of play and recre-ation. In Borneo, for example, calisthenics displace traditional sports such as leg wrestling and spear throwing. No activity can be introduced without displacing a former one, and the former ones have their place; in this instance they provide a social identity and self-esteem. Making schoolchildren learn new activities may add to the self-esteem of the teacher's society, but it may also reduce that of the pupil's society (Appell 1975a).

Another example involves the growing articulation of rural agricul-tural societies to the world market system. This is often encouraged in development without full consideration of the consequences. Once the populations in these societies become dependent on cash crops and exchanges within the world economic system, they lose their previous methods of adaptation to their local ecosystems. The result is a society that is less adaptable and more dependent than before. If the price for the farmers' cash crops decline on the world market, to the point where they can no longer afford to buy their food, the seriousness of the loss of their former subsistence food production technology becomes clear. In such situations, caught between the failure of the new production system and the loss or decline of the old, levels of nutrition tend to decline markedly.

A third example of the displacement of indigenous activities without adequate consideration of the costs involves indigenous methods of banking agricultural surpluses. Many of the societies of Borneo, for example, traditionally convert agricultural surpluses into brassware and ceramics. When a family has a poor agricultural year, this surplus can be reconverted into food stuffs. With modernization and development, however, this indigenous system of banking breaks down. As cash crops become more prevalent and as shops become more common in rural areas, the cash received from agricultural activities tends to be exchanged for perishables rather than durables. Surplus cash is used to buy candy, alcohol, soft drinks, clothing, and so forth and is thus drained off to outside markets. Consequently, when a bad harvest or some other misfortune (e.g., the illness of the head of the household) occurs, there is no "bank" to fall back upon. In none of the modernization schemes and resettlement schemes with which I am acquainted have I found any attempt to find a replacement for this indigenous system of banking, after it has disappeared.

These three examples show that one long-term effect of development and modernization is to make village societies more dependent on external values and forces and, hence, more vulnerable to factors beyond their control.

Limited Capacity for Adaptation

Every population has limited resources available to deal with the demands of social change. Demands vary according to the timing, quantity, and quality of change, but until the new demands are coped with and change is integrated into the social system, the adaptive resources of the population are committed and are not available to deal with other challenges. Unfortunately, there are few empirical studies of this and very little theory to build on or test. We do know that any society consists of interlinked hierarchical systems: the social system, the psychological system, and the physiological system. When demands for coping override the resources available in the social system, the individual will shut down activity in that system and shunt the problem of coping to another system. Typically, coping is shunted to the psychological or physiological systems. As a result, social change may create impairment not only in the behavioral repertoire of a population, but also in the physiological and psychological systems (Appell 1986; Dohrenwend and Dohrenwend 1974; Gunderson and Rahe 1974).

Physiological, Psychological, and Behavioral Impairment

Social change and its accompanying stress produce health impairment in the population at risk, whether the change is welcome or not (Gerstein et al., 1974). In a cross-cultural study of the stresses that accompany life crises and life changes, it was found that the death of a spouse produced the most stress. If this event is arbitrarily valued at 100, other life events can be scaled according to the amount of social readjustment required, as in Table 10.1 (from Holmes and Masuda 1974; and Holmes and Rahe 1967). The higher the total indice of social readjustment experienced by an individual at a given time, the greater the likelihood of health impairment (Dohrenwend and Dohrenwend 1974; Gunderson and Rahe 1974).

For the sake of illustration, this scale can be applied to a village moving from a swidden economy to an irrigated rice or cash crop economy. This would involve a change in work (valued at 36); a change in living conditions (26) and residence (20) as a new village organization evolves; probable changes in personal habits (24) and social activities (18); and a change in eating habits as subsidiary crops and vegetables planted in

Table 10.1. Costs in Stress of Life Crises/Changes

Event	Cost
Death of a spouse	100
Personal injury or illness	53
Marriage	50
Loss of job	47
Change in health of family member	45
Change in line of work	36
Change in living conditions	26
Change in personal habits	24
Change in residence	20
Change in social activities	18
Change in eating habits	15
Vacation	13

Adapted from Holmes and Masuda (1974), and Holmes and Rahe (1967).

swidden fields are lost (15). This totals to a measure of social readjustment of 139, almost one and one-half times the death of a spouse. Nor have we yet included para-psychological events such as accidents or behavioral impairments (e.g., increased arguments, divorce, impaired child rearing, etc.) that arise in a population attempting to cope with social change (Mazer 1965). Nor, finally, can the impact of social change be fully accounted for until the second and third generations have matured. Only then are the biosocial impairments that occurred during infancy and youth, when the changes occurred and the stress was experienced, fully revealed.

Again, we have no full inventory of the costs of change, only partial studies. The developing nations, currently experiencing massive social changes, are particularly well placed to contribute to, and to reap the rewards of, this critical area of scientific research.

Erosion of Support and Maintenance Systems

One of the characteristics of change, particularly of those changes that can be glossed under the rubric of "modernization," is that the indigenous support and maintenance systems are eroded to such an extent that they can no longer fulfill their function. "Support systems" refers to those indigenous social institutions that provide aid, assistance, and succor when one's health and hence self-reliance are impaired. "Maintenance systems" refers to systems of social control, which include informal networks of gossip and exchange, religious prohibitions, and formal sanctions. The problem is that these traditional systems are quickly eroded, but the support and maintenance systems of the modern world (social workers and counselors, employment and welfare agencies, consumer organizations, etc.) are the last institutions to be installed in the course of modernization. During a period of change and modernization, therefore, a population at risk has the least access to support and maintenance mechanisms, at precisely the time when they need them most. The traditional mechanisms typically receive no support from development planners. In fact, they may be the first targets of introduced change under the mistaken assumption that they are irrational, uneconomic, and so forth. For example, when Western medicine is introduced, indigenous methods of curing are often disparaged and discouraged. Local practitioners and curers, who at the very least provide psychological support and care, are typically pushed aside. Similarly, the system of exchanges in the society may be disrupted, such that behavior is no longer constrained by the fear of rupturing systems of reciprocity. When help is needed, after the old ties have broken, it will not be available.

We can look briefly at an example of the early stages of this process. The tribal longhouses of Borneo are similar in structure and function to Western condominiums, although this socio-jural institution evolved in Borneo centuries, if not millennia, before it did in the West. Despite this, there persists among most administrators the notion that the longhouse way of life is a sign of backwardness: it is not "modern." The local governments in Borneo have tried to induce longhouse-dwelling families to move into detached, single-family dwellings, in the errone-ous belief that this is necessary to encourage entrepreneurial behavior. Such reorganization destroys an entire integrated system of support and maintenance. When one is ill, there are no neighbors at hand to help prepare food. Work in distant fields is problematic, because shared responsibility for infant care is more difficult. There is no longer a pool of readily available workers to set up labor exchanges for field work. There is no longer a network of gossip to store the critical information of a pre-Gutenberg society. Nor is there the mutual protection, of life and property, that characterizes the longhouse.

Psychological Loss and Compensation

Change produces in individuals a set of social and psychological reac-tions that will be referred to here as the "social separation syndrome." This syndrome consists in role conflict and ambiguity, and a threat to one's self-esteem and social identity, combined with a psychological reaction that has been equated with the grief felt over the loss of a signif-icant other (Fried 1969; Marris 1974; Parkes 1971, 1972). When a pop-ulation undergoes major changes in its social space, its socioeconomic structure, or its assumptions about the world, it experiences the same grief, or what may be called "social bereavement." If the traumas of such losses are not successfully worked through and healed, the popula-tion will fail to reintegrate, losing its capacity to cope and becoming apathetic, depressed, or angry. As with individual grief, so with major social losses, the completion of the development cycle of bereavement requires that the past be conceived of as a meaningful and an important experience on which to build the future (Parkes 1972). If the past is de-stroyed without proper valuation, the normal development of the social bereavement process is aborted.

Such destruction also threatens one's self-identity and esteem, both of which are intimately interlinked. A social identity is built up through a complex set of interactions that include not only social roles but ethnic and locational identity as well. If these are eroded by change (Good-enough 1963), and role conflict and ambiguity increase, individuals may lose any sense of their personal identity or worth. If new roles and new identities are not yet available or amenable to construction, the population may remain in a social limbo for years. Self-identity and self-esteem are even more directly threatened in social change or development in which the traditional way of life is explicitly deprecated.

There is ample evidence that a loss of self-esteem, threats to social identity, and role conflict and ambiguity all contribute to health impairment. Bereavement itself is reported to have a physiological and psychological cost. In one study, the mortality rate among the bereaved during the first six months was found to be 40 percent higher than in a control group, and in another study it was found to be 70 percent higher (Parkes 1972:198). This results in a multiplier effect, change producing physiological and psychological health impairment which in turn produces illness in the population at risk. This means that in addition to coping with the actual facts of change, the population has to cope with growing illness, at the very time when its support and maintenance systems are eroding.

In understanding and coping with the social separation syndrome, anthropological inquiry serves an important function. Ethnographic research not only can contribute to the development of a positive self-evaluation (Appell 1974), it also can provide the materials whereby a population can view its own past, thereby providing a vital link with the changing present. Ethnographic museums serve a similar function, whereby the population at risk can see that its past was a meaningful and important experience on which to build its future. For the same reasons, the collection of indigenous oral literature and its introduction into school curricula, for example, is important.

Nutritional Status of the Population

There is growing evidence that populations undergoing change suffer a decline in nutritional status (Appell 1975a). Several interrelated processes are at work. The tendency for nutritional levels to decline in the shift from subsistence agriculture to market-oriented cash cropping was noted earlier. Some of this decline is due to the disruption of traditional consumption patterns. This may be periodic, due to the greater vulnerability (in terms of returns on one's labor) that attends production for a market as opposed to household consumption, or it may be structural (involving, for example, the consumption of an increasingly disproportionate share of the household's food resources by some of its members), due to the high caloric demands of labor in some types of cash-cropping systems (cf. Gross and Underwood 1971).

A decline in nutrition following a shift from subsistence to market-oriented agriculture may also be due, not to the pattern of consumption, but to the nature of what is consumed. Production for the market necessarily leads to greater consumption of marketed foodstuffs, which tend to have lower nutritional values than the foodstuffs produced and consumed within a system of subsistence agriculture. Some of the most notorious examples of problematic market-foods involve nursing formulas and food for infants. These, the consumption of which is encouraged with slick, often misleading advertising campaigns, are expensive (compared with their traditional substitutes) in relation to their nutritional content and require a level of knowledge, hygiene, and storage that is typically unavailable (Jelliffe 1971; Raphael 1976). As a result, the incidence of infant malnutrition, disease, and death tends to rise in direct correlation with their use.

A final instance of this link between nutritional problems and social change involves difficulties with maintaining glucose homeostasis and the resultant increased demand for sugar intake that is commonly associated with social change (see Appell 1986 for a review of this literature). Stress, such as the psychosocial stress associated with social change, results in the increased metabolism of body sugars (see Selye 1956) and a related increased demand for highly palatable foods, such as those containing proportionately large amounts of sugar (cf. Rowland and Antelman 1976). This demand for sugars can be satisfied by alcohol or the complex sugars found in cane and beet sugars, both of which are relatively inexpensive and widely available. Less easily dealt with, however, are the nutritional and behavioral diseases associated with this spiraling demand for sugars. Nutritional status declines because these refined sugars do not contain the fibers and trace elements necessary to their proper digestion (cf. Schroeder 1973). One disease associated with increased sugar demand and consumption is diabetes (see Eaton 1977 for a review of this literature). A second is hypoglycemia, a condition of low blood sugar (Bolton 1976a). Hypoglycemia, in turn, has been found to be associated with a variety of behavioral disorders, such as increased aggression (Bolton 1973, 1976a, 1976b; Bolton and Valdheim 1973). This is not a one-way, cause-and-effect situation, but a complex interrelationship between social environment and physiology.

A continuing assessment of the nutritional status of populations undergoing change is warranted. This can be done, with the assistance of health services, in conjunction with ethnographic investigations and other anthropological research.

Conclusions

The argument of this paper has three themes: (1) the importance of preserving human knowledge, hard won over thousands of years in the fight for survival in various ecosystems; (2) the dysfunctional aspects of social change; and (3) the importance of fully accounting for these costs in modernization and development.

It is important to reemphasize that the ethnographic recording of accumulated knowledge serves two critical functions. First, it preserves what is useful for the society's survival. Second, the very act of ethnographic research helps resolve the anxieties inherent in the social separation syndrome that accompanies all development, all modernization, all social change. In order for a population to resolve the conflicts of social bereavement and the threats to self-esteem and social identity that are associated with change, it must have access to ethnographic accounts of its culture. Only when a population has a positive valuation of its sociocultural system, providing a link between the past and the future, can the trauma of social separation be minimized. Only then can the population move into a new life with a minimum of the behavioral, psychological, and physiological impairments that usually accompany social change. Anthropology thus serves two important functions when it engages in baseline ethnographic studies, before modernization and development begin. Once social change is underway, the function of anthropological inquiry is to establish its full costs.

At present, these costs (viz., the loss of knowledge and the dysfunctions arising from social change) are seldom considered in development, and this results in failures of development. Social scientists are at fault for (to date) providing planners with only partial social models that do not include these social costs. The social scientists are also at fault for not using a language of costs more congruent with the language of the planners. In one sense, the development planner and the social scientist deal with two different means of reckoning. One is based on money and the other is based on certain limited aspects of social behavior. Before the planner can be convinced of the pernicious costs of development, the social scientist must develop more adequate models and translate them into the language of costs used by the planner.

I suggest that we can, in fact, estimate the costs of destroying a social system as precisely as policy makers typically estimate the other costs of development. We can estimate the costs of the loss of accumulated human knowledge and we can estimate, more closely, the costs of social change in a population at risk. The available evidence now points to the conclusion that social change, unless properly managed, can be detrimental to social and physical health. We may soon be able to calculate the potential impact of social change on a society as precisely as epidemiologists can calculate the impact of smoking. Once this is possible, and once we can add these newly figured costs to the other costs of development schemes, we will be better able to say which are "economical" and desirable, which "uneconomical" and undesirable.

More basic research is needed. The impact of social change will vary with the structure of the society at risk, the nature of the social change being implemented, and the manner in which it is managed. Anthropologists must study this in collaboration with social psychologists, epidemiologists, and medical statisticians. More basic anthropological research is especially needed on disappearing cultures, not only for their contributions to our understanding of humankind and their potential contributions to human survival, but also as a base against which social change can be planned, managed, and productively achieved. Enough empirical data is now available to build a theory to direct and inform this research. I have tried to sketch out some of the essential elements of such a theory in this paper.

References Cited

Appell, G. N.
1970   "Genetic Erosion of the Indigenous Cultivars of Borneo." *Plant Introduction Newsletter* 23:25–26.

1974   *Basic Issues in the Dilemmas and Ethical Conflicts in Anthropological Inquiry.* Position Papers on the Dilemmas and Ethical Conflicts in Anthropological Inquiry, no. 19. New York: MSS Modular Publication.

1975a   "The Pernicious Effects of Development." *Fields Within Fields* 14:31–41.

1975b   "Indigenous Man: Creator, Inventor, Discoverer." *News from Survival International* 9:10–12.

1975c   "Indigenous Man: Chemotherapeutic Explorations." *News from Survival International* 10:7–10.

1977   "The Status of Social Science Research in Sarawak and Its Relevance for Development." *Studies in Third World Societies* 2:3–90.

1986   "The Health Consequences of Social Change: A Set of Postulates for Developing General Adaptation Theory." *Sarawak Museum Journal* 36:43–74.

Bolton, Ralph
1973   "Aggression and Hypoglycemia among the Qolla: A Study of Psychological Anthropology." *Ethnology* 12:227–257.

1976a   "Hostility in Fantasy: A Further Test of the Hypoglycemia-Aggression Hypothesis." *Aggressive Behavior* 2:257–274.

1976b   "Andean Coca Chewing: A Metabolic Perspective." *American Anthropologist* 78:630–634.

Bolton, Ralph, and Constance Valdheim
1973   "The Ecology of East African Homicide." *Behavior Science Notes* 8:319–342.

Dohrenwend, Barbara Snell, and Bruce P. Dohrenwend, editors
1974   *Stressful Life Events: Their Nature and Effects.* New York: Wiley & Sons.

Dove, Michael R.
1985   *Swidden Agriculture in Indonesia: The Subsistence Strategies of the Kaliman-
        tan Kantu'.* Berlin: Mouton.

Eaton, Cynthia
1977   "Diabetes, Culture Change, and Acculturation: A Biocultural Anal-
        ysis." Student Prize Paper, Northeastern Anthropological Associa-
        tion meetings.

Freeman, Derek
1970   *Report on the Iban.* London School of Economics Monographs on
        Social Anthropology no. 41. London: The Athlone Press.

Fried, Marc
1969   "Grieving for a Lost Home." In *Social Psychiatry*, vol. 1, edited by Ari
        Kiev, pp. 336–359. New York: Science House.

Gerstein, Joanna C., et al.
1974   "Child Behavior and Life Events: Undesirable Change or Change
        per se?" In *Stressful Life Events: Their Nature and Effects,* edited by
        B. S. Dohrenwend and B. P. Dohrenwend.

Goodenough, Ward Hunt
1963   *Cooperation in Change.* New York: Russell Sage Foundation.

Gross, D. R., and B. A. Underwood
1971   "Technological Change and Caloric Costs: Sisal Agriculture in
        Northeastern Brazil." *American Anthropologist* 73:725–740.

Gunderson, E. K. Eric, and Richard H. Rahe, eds.
1974   *Life Stress in Illness.* Springfield, Ill.: Charles C. Thomas.

Holmes, Thomas H., and Minoru Masuda
1974   "Life Change and Illness Susceptibility." In *Stressful Life Events: Their
        Nature and Effects,* edited by B. S. Dohrenwend and B. P.
        Dohrenwend.

Holmes, T. H., and R. H. Rahe
1967   "The Social Readjustment Rating Scale." *Journal of Psychosomatic
        Research* 11:213–218.

International Union for the Conservation of Nature and Natural Resources
1977   "The Prize and the Peril in South East Asia." *IUCN Bulletin* 8 (1): 1.

Jelliffe, D. B.
1971   "Commerciogenetic Malnutrition?" *Nutrition Reviews* 30:199–205.
        Reprinted in *Food Technology* 25:153–154.

Marris, Peter
1974   *Loss and Change.* London: Routledge & Kegan Paul.

Mazer, Milton
1965   "The Human Predicaments of an Island Population." *Science and Psy-
        choanalysis* 8:159–170.

Myers, Norman
    1977   "Garden of Eden to Weed Patch: The Earth's Vanishing Genetic
            Heritage. *NRDC* [*Natural Resources Defense Council*] *Newsletter* 6 (1): 1–
            15.

National Academy of Sciences
    1975   Underexploited Tropical Plants with Promising Economic Value.
            Report of an Ad Hoc Panel of the Advisory Committee on Technol-
            ogy Innovation, Board on Science and Technology for International
            Development, Commission on International Relations. Washington,
            D.C.: National Academy of Sciences.

Parkes, Colon Murray
    1971   "Psycho-social Transitions: A Field for Study." *Social Science and Med-
            icine* 5:101–115.

    1972   *Bereavement: Studies of Grief in Adult Life.* New York: International Uni-
            versities Press.

Raphael, Dana
    1976   "Warning: The Milk in this Package May Be Lethal for Your
            Infant." In *Medical Anthropology,* edited by F. X. Grolling, S. J.
            Haley, and H. B. Haley. The Hague: Mouton.

Raven, Peter H., Brent Berlin, and Dennis E. Breedlove
    1971   "The Origins of Taxonomy." *Science* 174:1210–1213.

Rowland, Neil E., and Seymour M. Antelman
    1976   "Stress-induced Hyperphagia and Obesity in Rats: A Possible
            Model for Understanding Human Obesity." *Science* 191:310–312.

Schroeder, Henry A.
    1973   *The Trace Elements and Man: Some Positive and Negative Aspects.* Old
            Greenwich, Conn.: Devin-Adair.

Selye, Hans
    1956   *The Stress of Life.* New York: McGraw-Hill.

CONTRIBUTORS

G. N. Appell, Ph.D., carried out research in Sabah (North Borneo) in 1959–1960, 1961–1963, and summer 1986, and in East Kalimantan in 1980–1981. He currently is senior research associate in the department of anthropology at Brandeis University in Waltham, Masachusetts, U.S.A.

Jane M. Atkinson, Ph.D., carried out research among the Wana of South Sulawesi in 1974–1976 and currently is associate professor in the department of sociology of Lewis and Clark College in Portland, Oregon, U.S.A.

Jeffrey D. Brewer, Ph.D., carried out research among the Bimanese of Sumbawa in 1975–1976 and currently is director of a USAID/Louis Berger development project in India.

Hans J. Daeng, B.A., a native of Flores and senior lecturer in the department of anthropology of Gadjah Mada University, Yogyakarta D.I.Y., Indonesia. He is currently studying for his Ph.D. in the department of anthropology at the University of Indonesia, Jakarta.

Michael R. Dove, Ph.D., carried out research among the Kantu' of West Kalimantan in 1974–1976, and among various tribal and peasant groups on Java, Sumatra, Sumbawa, Flores, and Kalimantan during 1979–1985. He is currently project anthropologist for the Winrock International Institute for Agricultural Development in Islamabad, Pakistan.

Carl L. Hoffman, Ph.D., carried out research among the Punan of East and South Kalimantan in 1980–1982 and currently is on the field staff of the Peace Corps in the Philippines.

Purwanta Iskandar, B.A., a native of Central Java, carried out research in Java, Sumatra, Sulawesi, Kalimantan, and Eastern Indonesia during 1976–1981. He is on the staff of the National Family Planning Board (BKKBN) in Jakarta, Indonesia, currently on leave to study for his M.A. in the department of sociology at the University of Southern California, Los Angeles, U.S.A.

Victor T. King, Ph.D., carried out field research among the Maloh of West Kalimantan in 1972–1973, and archival research in the Netherlands between 1974 and 1986. He is currently a lecturer in the department of sociology and social anthropology and the Centre for South-East Asian studies at the University of Hull, England.

P. M. Laksono, M.A., a native of Central Java, carried out research among the Javanese on Merapi volcano in Central Java in 1977 and 1979. He is lecturer in the department of anthropology and research associate in the Environmental Studies Center, both of Gadjah Mada University in Indonesia, currently on leave to study for his Ph.D. in the department of anthropology of Cornell University, Ithaca, New York, U.S.A.

Adriaan S. Rienks, M.A., carried out research in Central Java in 1978–1981 and 1982–1984, and is currently studying for his Ph.D. in anthropology at the Free University in Amsterdam, The Netherlands.

Reimar Schefold, Ph.D., carried out research among the Mentawai of Siberut in 1967–1969, 1974, and 1978. He currently is senior lecturer in the Institute of Cultural Anthropology of the Free University in Amsterdam, The Netherlands.

INDEX

Production Notes

This book was designed by Roger Eggers.
Composition and paging were done on the
Quadex Composing System and typesetting
on the Compugraphic 8400 by the design
and production staff of University of
Hawaii Press.

The text typeface is Baskerville and the
display typeface is Compugraphic Palatino.

Offset presswork and binding were done
by Vail-Ballou Press, Inc. Text paper
is Glatfelter Offset Vellum, basis 50.